UKRAINIAN
VOCABULARY

ENGLISH-UKRAINIAN

The most useful words
To expand your lexicon and sharpen
your language skills

7000 words

Ukrainian vocabulary for English speakers - 7000 words

By Andrey Taranov

T&P Books vocabularies are intended for helping you learn, memorize and review foreign words. The dictionary is divided into themes, covering all major spheres of everyday activities, business, science, culture, etc.

The process of learning words using T&P Books' theme-based dictionaries gives you the following advantages:

- Correctly grouped source information predetermines success at subsequent stages of word memorization
- Availability of words derived from the same root allowing memorization of word units (rather than separate words)
- Small units of words facilitate the process of establishing associative links needed for consolidation of vocabulary
- Level of language knowledge can be estimated by the number of learned words

T&P Books Publishing
www.tpbooks.com

This book is also available in E-book formats.
Please visit www.tpbooks.com or the major online bookstores.

UKRAINIAN VOCABULARY
for English speakers

T&P Books vocabularies are intended to help you learn, memorize, and review foreign words. The vocabulary contains over 7000 commonly used words arranged thematically.

- Vocabulary contains the most commonly used words
- Recommended as an addition to any language course
- Meets the needs of beginners and advanced learners of foreign languages
- Convenient for daily use, revision sessions, and self-testing activities
- Allows you to assess your vocabulary

Special features of the vocabulary

- Words are organized according to their meaning, not alphabetically
- Words are presented in three columns to facilitate the reviewing and self-testing processes
- Words in groups are divided into small blocks to facilitate the learning process
- The vocabulary offers a convenient and simple transcription of each foreign word

The vocabulary has 198 topics including:

Basic Concepts, Numbers, Colors, Months, Seasons, Units of Measurement, Clothing & Accessories, Food & Nutrition, Restaurant, Family Members, Relatives, Character, Feelings, Emotions, Diseases, City, Town, Sightseeing, Shopping, Money, House, Home, Office, Working in the Office, Import & Export, Marketing, Job Search, Sports, Education, Computer, Internet, Tools, Nature, Countries, Nationalities and more …

TABLE OF CONTENTS

REGIONAL GEOGRAPHY

MISCELLANEOUS

REGIONAL GEOGRAPHY

MISCELLANEOUS

PRONUNCIATION GUIDE

Letter	Ukrainian example	T&P phonetic alphabet	English example

Vowels

Letter	Ukrainian example	T&P phonetic alphabet	English example
А а	акт	[a]	shorter than in 'ask'
Е е	берет	[e], [ɛ]	absent, pet
Є є	модельєр	[ɛ]	man, bad
И и	ритм	[k]	clock, kiss
I i	компанія	[i]	shorter than in 'feet'
Ï ï	поїзд	[ji]	playing, spying
О о	око	[ɔ]	bottle, doctor
У у	буря	[u]	book
Ю ю	костюм	[ʲu]	cued, cute
Я я	маяк	[ja], [ʲa]	royal

Consonants

Letter	Ukrainian example	T&P phonetic alphabet	English example
Б б	бездна	[b]	baby, book
В в	вікно	[w]	vase, winter
Г г	готель	[h]	between [g] and [h]
Ґ ґ	ґудзик	[g]	game, gold
Д д	дефіс	[d]	day, doctor
Ж ж	жанр	[ʒ]	forge, pleasure
З з	зброя	[z]	zebra, please
Й й	йти	[j]	yes, New York
К к	крок	[k]	clock, kiss
Л л	лев	[l]	lace, people
М м	мати	[m]	magic, milk
Н н	назва	[n]	name, normal
П п	приз	[p]	pencil, private
Р р	радість	[r]	rice, radio
С с	сон	[s]	city, boss
Т т	тир	[t]	tourist, trip
Ф ф	фарба	[f]	face, food
Х х	холод	[h]	home, have
Ц ц	церква	[ts]	cats, tsetse fly
Ч ч	час	[tʃ]	church, French

Letter	Ukrainian example	T&P phonetic alphabet	English example
Ш ш	шуба	[ʃ]	machine, shark
Щ щ	щука	[ɕ]	sheep, shop
ь	камінь	[ʲ]	soft sign - no sound
ъ	ім'я	[ʲ]	hard sign, no sound

ABBREVIATIONS
used in the vocabulary

English abbreviations

ab.	-	about
adj	-	adjective
adv	-	adverb
anim.	-	animate
as adj	-	attributive noun used as adjective
e.g.	-	for example
etc.	-	et cetera
fam.	-	familiar
fem.	-	feminine
form.	-	formal
inanim.	-	inanimate
masc.	-	masculine
math	-	mathematics
mil.	-	military
n	-	noun
pl	-	plural
pron.	-	pronoun
sb	-	somebody
sing.	-	singular
sth	-	something
v aux	-	auxiliary verb
vi	-	intransitive verb
vi, vt	-	intransitive, transitive verb
vt	-	transitive verb

Ukrainian abbreviations

ж	-	feminine noun
мн	-	plural
с	-	neuter
ч	-	masculine noun

BASIC CONCEPTS

Basic concepts. Part 1

1. Pronouns

I, me	я	[ja]
you	ти	[ti]
he	він	[win]
she	вона	[wo'na]
it	воно	[wo'nɔ]
we	ми	[mi]
you (to a group)	ви	[wi]
they	вони	[wo'ni]

2. Greetings. Salutations. Farewells

Hello! (fam.)	Здрастуй!	['zdrastuj]
Hello! (form.)	Здрастуйте!	['zdrastujtɛ]
Good morning!	Доброго ранку!	['dɔbrɔɦo 'ranku]
Good afternoon!	Добрий день!	['dɔbrij dɛnʲ]
Good evening!	Добрий вечір!	['dɔbrij 'wɛtʃir]
to say hello	вітатися	[wi'tatisʲa]
Hi! (hello)	Привіт!	[pri'wit]
greeting (n)	привітання (c)	[priwi'tanʲa]
to greet (vt)	вітати	[wi'tati]
How are you?	Як справи?	[jak 'sprawi]
How are you? (form.)	Як у вас справи?	[jak u was 'sprawi]
What's new?	Що нового?	[ɕo no'wɔɦo]
Bye-Bye! Goodbye!	До побачення!	[do po'batʃɛnʲa]
See you soon!	До скорої зустрічі!	[do 'skɔroji 'zustritʃiʲ]
Farewell! (to a friend)	Прощавай!	[proɕa'waj]
Farewell! (form.)	Прощавайте!	[proɕa'wajtɛ]
to say goodbye	прощатися	[pro'ɕatisʲa]
So long!	Бувай!	[bu'waj]
Thank you!	Дякую!	['dʲakuʲu]
Thank you very much!	Щиро дякую!	['ɕiro 'dʲakuʲu]
You're welcome	Будь ласка	[budʲ 'laska]

| Don't mention it! | Не варто подяки | [nɛ 'warto po'dʲaki] |
| It was nothing | Нема за що | [nɛ'ma za ɕo] |

Excuse me! (fam.)	Вибач!	['wibatʃ]
Excuse me! (form.)	Вибачте!	['wibatʃtɛ]
to excuse (forgive)	вибачати	[wiba'tʃati]

to apologize (vi)	вибачатися	[wiba'tʃatisʲa]
My apologies	Мої вибачення	[moi 'wibatʃɛnʲa]
I'm sorry!	Вибачте!	['wibatʃtɛ]
to forgive (vt)	вибачати	[wiba'tʃati]
please (adv)	будь ласка	[budʲ 'laska]

Don't forget!	Не забудьте!	[nɛ za'budʲtɛ]
Certainly!	Звичайно!	[zwi'tʃajno]
Of course not!	Звичайно ні!	[zwi'tʃajno ni]
Okay! (I agree)	Згоден!	['zɦodɛn]
That's enough!	Досить!	['dositʲ]

3. Cardinal numbers. Part 1

0 zero	нуль	[nulʲ]
1 one	один	[o'din]
2 two	два	[dwa]
3 three	три	[tri]
4 four	чотири	[tʃo'tiri]

5 five	п'ять	[pʲatʲ]
6 six	шість	[ʃistʲ]
7 seven	сім	[sim]
8 eight	вісім	['wisim]
9 nine	дев'ять	['dɛwʲatʲ]

10 ten	десять	['dɛsʲatʲ]
11 eleven	одинадцять	[odi'nadtsʲatʲ]
12 twelve	дванадцять	[dwa'nadtsʲatʲ]
13 thirteen	тринадцять	[tri'nadtsʲatʲ]
14 fourteen	чотирнадцять	[tʃotir'nadtsʲatʲ]

15 fifteen	п'ятнадцять	[pʲat'nadtsʲatʲ]
16 sixteen	шістнадцять	[ʃist'nadtsʲatʲ]
17 seventeen	сімнадцять	[sim'nadtsʲatʲ]
18 eighteen	вісімнадцять	[wisim'nadtsʲatʲ]
19 nineteen	дев'ятнадцять	[dɛwʲat'nadtsʲatʲ]

20 twenty	двадцять	['dwadtsʲatʲ]
21 twenty-one	двадцять один	['dwadtsʲatʲ o'din]
22 twenty-two	двадцять два	['dwadtsʲatʲ dwa]
23 twenty-three	двадцять три	['dwadtsʲatʲ tri]
30 thirty	тридцять	['tridtsʲatʲ]

31 thirty-one	тридцять один	['tridtsʲatʲ oʹdin]
32 thirty-two	тридцять два	['tridtsʲatʲ dwa]
33 thirty-three	тридцять три	['tridtsʲatʲ tri]
40 forty	сорок	['sɔrok]
41 forty-one	сорок один	['sɔrok oʹdin]
42 forty-two	сорок два	['sɔrok dwa]
43 forty-three	сорок три	['sɔrok tri]
50 fifty	п'ятдесят	[pʲʹatdɛ'sʲat]
51 fifty-one	п'ятдесят один	[pʲʹatdɛ'sʲat oʹdin]
52 fifty-two	п'ятдесят два	[pʲʹatdɛ'sʲat dwa]
53 fifty-three	п'ятдесят три	[pʲʹatdɛ'sʲat tri]
60 sixty	шістдесят	[ʃizdɛ'sʲat]
61 sixty-one	шістдесят один	[ʃizdɛ'sʲat oʹdin]
62 sixty-two	шістдесят два	[ʃizdɛ'sʲat dwa]
63 sixty-three	шістдесят три	[ʃizdɛ'sʲat tri]
70 seventy	сімдесят	[simdɛ'sʲat]
71 seventy-one	сімдесят один	[simdɛ'sʲat odin]
72 seventy-two	сімдесят два	[simdɛ'sʲat dwa]
73 seventy-three	сімдесят три	[simdɛ'sʲat tri]
80 eighty	вісімдесят	[wisimdɛ'sʲat]
81 eighty-one	вісімдесят один	[wisimdɛ'sʲat oʹdin]
82 eighty-two	вісімдесят два	[wisimdɛ'sʲat dwa]
83 eighty-three	вісімдесят три	[wisimdɛ'sʲat tri]
90 ninety	дев'яносто	[dɛwʲʹa'nɔsto]
91 ninety-one	дев'яносто один	[dɛwʲʹa'nɔsto oʹdin]
92 ninety-two	дев'яносто два	[dɛwʲʹa'nɔsto dwa]
93 ninety-three	дев'яносто три	[dɛwʲʹa'nɔsto tri]

4. Cardinal numbers. Part 2

100 one hundred	сто	[sto]
200 two hundred	двісті	['dwisti]
300 three hundred	триста	['trista]
400 four hundred	чотириста	[tʃo'tirista]
500 five hundred	п'ятсот	[pʲʹa'tsot]
600 six hundred	шістсот	[ʃist'sot]
700 seven hundred	сімсот	[sim'sot]
800 eight hundred	вісімсот	[wisim'sot]
900 nine hundred	дев'ятсот	[dɛwʲʹa'tsot]
1000 one thousand	тисяча	['tisʲatʃa]
2000 two thousand	дві тисячі	[dwi 'tisʲatʃi]
3000 three thousand	три тисячі	[tri 'tisʲatʃi]

10000 ten thousand	десять тисяч	[ˈdɛsʲatʲ ˈtisʲatʃ]
one hundred thousand	сто тисяч	[sto ˈtisʲatʃ]
million	мільйон (ч)	[milʲˈjon]
billion	мільярд (ч)	[miˈljard]

5. Numbers. Fractions

fraction	дріб (ч)	[drib]
one half	одна друга	[odˈna ˈdruɦa]
one third	одна третя	[odˈna ˈtrɛtʲa]
one quarter	одна четверта	[odˈna tʃɛtˈwɛrta]
one eighth	одна восьма	[odˈna ˈwosʲma]
one tenth	одна десята	[odˈna dɛˈsʲata]
two thirds	дві третіх	[dwi ˈtrɛtih]
three quarters	три четвертих	[tri tʃɛtˈwɛrtih]

6. Numbers. Basic operations

subtraction	віднімання (с)	[widniˈmanʲa]
to subtract (vi, vt)	віднімати	[widniˈmati]
division	ділення (с)	[ˈdilɛnʲa]
to divide (vt)	ділити	[diˈliti]
addition	додавання (с)	[dodaˈwanʲa]
to add up (vt)	додати	[doˈdati]
to add (vi, vt)	прибавляти	[pribawˈlʲati]
multiplication	множення (с)	[ˈmnɔʒɛnʲa]
to multiply (vt)	множити	[ˈmnɔʒiti]

7. Numbers. Miscellaneous

digit, figure	цифра (ж)	[ˈtsifra]
number	число (с)	[tʃisˈlɔ]
numeral	числівник (ч)	[tʃisˈliwnik]
minus sign	мінус (ч)	[ˈminus]
plus sign	плюс (ч)	[plʲus]
formula	формула (ж)	[ˈfɔrmula]
calculation	обчислення (с)	[obˈtʃislɛnʲa]
to count (vi, vt)	рахувати	[rahuˈwati]
to count up	підраховувати	[pidraˈhɔwuwati]
to compare (vt)	порівнювати	[poˈriwnʲuwati]
How much?	Скільки?	[ˈskilʲki]
sum, total	сума (ж)	[ˈsuma]

| result | **результат** (ч) | [rɛzulʲ'tat] |
| remainder | **залишок** (ч) | ['zaliʃok] |

a few (e.g., ~ years ago)	**декілька**	['dɛkilʲka]
little (I had ~ time)	**небагато…**	[nɛba'ɦato]
the rest	**решта** (ж)	['rɛʃta]
one and a half	**півтора**	[piwto'ra]
dozen	**дюжина** (ж)	['dʲuʒina]

in half (adv)	**навпіл**	['nawpilʲ]
equally (evenly)	**порівну**	['pɔriwnu]
half	**половина** (ж)	[polo'wina]
time (three ~s)	**раз** (ч)	[raz]

8. The most important verbs. Part 1

to advise (vt)	**радити**	['raditi]
to agree (say yes)	**погоджуватися**	[po'ɦɔdʒuwatisʲa]
to answer (vi, vt)	**відповідати**	[widpowi'dati]
to apologize (vi)	**вибачатися**	[wiba'tʃatisʲa]
to arrive (vi)	**приїжджати**	[prijiʒ'ʒati]

to ask (~ oneself)	**запитувати**	[za'pituwati]
to ask (~ sb to do sth)	**просити**	[pro'siti]
to be (vi)	**бути**	['buti]

to be afraid	**боятися**	[boʲ'atisʲa]
to be hungry	**хотіти їсти**	[ho'titi 'jisti]
to be interested in …	**цікавитися**	[tsi'kawitisʲa]
to be needed	**бути потрібним**	['buti po'tribnim]
to be surprised	**дивуватись**	[diwu'watisʲ]

to be thirsty	**хотіти пити**	[ho'titi 'piti]
to begin (vt)	**починати**	[potʃi'nati]
to belong to …	**належати**	[na'lɛʒati]
to boast (vi)	**хвалитися**	[hwa'litisʲa]
to break (snap a branch, toy, etc.)	**ламати**	[la'mati]

to call (~ for help)	**кликати**	['klikati]
can (v aux)	**могти**	[moɦ'ti]
to catch (vt)	**ловити**	[lo'witi]
to change (vt)	**змінювати**	['zminʲuwati]
to choose (select)	**вибирати**	[wibi'rati]

to come down (~ the stairs)	**спускатися**	[spus'katisʲa]
to compare (vt)	**порівнювати**	[po'riwnʲuwati]
to complain (vi, vt)	**скаржитися**	['skarʒitisʲa]
to confuse (mix up)	**плутати**	['plutati]

| to continue (vt) | продовжувати | [pro'dɔwʒuwati] |
| to control (vt) | контролювати | [kontrolʲu'wati] |

to cook (~ dinner, etc.)	готувати	[ɦotu'wati]
to cost (vt)	коштувати	['kɔʃtuwati]
to count (add up)	лічити	[li'ʧiti]
to count on ...	розраховувати на...	[rozra'ɦowuwati na]
to create (vt)	створити	[stwo'riti]
to cry (weep)	плакати	['plakati]

9. The most important verbs. Part 2

to deceive (vi, vt)	обманювати	[ob'manʲuwati]
to decorate (~ a tree, street)	прикрашати	[prikra'ʃati]
to defend (a country, etc.)	захищати	[zahi'ɕati]
to demand (request firmly)	вимагати	[wima'ɦati]
to dig (vt)	рити	['riti]

to discuss (vt)	обговорювати	[obɦo'worʲuwati]
to do (vt)	робити	[ro'biti]
to doubt (have doubts)	сумніватися	[sumni'watisʲa]
to drop (let fall)	упускати	[upus'kati]
to enter (~ a room, etc.)	входити	['whɔditi]

to excuse (forgive)	вибачати	[wɨba'ʧati]
to exist (vi)	існувати	[isnu'wati]
to expect (foresee)	передбачити	[pɛrɛd'baʧiti]
to explain (vt)	пояснювати	[poʲlasnʲuwati]
to fall (vi)	падати	['padati]

to find (vt)	знаходити	[zna'ɦɔditi]
to finish (vt)	закінчувати	[za'kinʧuwati]
to fly (vi)	летіти	[lɛ'titi]
to follow ... (come after)	іти слідом	[i'ti 'slidom]
to forget (vi, vt)	забувати	[zabu'wati]

to forgive (vt)	прощати	[pro'ɕati]
to give (vt)	давати	[da'wati]
to give a hint	підказати	[pidka'zati]
to go (on foot)	йти	[jti]

to go for a swim	купатися	[ku'patisʲa]
to go out (for dinner, etc.)	виходити	[wi'ɦɔditi]
to guess (e.g., ~ a riddle)	вгадати	[wɦa'dati]

to have (vt)	мати	['mati]
to have breakfast	снідати	['snidati]
to have dinner	вечеряти	[wɛ'ʧɛrʲati]

| to have lunch | обідати | [o'bidati] |
| to hear (vt) | чути | ['tʃuti] |

to help (vt)	допомагати	[dopoma'ɦati]
to hide (vt)	ховати	[ho'wati]
to hope (vi, vt)	сподіватися	[spodi'watisʲa]
to hunt (vi, vt)	полювати	[polʲu'wati]
to hurry (vi)	поспішати	[pospi'ʃati]

10. The most important verbs. Part 3

to inform (vt)	інформувати	[informu'wati]
to insist (vi, vt)	наполягати	[napolʲa'ɦati]
to insult (vt)	ображати	[obra'ʒati]
to invite (vt)	запрошувати	[za'proʃuwati]
to joke (vi)	жартувати	[ʒartu'wati]

to keep (vt)	зберігати	[zbɛri'ɦati]
to keep silent, to hush	мовчати	[mow'tʃati]
to kill (vt)	убивати	[ubi'wati]
to know (sb)	знати	['znati]
to know (sth)	знати	['znati]
to laugh (vi)	сміятися	[smi'atisʲa]

to liberate (~ a city, etc.)	звільняти	[zwilʲ'nʲati]
to like (enjoy, favor; I like …)	подобатися	[po'dɔbatisʲa]
to look for … (search)	шукати	[ʃu'kati]
to love (sb)	кохати	[ko'ɦati]
to make a mistake	помилятися	[pomi'lʲatisʲa]

to manage, to run	керувати	[kɛru'wati]
to mean (signify)	означати	[ozna'tʃati]
to mention (talk about)	згадувати	['zɦaduwati]
to miss (~ school, etc.)	пропускати	[propus'kati]
to notice (see)	помічати	[pomi'tʃati]

to object (vi, vt)	заперечувати	[zapɛ'rɛtʃuwati]
to observe (see)	спостерігати	[spostɛri'ɦati]
to open (vt)	відчинити	[widtʃi'niti]
to order (meal, etc.)	замовляти	[zamow'lʲati]
to order (mil.)	наказувати	[na'kazuwati]
to own (possess)	володіти	[wolo'diti]

to participate (vi)	брати участь	['brati 'utʃastʲ]
to pay (vi, vt)	платити	[pla'titi]
to permit (vt)	дозволяти	[dozwo'lʲati]
to plan (vt)	планувати	[planu'wati]
to play (children)	грати	['ɦrati]
to pray (vi, vt)	молитися	[mo'litisʲa]

to prefer (vt)	воліти	[wo'liti]
to promise (vt)	обіцяти	[obi'tsʲati]
to pronounce (vt)	вимовляти	[wimow'lʲati]
to propose (vt)	пропонувати	[proponu'wati]
to punish (vt)	покарати	[poka'rati]

11. The most important verbs. Part 4

to read (vi, vt)	читати	[tʃi'tati]
to recommend (vt)	рекомендувати	[rɛkomɛndu'wati]
to refuse (vi, vt)	відмовлятися	[widmow'lʲatisʲa]
to regret (be sorry)	жалкувати	[ʒalku'wati]
to rent (sth from sb)	зняти	['znʲati]

to repeat (say again)	повторювати	[pow'torʲuwati]
to reserve, to book	резервувати	[rɛzɛrwu'wati]
to run (vi)	бігти	['biɦti]
to save (rescue)	рятувати	[rʲatu'wati]
to say (~ thank you)	сказати	[ska'zati]

to scold (vt)	лаяти	['laʲati]
to see (vt)	бачити	['batʃiti]
to sell (vt)	продавати	[proda'wati]
to send (vt)	відправляти	[widpraw'lʲati]
to shoot (vi)	стріляти	[stri'lʲati]

to shout (vi)	кричати	[kri'tʃati]
to show (vt)	показувати	[po'kazuwati]
to sign (~ a document)	підписувати	[pid'pisuwati]
to sit down (vi)	сідати	[si'dati]

to smile (vi)	посміхатися	[posmi'hatisʲa]
to speak (vi, vt)	говорити	[ɦowo'riti]
to steal (money, etc.)	красти	['krasti]
to stop (~ to rest)	зупинятися	[zupi'nʲatisʲa]
to stop (please ~ calling me)	припиняти	[pripi'nʲati]

to study (vt)	вивчати	[wiw'tʃati]
to swim (vi)	плавати	['plawati]
to take (vt)	брати	['brati]
to think (vi, vt)	думати	['dumati]
to threaten (vt)	погрожувати	[poɦ'rɔʒuwati]

to touch (with hands)	торкати	[tor'kati]
to translate (vt)	перекладати	[pɛrɛkla'dati]
to trust (vt)	довіряти	[dowi'rʲati]
to try (attempt)	пробувати	['prɔbuwati]
to turn (e.g., ~ left)	повертати	[powɛr'tati]
to underestimate (vt)	недооцінювати	[nɛdoo'tsinʲuwati]

to understand (vt)	**розуміти**	[rozu'miti]
to unite (vt)	**об'єднувати**	[o'b'ɛdnuwati]
to wait (vt)	**чекати**	[ʧɛ'kati]

to want (wish, desire)	**хотіти**	[ho'titi]
to warn (vt)	**попереджувати**	[popɛ'rɛdʒuwati]
to work (vi)	**працювати**	[praʦʲu'wati]
to write (vt)	**писати**	[pi'sati]
to write down	**записувати**	[za'pisuwati]

12. Colors

color	**колір** (ч)	['kɔlir]
shade (tint)	**відтінок** (ч)	[wid'tinok]
hue	**тон** (ч)	[ton]
rainbow	**веселка** (ж)	[wɛ'sɛlka]

white (adj)	**білий**	['bilij]
black (adj)	**чорний**	['ʧɔrnij]
gray (adj)	**сірий**	['sirij]

green (adj)	**зелений**	[zɛ'lɛnij]
yellow (adj)	**жовтий**	['ʒɔwtij]
red (adj)	**червоний**	[ʧɛr'wɔnij]

blue (adj)	**синій**	['sinij]
light blue (adj)	**блакитний**	[bla'kitnij]
pink (adj)	**рожевий**	[ro'ʒɛwij]
orange (adj)	**помаранчевий**	[poma'ranʧɛwij]
violet (adj)	**фіолетовий**	[fio'lɛtowij]
brown (adj)	**коричневий**	[ko'riʧnɛwij]
golden (adj)	**золотий**	[zolo'tij]
silvery (adj)	**сріблястий**	[srib'lʲastij]

beige (adj)	**бежевий**	['bɛʒɛwij]
cream (adj)	**кремовий**	['krɛmowij]
turquoise (adj)	**бірюзовий**	[biru'zɔwij]
cherry red (adj)	**вишневий**	[wiʃ'nɛwij]
lilac (adj)	**бузковий**	[buz'kɔwij]
crimson (adj)	**малиновий**	[ma'linowij]

light (adj)	**світлий**	['switlij]
dark (adj)	**темний**	['tɛmnij]
bright, vivid (adj)	**яскравий**	[jas'krawij]

colored (e.g., ~ pencils)	**кольоровий**	[kolʲo'rɔwij]
color (e.g., ~ film)	**кольоровий**	[kolʲo'rɔwij]
black-and-white (adj)	**чорно-білий**	['ʧɔrno 'bilij]
plain (one-colored)	**однобарвний**	[odno'barwnij]
multicolored (adj)	**різнобарвний**	[rizno'barwnij]

13. Questions

Who?	Хто?	[hto]
What?	Що?	[ɕɔ]
Where? (at, in)	Де?	[dɛ]
Where (to)?	Куди?	[ku'di]
Where from?	Звідки?	['zwidki]
When?	Коли?	[ko'li]
Why? (What for?)	Навіщо?	[na'wiɕo]
Why? (~ are you crying?)	Чому?	[ʧo'mu]
What for?	Для чого?	[dlʲa 'ʧɔho]
How? (in what way)	Як?	[jak]
What? (What kind of …?)	Який?	[ja'kij]
Which?	Котрий?	[kot'rij]
To whom?	Кому?	[ko'mu]
About whom?	Про кого?	[pro 'kɔho]
About what?	Про що?	[pro ɕo]
With whom?	З ким?	[z kim]
How many? How much?	Скільки?	['skilʲki]
Whose?	Чий?	[ʧij]
Whose? (fem.)	Чия?	[ʧiʲʲa]
Whose? (pl)	Чиї?	['ʧiji]

14. Function words. Adverbs. Part 1

Where? (at, in)	Де?	[dɛ]
here (adv)	тут	[tut]
there (adv)	там	[tam]
somewhere (to be)	десь	[dɛsʲ]
nowhere (not in any place)	ніде	[ni'dɛ]
by (near, beside)	біля	['bilʲa]
by the window	біля вікна	['bilʲa wik'na]
Where (to)?	Куди?	[ku'di]
here (e.g., come ~!)	сюди	[sʲu'di]
there (e.g., to go ~)	туди	[tu'di]
from here (adv)	звідси	['zwidsi]
from there (adv)	звідти	['zwidti]
close (adv)	близько	['blizʲko]
far (adv)	далеко	[da'lɛko]
near (e.g., ~ Paris)	біля	['bilʲa]
nearby (adv)	поряд	['pɔrʲad]

not far (adv)	**недалеко**	[nɛda'lɛko]
left (adj)	**лівий**	['liwij]
on the left	**зліва**	['zliwa]
to the left	**ліворуч**	[li'wɔrutʃ]
right (adj)	**правий**	['prawij]
on the right	**справа**	['sprawa]
to the right	**праворуч**	[pra'wɔrutʃ]
in front (adv)	**спереду**	['spɛrɛdu]
front (as adj)	**передній**	[pɛ'rɛdnij]
ahead (the kids ran ~)	**уперед**	[upɛ'rɛd]
behind (adv)	**позаду**	[po'zadu]
from behind	**ззаду**	['zzadu]
back (towards the rear)	**назад**	[na'zad]
middle	**середина** (ж)	[sɛ'rɛdina]
in the middle	**посередині**	[posɛ'rɛdini]
at the side	**збоку**	['zbɔku]
everywhere (adv)	**скрізь**	[skrizʲ]
around (in all directions)	**навколо**	[naw'kɔlo]
from inside	**зсередини**	[zsɛ'rɛdinɨ]
somewhere (to go)	**кудись**	[ku'disʲ]
straight (directly)	**прямо**	['prʲamo]
back (e.g., come ~)	**назад**	[na'zad]
from anywhere	**звідки-небудь**	['zwidki 'nɛbudʲ]
from somewhere	**звідкись**	['zwidkisʲ]
firstly (adv)	**по-перше**	[po 'pɛrʃɛ]
secondly (adv)	**по-друге**	[po 'druhɛ]
thirdly (adv)	**по-третє**	[po 'trɛtɛ]
suddenly (adv)	**раптом**	['raptom]
at first (in the beginning)	**спочатку**	[spo'tʃatku]
for the first time	**уперше**	[u'pɛrʃɛ]
long before …	**задовго до…**	[za'dɔwɦo do]
anew (beginning over again)	**заново**	['zanowo]
for good (adv)	**назовсім**	[na'zɔwsim]
never (adv)	**ніколи**	[ni'kɔli]
again (adv)	**знову**	['znɔwu]
now (at present, currently)	**тепер**	[tɛ'pɛr]
often (adv)	**часто**	['tʃasto]
then (adv)	**тоді**	[to'di]
urgently (quickly)	**терміново**	[tɛrmi'nɔwo]
usually (adv)	**звичайно**	[zwi'tʃajno]
by the way, …	**до речі,…**	[do 'rɛtʃi]

possibly	можливо	[moʒ'liwo]
probably (adv)	мабуть	[ma'butʲ]
maybe (adv)	може бути	['mɔʒɛ 'buti]
besides ...	крім того,...	[krim 'toɦo]
that's why ...	тому	['tomu]
in spite of ...	незважаючи на...	[nɛzwa'ʒaʲutʃi na]
thanks to ...	завдяки...	[zawdʲa'ki]

what (pron.)	що	[ɕo]
that (conj.)	що	[ɕo]
something	щось	[ɕosʲ]
anything (something)	що-небудь	[ɕo 'nɛbudʲ]
nothing	нічого	[ni'tʃɔɦo]

who (pron.)	хто	[hto]
someone	хтось	[htosʲ]
somebody	хто-небудь	[hto 'nɛbudʲ]

nobody	ніхто	[nih'tɔ]
nowhere (a voyage to ~)	нікуди	['nikudi]
nobody's	нічий	[ni'tʃij]
somebody's	чий-небудь	[tʃij 'nɛbudʲ]

so (I'm ~ glad)	так	[tak]
also (as well)	також	[ta'kɔʒ]
too (as well)	теж	[tɛʒ]

15. Function words. Adverbs. Part 2

Why?	Чому?	[tʃo'mu]
for some reason	чомусь	[tʃo'musʲ]
because ...	тому, що...	['tomu, ɕo ...]
for some purpose	навіщось	[na'wiɕosʲ]

and	і	[i]
or	або	[a'bɔ]
but	але	[a'lɛ]
for (e.g., ~ me)	для	[dlʲa]

too (~ many people)	занадто	[za'nadto]
only (exclusively)	тільки	['tilʲki]
exactly (adv)	точно	['tɔtʃno]
about (more or less)	близько	['blizʲko]

approximately (adv)	приблизно	[prib'lizno]
approximate (adj)	приблизний	[prib'liznij]
almost (adv)	майже	['majʒɛ]
the rest	решта (ж)	['rɛʃta]
the other (second)	інший	['inʃij]
other (different)	інший	['inʃij]

each (adj)	кожен	['kɔʒɛn]
any (no matter which)	будь-який	[budʲ ja'kij]
many (adj)	багато	[ba'ɦato]
much (adv)	багато	[ba'ɦato]
many, much (a lot of)	багато	[ba'ɦato]
many people	багато хто	[ba'ɦato hto]
all (everyone)	всі	[wsi]

in return for …	в обмін на…	[w 'ɔbmin na]
in exchange (adv)	натомість	[na'tɔmistʲ]
by hand (e.g., made ~)	вручну	[wrutʃ'nu]
hardly (unlikely)	навряд чи	[naw'rʲad tʃi]

probably (adv)	мабуть	[ma'butʲ]
on purpose (intentionally)	навмисно	[naw'misno]
by accident (adv)	випадково	[wipad'kɔwo]

very (adv)	дуже	['duʒɛ]
for example (adv)	наприклад	[na'priklad]
between	між	[miʒ]
among	серед	['sɛrɛd]
so much (such a lot)	стільки	['stilʲki]
especially (adv)	особливо	[osob'liwo]

Basic concepts. Part 2

16. Opposites

rich (adj)	багатий	[ba'ɦatij]
poor (adj)	бідний	['bidnij]
ill, sick (adj)	хворий	['hwɔrij]
well (not sick)	здоровий	[zdo'rɔwij]
big (adj)	великий	[wɛ'likij]
small (adj)	маленький	[ma'lɛnʲkij]
quickly (adv)	швидко	['ʃwidko]
slowly (adv)	повільно	[po'wilʲno]
fast (adj)	швидкий	[ʃwid'kij]
slow (adj)	повільний	[po'wilʲnij]
glad (adj)	веселий	[wɛ'sɛlij]
sad (adj)	сумний	[sum'nij]
together (adv)	разом	['razom]
separately (adv)	окремо	[ok'rɛmo]
aloud (to read ~)	вголос	['wɦɔlos]
silently (to oneself)	про себе	[pro 'sɛbɛ]
tall (adj)	високий	[wi'sɔkij]
low (adj)	низький	[nizʲ'kij]
deep (adj)	глибокий	[ɦli'bɔkij]
shallow (adj)	мілкий	[mil'kij]
yes	так	[tak]
no	ні	[ni]
distant (in space)	далекий	[da'lɛkij]
nearby (adj)	близький	[blizʲ'kij]
far (adv)	далеко	[da'lɛko]
nearby (adv)	поруч	['pɔrutʃ]
long (adj)	довгий	['dɔwɦij]
short (adj)	короткий	[ko'rɔtkij]

| good (kindhearted) | добрий | ['dɔbrij] |
| evil (adj) | злий | ['zlij] |

| married (adj) | одружений | [od'ruʒɛnij] |
| single (adj) | холостий | [holos'tij] |

| to forbid (vt) | заборонити | [zaboro'niti] |
| to permit (vt) | дозволити | [doz'wɔliti] |

| end | кінець (ч) | [ki'nɛts] |
| beginning | початок (ч) | [po'tʃatok] |

| left (adj) | лівий | ['liwij] |
| right (adj) | правий | ['prawij] |

| first (adj) | перший | ['pɛrʃij] |
| last (adj) | останній | [os'tanij] |

| crime | злочин (ч) | ['zlɔtʃin] |
| punishment | кара (ж) | ['kara] |

| to order (vt) | наказати | [naka'zati] |
| to obey (vi, vt) | підкоритися | [pidko'ritisʲa] |

| straight (adj) | прямий | [prʲa'mij] |
| curved (adj) | кривий | [kri'wij] |

| paradise | рай (ч) | [raj] |
| hell | пекло (с) | ['pɛklo] |

| to be born | народитися | [naro'ditisʲa] |
| to die (vi) | померти | [po'mɛrti] |

| strong (adj) | сильний | ['siɫʲnij] |
| weak (adj) | слабкий | [slab'kij] |

| old (adj) | старий | [sta'rij] |
| young (adj) | молодий | [molo'dij] |

| old (adj) | старий | [sta'rij] |
| new (adj) | новий | [no'wij] |

| hard (adj) | твердий | [twɛr'dij] |
| soft (adj) | м'який | [mʲʲa'kij] |

| warm (tepid) | теплий | ['tɛplij] |
| cold (adj) | холодний | [ho'lɔdnij] |

| fat (adj) | товстий | [tows'tij] |
| thin (adj) | худий | [hu'dij] |

| narrow (adj) | вузький | [wuzʲ'kij] |

| wide (adj) | широкий | [ʃɪˈrɔkij] |

| good (adj) | добрий | [ˈdɔbrij] |
| bad (adj) | поганий | [poˈɦanij] |

| brave (adj) | хоробрий | [hoˈrɔbrij] |
| cowardly (adj) | боягузливий | [bojaˈɦuzłiwij] |

17. Weekdays

Monday	понеділок (ч)	[ponɛˈdilok]
Tuesday	вівторок (ч)	[wiwˈtɔrok]
Wednesday	середа (ж)	[sɛrɛˈda]
Thursday	четвер (ч)	[ʧɛtˈwɛr]
Friday	п'ятниця (ж)	[ˈpʲatnitsʲa]
Saturday	субота (ж)	[suˈbota]
Sunday	неділя (ж)	[nɛˈdilʲa]

today (adv)	сьогодні	[sʲoˈɦodni]
tomorrow (adv)	завтра	[ˈzawtra]
the day after tomorrow	післязавтра	[pislʲaˈzawtra]
yesterday (adv)	вчора	[ˈwʧɔra]
the day before yesterday	позавчора	[pozawˈʧɔra]

day	день (ч)	[dɛnʲ]
working day	робочий день (ч)	[roˈbɔʧij dɛnʲ]
public holiday	святковий день (ч)	[swʲatˈkɔwij dɛnʲ]
day off	вихідний день (ч)	[wihidˈnij dɛnʲ]
weekend	вихідні (мн)	[wihidˈni]
all day long	весь день	[wɛsʲ dɛnʲ]
the next day (adv)	на наступний день	[na naˈstupnij dɛnʲ]
two days ago	2 дні тому	[dwa dni ˈtɔmu]
the day before	напередодні	[napɛrɛˈdɔdni]
daily (adj)	щоденний	[ɕoˈdɛnij]
every day (adv)	щодня	[ɕodˈnʲa]

week	тиждень (ч)	[ˈtiʒdɛnʲ]
last week (adv)	на минулому тижні	[na miˈnulomu ˈtiʒni]
next week (adv)	на наступному тижні	[na naˈstupnomu ˈtiʒni]
weekly (adj)	щотижневий	[ɕotiʒˈnɛwij]
every week (adv)	щотижня	[ɕoˈtiʒnʲa]
twice a week	два рази на тиждень	[dwa ˈrazi na ˈtiʒdɛnʲ]
every Tuesday	кожен вівторок	[ˈkɔʒɛn wiwˈtɔrok]

18. Hours. Day and night

| morning | ранок (ч) | [ˈranok] |
| in the morning | вранці | [ˈwrantsi] |

noon, midday	полудень (ч)	['pɔludɛnʲ]
in the afternoon	після обіду	['pislʲa o'bidu]
evening	вечір (ч)	['wɛtʃir]
in the evening	увечері	[u'wɛtʃɛri]
night	ніч (ж)	[nitʃ]
at night	уночі	[uno'tʃi]
midnight	північ (ж)	['piwnitʃ]

second	секунда (ж)	[sɛ'kunda]
minute	хвилина (ж)	[hwi'lina]
hour	година (ж)	[ɦo'dina]
half an hour	півгодини (мн)	[piwɦo'dini]
a quarter-hour	чверть (ж) години	[tʃwɛrtʲ ɦo'dini]
fifteen minutes	15 хвилин	[pʲat'nadtsʲatʲ hwi'lin]
24 hours	доба (ж)	[do'ba]

sunrise	схід (ч) сонця	[shid 'sɔntsʲa]
dawn	світанок (ч)	[swi'tanok]
early morning	ранній ранок (ч)	['ranij 'ranok]
sunset	захід (ч)	['zahid]

early in the morning	рано вранці	['rano 'wrantsi]
this morning	сьогодні вранці	[sʲo'ɦodni 'wrantsi]
tomorrow morning	завтра вранці	['zawtra 'wrantsi]
this afternoon	сьогодні вдень	[sʲo'ɦodni wdɛnʲ]
in the afternoon	після обіду	['pislʲa o'bidu]
tomorrow afternoon	завтра після обіду	['zawtra 'pislʲa o'bidu]
tonight (this evening)	сьогодні увечері	[sʲo'ɦodni u'wɛtʃɛri]
tomorrow night	завтра увечері	['zawtra u'wɛtʃɛri]

at 3 o'clock sharp	рівно о третій годині	['riwno o t'rɛtij ɦo'dini]
about 4 o'clock	біля четвертої години	['bilʲa tʃɛt'wɛrtoji ɦo'dini]
by 12 o'clock	до дванадцятої години	[do dwa'nadtsʲatoji ɦo'dini]
in 20 minutes	за двадцять хвилин	[za 'dwadtsʲatʲ hwi'lin]
in an hour	за годину	[za ɦo'dinu]
on time (adv)	вчасно	['wtʃasno]

a quarter to …	без чверті	[bɛz 'tʃwɛrti]
within an hour	протягом години	['protʲaɦom ɦo'dini]
every 15 minutes	кожні п'ятнадцять хвилин	['kɔʒni pʲat'nadtsʲatʲ hwi'lin]
round the clock	цілодобово	[tsilodo'bɔwo]

19. Months. Seasons

January	січень (ч)	['sitʃɛnʲ]
February	лютий (ч)	['lʲutij]
March	березень (ч)	['bɛrɛzɛnʲ]
April	квітень (ч)	['kwitɛnʲ]
May	травень (ч)	['trawɛnʲ]

June	червень (ч)	['ʧɛrwɛnʲ]
July	липень (ч)	['lipɛnʲ]
August	серпень (ч)	['sɛrpɛnʲ]
September	вересень (ч)	['wɛrɛsɛnʲ]
October	жовтень (ч)	['ʒɔwtɛnʲ]
November	листопад (ч)	[lʲisto'pad]
December	грудень (ч)	['ɦrudɛnʲ]

spring	весна (ж)	[wɛs'na]
in spring	навесні	[nawɛs'nʲi]
spring (as adj)	весняний	[wɛs'nʲanʲij]

summer	літо (с)	['lʲito]
in summer	влітку	['wlʲitku]
summer (as adj)	літній	['lʲitnʲij]

fall	осінь (ж)	['ɔsʲinʲ]
in fall	восени	[wosɛ'nʲi]
fall (as adj)	осінній	[o'sʲinʲij]

winter	зима (ж)	[zʲi'ma]
in winter	взимку	['wzʲimku]
winter (as adj)	зимовий	[zʲi'mɔwij]

month	місяць (ч)	['mʲisʲaʦ]
this month	в цьому місяці	[w ʦʲomu 'mʲisʲaʦi]
next month	в наступному місяці	[w na'stupnomu 'mʲisʲaʦi]
last month	в минулому місяці	[w mʲi'nulomu 'mʲisʲaʦi]

a month ago	місяць тому	['mʲisʲaʦ 'tomu]
in a month (a month later)	через місяць	['ʧɛrɛz 'mʲisʲaʦ]
in 2 months (2 months later)	через 2 місяці	['ʧɛrɛz dwa 'mʲisʲaʦi]
the whole month	весь місяць	[wɛsʲ 'mʲisʲaʦ]
all month long	цілий місяць	['ʦʲilij 'mʲisʲaʦ]

monthly (~ magazine)	щомісячний	[ɕo'mʲisʲaʧnij]
monthly (adv)	щомісяця	[ɕo'mʲisʲaʦʲa]
every month	кожний місяць	['kɔʒnij 'mʲisʲaʦ]
twice a month	два рази на місяць	[dwa 'razi na 'mʲisʲaʦ]

year	рік (ч)	[rik]
this year	в цьому році	[w ʦʲomu 'rɔʦi]
next year	в наступному році	[w na'stupnomu 'rɔʦi]
last year	в минулому році	[w mʲi'nulomu 'rɔʦi]

a year ago	рік тому	[rik 'tomu]
in a year	через рік	['ʧɛrɛz rik]
in two years	через два роки	['ʧɛrɛz dwa 'rɔki]
the whole year	увесь рік	[u'wɛsʲ rik]
all year long	цілий рік	['ʦʲilij rik]
every year	кожен рік	['kɔʒɛn 'rik]

annual (adj)	щорічний	[ɕo'ritʃnij]
annually (adv)	щороку	[ɕo'rɔku]
4 times a year	чотири рази на рік	[tʃo'tiri 'razi na rik]

date (e.g., today's ~)	число (c)	[tʃis'lɔ]
date (e.g., ~ of birth)	дата (ж)	['data]
calendar	календар (ч)	[kalɛn'dar]

half a year	півроку	[piw'rɔku]
six months	півріччя (c)	[piw'ritʃʲa]
season (summer, etc.)	сезон (ч)	[sɛ'zɔn]
century	вік (ч)	[wik]

20. Time. Miscellaneous

time	час (c)	[tʃas]
moment	мить (ж)	[mitʲ]
instant (n)	мить (ж)	[mitʲ]
instant (adj)	миттєвий	[mit'tɛwij]
lapse (of time)	відрізок (ч)	[wid'rizok]
life	життя (c)	[ʒit'tʲa]
eternity	вічність (ж)	['witʃnistʲ]

epoch	епоха (ж)	[ɛ'pɔha]
era	ера (ж)	['ɛra]
cycle	цикл (ч)	['tsikl]
period	період (ч)	[pɛ'riod]
term (short-~)	термін (ч)	['tɛrmin]

the future	майбутнє (c)	[maj'butnɛ]
future (as adj)	майбутній	[maj'butnij]
next time	наступного разу	[na'stupnoɦo 'razu]
the past	минуле (c)	[mi'nulɛ]
past (recent)	минулий	[mi'nulij]
last time	минулого разу	[mi'nuloɦo 'razu]

later (adv)	пізніше	[piz'niʃɛ]
after (prep.)	після	['pislʲa]
nowadays (adv)	сьогодення	[sʲoɦo'dɛnʲa]
now (at this moment)	зараз	['zaraz]
immediately (adv)	негайно	[nɛ'ɦajno]
soon (adv)	незабаром	[nɛza'barom]
in advance (beforehand)	завчасно	[zaw'tʃasno]

a long time ago	давно	[daw'nɔ]
recently (adv)	нещодавно	[nɛɕo'dawno]
destiny	доля (ж)	['dɔlʲa]
memories (childhood ~)	пам'ять (ж)	['pamʲatʲ]
archives	архів (ч)	[ar'hiw]
during ...	під час	[pid 'tʃas]

long, a long time (adv)	довго	['dɔwɦo]
not long (adv)	недовго	[nɛ'dɔwɦo]
early (in the morning)	рано	['rano]
late (not early)	пізно	['pizno]

forever (for good)	назавжди	[na'zawʒdi]
to start (begin)	починати	[potʃi'nati]
to postpone (vt)	перенести	[pɛrɛ'nɛsti]

at the same time	одночасно	[odno'tʃasno]
permanently (adv)	постійно	[pos'tijno]
constant (noise, pain)	постійний	[pos'tijnij]
temporary (adj)	тимчасовий	[timtʃa'sɔwij]

sometimes (adv)	інколи	['inkoli]
rarely (adv)	рідко	['ridko]
often (adv)	часто	['tʃasto]

21. Lines and shapes

square	квадрат (ч)	[kwad'rat]
square (as adj)	квадратний	[kwad'ratnij]
circle	коло (с)	['kɔlo]
round (adj)	круглий	['kruɦlij]
triangle	трикутник (ч)	[tri'kutnik]
triangular (adj)	трикутний	[tri'kutnij]

oval	овал (ч)	[o'wal]
oval (as adj)	овальний	[o'walʲnij]
rectangle	прямокутник (ч)	[prʲamo'kutnik]
rectangular (adj)	прямокутний	[prʲamo'kutnij]

pyramid	піраміда (ж)	[pira'mida]
rhombus	ромб (ч)	[romb]
trapezoid	трапеція (ж)	[tra'pɛtsiʲa]
cube	куб (ч)	[kub]
prism	призма (ж)	['prizma]

circumference	коло (с)	['kɔlo]
sphere	сфера (ж)	['sfɛra]
ball (solid sphere)	куля (ж)	['kulʲa]
diameter	діаметр (ч)	[di'amɛtr]
radius	радіус (ч)	['radius]
perimeter (circle's ~)	периметр (ч)	[pɛ'rimɛtr]
center	центр (ч)	[tsɛntr]

horizontal (adj)	горизонтальний	[ɦorizon'talʲnij]
vertical (adj)	вертикальний	[wɛrti'kalʲnij]
parallel (n)	паралель (ж)	[para'lɛlʲ]
parallel (as adj)	паралельний	[para'lɛlʲnij]

line	лінія (ж)	['liniʲa]
stroke	риса (ж)	['risa]
straight line	пряма лінія (ж)	[prʲa'ma 'liniʲa]
curve (curved line)	крива лінія (ж)	[kri'wa 'liniʲa]
thin (line, etc.)	тонкий	[ton'kij]
contour (outline)	контур (ч)	['kɔntur]

intersection	перетин (ч)	[pɛ'rɛtin]
right angle	прямий кут (ч)	[prʲa'mij kut]
segment	сегмент (ч)	[sɛɦ'mɛnt]
sector (circular ~)	сектор (ч)	['sɛktor]
side (of a triangle, etc.)	бік (ч)	[bik]
angle	кут (ч)	[kut]

22. Units of measurement

weight	вага (ж)	[wa'ɦa]
length	довжина (ж)	[dowʒi'na]
width	ширина (ж)	[ʃiri'na]
height	висота (ж)	[wiso'ta]
depth	глибина (ж)	[ɦlibi'na]
volume	об'єм (ч)	[o'bʲɛm]
area	площа (ж)	['plɔça]

gram	грам (ч)	[ɦram]
milligram	міліграм (ч)	[mili'ɦram]
kilogram	кілограм (ч)	[kilo'ɦram]
ton	тонна (ж)	['tɔna]
pound	фунт (ч)	['funt]
ounce	унція (ж)	['untsiʲa]

meter	метр (ч)	[mɛtr]
millimeter	міліметр (ч)	[mili'mɛtr]
centimeter	сантиметр (ч)	[santi'mɛtr]
kilometer	кілометр (ч)	[kilo'mɛtr]
mile	миля (ж)	['milʲa]

inch	дюйм (ч)	[dʲujm]
foot	фут (ч)	[fut]
yard	ярд (ч)	[jard]

square meter	квадратний метр (ч)	[kwad'ratnij mɛtr]
hectare	гектар (ч)	[ɦɛk'tar]

liter	літр (ч)	[litr]
degree	градус (ч)	['ɦradus]
volt	вольт (ч)	[wolʲt]
ampere	ампер (ч)	[am'pɛr]
horsepower	кінська сила (ж)	['kinsʲka 'sila]
quantity	кількість (ж)	['kilʲkistʲ]

a little bit of …	небагато… (ж)	[nɛba'ɦato]
half	половина (ж)	[polo'wina]
dozen	дюжина (ж)	['dʲuʒina]
piece (item)	штука (ж)	['ʃtuka]

| size | розмір (ч) | ['rɔzmir] |
| scale (map ~) | масштаб (ч) | [masʃ'tab] |

minimal (adj)	мінімальний	[mini'malʲnij]
the smallest (adj)	найменший	[naj'mɛnʃij]
medium (adj)	середній	[sɛ'rɛdnij]
maximal (adj)	максимальний	[maksi'malʲnij]
the largest (adj)	найбільший	[naj'bilʲʃij]

23. Containers

canning jar (glass ~)	банка (ж)	['banka]
can	банка (ж)	['banka]
bucket	відро (с)	[wid'rɔ]
barrel	бочка (ж)	['bɔtʃka]

wash basin (e.g., plastic ~)	таз (ч)	[taz]
tank (receptacle)	бак (ч)	[bak]
hip flask	фляжка (ж)	['flʲaʒka]
jerrycan	каністра (ж)	[ka'nistra]
tank (e.g., tank car)	цистерна (ж)	[tsis'tɛrna]

mug	кухоль (ч)	['kuholʲ]
cup (of coffee, etc.)	чашка (ж)	['tʃaʃka]
saucer	блюдце (с)	['blʲudtsɛ]
glass (tumbler)	склянка (ж)	['sklʲanka]
wine glass	келих (ч)	['kɛlih]
stock pot (deep crock)	каструля (ж)	[kas'trulʲa]

| bottle (~ of wine) | пляшка (ж) | ['plʲaʃka] |
| neck (of a bottle, etc.) | горлечко | ['ɦɔrlɛtʃko] |

carafe (decanter)	карафа (ж)	[ka'rafa]
pitcher	глечик (ч)	['ɦlɛtʃik]
vessel (container)	посудина (ж)	[po'sudina]
pot (crock, stoneware ~)	горщик (ч)	['ɦɔrɕik]
vase	ваза (ж)	['waza]

flacon, bottle (perfume ~)	флакон (ч)	[fla'kɔn]
vial, small bottle	пляшечка (ж)	['plʲaʃɛtʃka]
tube (of toothpaste)	тюбик (ч)	['tʲubik]

sack (bag)	мішок (ч)	[mi'ʃɔk]
bag (paper ~, plastic ~)	пакет (ч)	[pa'kɛt]
pack (of cigarettes, etc.)	пачка (ж)	['patʃka]

box (e.g., shoebox)	коробка (ж)	[ko'rɔbka]
crate	ящик (ч)	['jaçik]
basket	кошик (ч)	['kɔʃik]

24. Materials

material	матеріал (ч)	[matɛri'al]
wood (n)	дерево (с)	['dɛrɛwo]
wood-, wooden (adj)	дерев'яний	[dɛrɛ'w'janij]

| glass (n) | скло (с) | ['sklo] |
| glass (as adj) | скляний | [sklʲa'nij] |

| stone (n) | камінь (ч) | ['kaminʲ] |
| stone (as adj) | кам'яний | [kam'ʲa'nij] |

| plastic (n) | пластмаса (ж) | [plast'masa] |
| plastic (as adj) | пластмасовий | [plast'masowij] |

| rubber (n) | гума (ж) | ['ɦuma] |
| rubber (as adj) | гумовий | ['ɦumowij] |

| cloth, fabric (n) | тканина (ж) | [tka'nina] |
| fabric (as adj) | з тканини | [z tka'nini] |

| paper (n) | папір (ч) | [pa'pir] |
| paper (as adj) | паперовий | [papɛ'rɔwij] |

| cardboard (n) | картон (ч) | [kar'tɔn] |
| cardboard (as adj) | картонний | [kar'tɔnij] |

polyethylene	поліетилен (ч)	[poliɛti'lɛn]
cellophane	целофан (ч)	[ʦɛlo'fan]
linoleum	лінолеум (ч)	[li'nɔlɛum]
plywood	фанера (ж)	[fa'nɛra]

porcelain (n)	фарфор (ч)	['farfor]
porcelain (as adj)	порцеляновий	[porʦɛ'lʲanowij]
clay (n)	глина (ж)	['ɦlina]
clay (as adj)	глиняний	['ɦlinʲanij]
ceramic (n)	кераміка (ж)	[kɛ'ramika]
ceramic (as adj)	керамічний	[kɛra'miʧnij]

25. Metals

metal (n)	метал (ч)	[mɛ'tal]
metal (as adj)	металевий	[mɛta'lɛwij]
alloy (n)	сплав (ч)	[splaw]

gold (n)	золото (с)	['zɔloto]
gold, golden (adj)	золотий	[zolo'tij]
silver (n)	срібло (с)	['sriblo]
silver (as adj)	срібний	['sribnij]

iron (n)	залізо (с)	[za'lizo]
iron-, made of iron (adj)	залізний	[za'liznij]
steel (n)	сталь (ж)	[stalʲ]
steel (as adj)	сталевий	[sta'lɛwij]
copper (n)	мідь (ж)	[midʲ]
copper (as adj)	мідний	['midnij]

aluminum (n)	алюміній (ч)	[alʲu'minij]
aluminum (as adj)	алюмінієвий	[alʲu'miniɛwij]
bronze (n)	бронза (ж)	['brɔnza]
bronze (as adj)	бронзовий	['brɔnzowij]

brass	латунь (ж)	[la'tunʲ]
nickel	нікель (ч)	['nikɛlʲ]
platinum	платина (ж)	['platina]
mercury	ртуть (ж)	[rtutʲ]
tin	олово (с)	['ɔlowo]
lead	свинець (ч)	[swi'nɛts]
zinc	цинк (ч)	['tsink]

HUMAN BEING

Human being. The body

human being	людина (ж)	[lʲu'dina]
man (adult male)	чоловік (ч)	[tʃolo'wik]
woman	жінка (ж)	['ʒinka]
child	дитина (ж)	[di'tina]
girl	дівчинка (ж)	['diwtʃinka]
boy	хлопчик (ч)	['hlɔptʃik]
teenager	підліток (ч)	['pidlitok]
old man	старий (ч)	[sta'rij]
old woman	стара жінка (ж)	[sta'ra 'ʒinka]

organism (body)	організм (ч)	[orɦa'nizm]
heart	серце (с)	['sɛrtsɛ]
blood	кров (ж)	[krow]
artery	артерія (ж)	[ar'tɛriʲa]
vein	вена (ж)	['wɛna]
brain	мозок (ч)	['mɔzok]
nerve	нерв (ч)	[nɛrw]
nerves	нерви (мн)	['nɛrwi]
vertebra	хребець (ч)	[hrɛ'bɛts]
spine (backbone)	хребет (ч)	[hrɛ'bɛt]
stomach (organ)	шлунок (ч)	['ʃlunok]
intestines, bowels	кишечник (ч)	[ki'ʃɛtʃnik]
intestine (e.g., large ~)	кишка (ж)	['kiʃka]
liver	печінка (ж)	[pɛ'tʃinka]
kidney	нирка (ж)	['nirka]
bone	кістка (ж)	['kistka]
skeleton	скелет (ч)	[skɛ'lɛt]
rib	ребро (с)	[rɛb'rɔ]
skull	череп (ч)	['tʃɛrɛp]
muscle	м'яз (ч)	['mʲʲaz]
biceps	біцепс (ч)	['bitsɛps]

triceps	трицепс (ч)	['triˠsɛps]
tendon	сухожилля (с)	[suho'ʒilʲa]
joint	суглоб (ч)	[suɦ'lɔb]
lungs	легені (мн)	[lɛ'ɦɛni]
genitals	статеві органи (мн)	[sta'tɛwi 'ɔrɦani]
skin	шкіра (ж)	['ʃkira]

28. Head

head	голова (ж)	[ɦolo'wa]
face	обличчя (с)	[ob'litʃʲa]
nose	ніс (ч)	[nis]
mouth	рот (ч)	[rot]

eye	око (с)	['ɔko]
eyes	очі (мн)	['ɔtʃi]
pupil	зіниця (ж)	[zi'nitsʲa]
eyebrow	брова (ж)	[bro'wa]
eyelash	вія (ж)	['wiʲa]
eyelid	повіка (ж)	[po'wika]

tongue	язик (ч)	[ja'zik]
tooth	зуб (ч)	[zub]
lips	губи (мн)	['ɦubi]
cheekbones	вилиці (мн)	['wilitsi]
gum	ясна (мн)	['ʲasna]
palate	піднебіння (с)	[pidnɛ'binʲa]

nostrils	ніздрі (мн)	['nizdri]
chin	підборіддя (с)	[pidbo'riddʲa]
jaw	щелепа (ж)	[ɕɛ'lɛpa]
cheek	щока (ж)	[ɕo'ka]

forehead	чоло (с)	[tʃo'lɔ]
temple	скроня (ж)	['skrɔnʲa]
ear	вухо (с)	['wuɦo]
back of the head	потилиця (ж)	[po'tilitsʲa]
neck	шия (ж)	['ʃʲa]
throat	горло (с)	['ɦɔrlo]

hair	волосся (с)	[wo'lɔssʲa]
hairstyle	зачіска (ж)	['zatʃiska]
haircut	стрижка (ж)	['striʒka]
wig	парик (ч)	[pa'rik]

mustache	вуса (мн)	['wusa]
beard	борода (ж)	[boro'da]
to have (a beard, etc.)	носити	[no'siti]
braid	коса (ж)	[ko'sa]
sideburns	бакенбарди (мн)	[bakɛn'bardi]

red-haired (adj)	рудий	[ru'dij]
gray (hair)	сивий	['siwij]
bald (adj)	лисий	['lisij]
bald patch	лисина (ж)	['lisina]

| ponytail | хвіст (ч) | [hwist] |
| bangs | чубчик (ч) | ['tʃubtʃik] |

29. Human body

hand	кисть (ж)	[kistʲ]
arm	рука (ж)	[ru'ka]
finger	палець (ч)	['palɛts]
toe	палець	['palɛtsʲ]
thumb	великий палець (ч)	[wɛ'likij 'palɛts]
little finger	мізинець (ч)	[mi'zinɛts]
nail	ніготь (ч)	['niɦotʲ]

fist	кулак (ч)	[ku'lak]
palm	долоня (ж)	[do'lɔnʲa]
wrist	зап'ясток (ч)	[za'pʲʲastok]
forearm	передпліччя (с)	[pɛrɛdp'litʃʲa]
elbow	лікоть (ч)	['likotʲ]
shoulder	плече (с)	[plɛ'tʃɛ]

leg	гомілка (ж)	[ɦo'milka]
foot	ступня (ж)	[stup'nʲa]
knee	коліно (с)	[ko'lino]
calf	литка (ж)	['litka]
hip	стегно (с)	[stɛɦ'nɔ]
heel	п'ятка (ж)	['pʲʲatka]

body	тіло (с)	['tilo]
stomach	живіт (ч)	[ʒi'wit]
chest	груди (мн)	['ɦrudi]
breast	груди (мн)	['ɦrudi]
flank	бік (ч)	[bik]
back	спина (ж)	['spina]
lower back	поперек (ч)	[popɛ'rɛk]
waist	талія (ж)	['taliʲa]

navel (belly button)	пупок (ч)	[pu'pɔk]
buttocks	сідниці (мн)	[sid'nitsi]
bottom, behind	зад (ч)	[zad]

beauty mark	родимка (ж)	['rɔdimka]
birthmark (café au lait spot, mole)	родима пляма (ж)	[ro'dima 'plʲama]
tattoo	татуювання (с)	[tatuʲu'wanʲa]
scar	рубець (ч)	[ru'bɛts]

Clothing & Accessories

30. Outerwear. Coats

clothes	одяг (ч)	['ɔdʲaɦ]
outerwear	верхній одяг (ч)	['wɛrhnij 'ɔdʲaɦ]
winter clothing	зимовий одяг (ч)	[zi'mɔwij 'ɔdʲaɦ]

coat (overcoat)	пальто (с)	[palʲ'tɔ]
fur coat	шуба (ж)	['ʃuba]
fur jacket	кожушок (ч)	[kɔʒu'ʃɔk]
down coat	пуховик (ч)	[puho'wik]

jacket (e.g., leather ~)	куртка (ж)	['kurtka]
raincoat (trenchcoat, etc.)	плащ (ч)	[plaɕ]
waterproof (adj)	непромокальний	[nɛpromo'kalʲnij]

31. Men's & women's clothing

shirt (button shirt)	сорочка (ж)	[so'rɔʧka]
pants	штани (мн)	[ʃta'ni]
jeans	джинси (мн)	['dʒinsi]
suit jacket	піджак (ч)	[pi'dʒak]
suit	костюм (ч)	[kos'tʲum]

dress (frock)	сукня (ж)	['suknʲa]
skirt	спідниця (ж)	[spid'nitsʲa]
blouse	блузка (ж)	['bluzka]
knitted jacket (cardigan, etc.)	кофта (ж)	['kɔfta]
jacket (top part of a suit)	жакет (ч)	[ʒa'kɛt]

T-shirt	футболка (ж)	[fut'bɔlka]
shorts	шорти (мн)	['ʃɔrti]
tracksuit	спортивний костюм (ч)	[spor'tiwnij kos'tʲum]
bathrobe	халат (ч)	[ha'lat]
pajamas	піжама (ж)	[pi'ʒama]

| sweater | светр (ч) | [swɛtr] |
| pullover | пуловер (ч) | [pulo'wɛr] |

vest	жилет (ч)	[ʒi'lɛt]
tailcoat	фрак (ч)	[frak]
tuxedo	смокінг (ч)	['smɔkinɦ]

uniform	форма (ж)	['fɔrma]
workwear	робочий одяг (ч)	[ro'bɔtʃij 'ɔdʲaɦ]
overalls	комбінезон (ч)	[kombinɛ'zɔn]
coat (e.g., doctor's smock)	халат (ч)	[ha'lat]

32. Clothing. Underwear

underwear	білизна (ж)	[bi'lizna]
boxers, briefs	труси (мн)	[tru'si]
panties	жіноча білизна	[ʒi'nɔtʃa biliz'na]
undershirt (A-shirt)	майка (ж)	['majka]
socks	шкарпетки (мн)	[ʃkar'pɛtki]
nightdress	нічна сорочка (ж)	[nitʃ'na so'rɔtʃka]
bra	бюстгальтер (ч)	[bʲust'ɦalʲtɛr]
knee highs (knee-high socks)	гольфи (мн)	['ɦɔlʲfi]
pantyhose	колготки (мн)	[kol'ɦɔtki]
stockings (hosiery)	панчохи (мн)	[pan'tʃɔhi]
bathing suit	купальник (ч)	[ku'palʲnik]

33. Headwear

hat	шапка (ж)	['ʃapka]
fedora	капелюх (ч)	[kapɛ'lʲuh]
baseball cap	бейсболка (ж)	[bɛjs'bɔlka]
flatcap	кашкет (ч)	[kaʃ'kɛt]
beret	берет (ч)	[bɛ'rɛt]
hood	каптур (ч)	[kap'tur]
panama hat	панамка (ж)	[pa'namka]
knit cap (knitted hat)	в'язана шапочка (ж)	['wʲazana 'ʃapotʃka]
headscarf	хустка (ж)	['hustka]
women's hat	капелюшок (ч)	[kapɛ'lʲuʃok]
hard hat	каска (ж)	['kaska]
garrison cap	пілотка (ж)	[pi'lɔtka]
helmet	шолом (ч)	[ʃo'lɔm]
derby	котелок (ч)	[kotɛ'lɔk]
top hat	циліндр (ч)	[tsi'lindr]

34. Footwear

footwear	взуття (с)	[wzut'tʲa]
shoes (men's shoes)	черевики (мн)	[tʃɛrɛ'wiki]

shoes (women's shoes)	туфлі (мн)	['tufli]
boots (e.g., cowboy ~)	чоботи (мн)	['tʃɔboti]
slippers	капці (мн)	['kaptsi]
tennis shoes (e.g., Nike ~)	кросівки (мн)	[kro'siwki]
sneakers (e.g., Converse ~)	кеди (мн)	['kɛdi]
sandals	сандалі (мн)	[san'dali]
cobbler (shoe repairer)	чоботар (ч)	[tʃobo'tar]
heel	каблук (ч)	[kab'luk]
pair (of shoes, etc.)	пара (ж)	['para]
shoestring	шнурок (ч)	[ʃnu'rɔk]
to lace (vt)	шнурувати	[ʃnuru'wati]
shoehorn	ріжок (ч) для взуття	[ri'ʒɔk dlʲa wzu'tʲa]
shoe polish	крем (ч) для взуття	[krɛm dlʲa wzut'tʲa]

35. Textile. Fabrics

cotton (n)	бавовна (ж)	[ba'wɔwna]
cotton (as adj)	з бавовни	[z ba'wɔwni]
flax (n)	льон (ч)	[lʲon]
flax (as adj)	з льону	[z lʲonu]
silk (n)	шовк (ч)	['ʃɔwk]
silk (as adj)	шовковий	[ʃow'kɔwij]
wool (n)	вовна (ж)	['wɔwna]
wool (as adj)	вовняний	['wɔwnʲanij]
velvet	оксамит (ч)	[oksa'mit]
suede	замша (ж)	['zamʃa]
corduroy	вельвет (ч)	[wɛlʲ'wɛt]
nylon (n)	нейлон (ч)	[nɛj'lɔn]
nylon (as adj)	з нейлону	[z nɛj'lɔnu]
polyester (n)	поліестер (ч)	[poli'ɛstɛr]
polyester (as adj)	поліестровий	[poli'ɛstrowij]
leather (n)	шкіра (ж)	['ʃkira]
leather (as adj)	зі шкіри	[zi 'ʃkiri]
fur (n)	хутро (с)	['hutro]
fur (as adj)	хутряний	[hu'trʲanij]

36. Personal accessories

gloves	рукавички (мн)	[ruka'witʃki]
mittens	рукавиці (мн)	[ruka'witsi]

scarf (muffler)	шарф (ч)	[ʃarf]
glasses (eyeglasses)	окуляри (мн)	[okuˈlʲari]
frame (eyeglass ~)	оправа (ж)	[opˈrawa]
umbrella	парасолька (ж)	[paraˈsɔlʲka]
walking stick	ціпок (ч)	[tsiˈpɔk]
hairbrush	щітка (ж) для волосся	[ˈɕitka dlʲa woˈlɔssʲa]
fan	віяло (с)	[ˈwiʲalo]
tie (necktie)	краватка (ж)	[kraˈwatka]
bow tie	краватка-метелик (ж)	[kraˈwatka mɛˈtɛlik]
suspenders	підтяжки (мн)	[pidˈtʲaʒki]
handkerchief	носовичок (ч)	[nosowiˈtʃɔk]
comb	гребінець (ч)	[ɦrɛbiˈnɛts]
barrette	заколка (ж)	[zaˈkɔlka]
hairpin	шпилька (ж)	[ˈʃpilʲka]
buckle	пряжка (ж)	[ˈprʲaʒka]
belt	ремінь (ч)	[ˈrɛminʲ]
shoulder strap	ремінь (ч)	[ˈrɛminʲ]
bag (handbag)	сумка (ж)	[ˈsumka]
purse	сумочка (ж)	[ˈsumotʃka]
backpack	рюкзак (ч)	[rʲukˈzak]

37. Clothing. Miscellaneous

fashion	мода (ж)	[ˈmɔda]
in vogue (adj)	модний	[ˈmɔdnij]
fashion designer	модельєр (ч)	[modɛˈljɛr]
collar	комір (ч)	[ˈkɔmir]
pocket	кишеня (ж)	[kiˈʃɛnʲa]
pocket (as adj)	кишеньковий	[kiʃɛnʲˈkɔwij]
sleeve	рукав (ч)	[ruˈkaw]
hanging loop	петля (ж)	[pɛtˈlʲa]
fly (zippered opening on trousers)	ширинка (ж)	[ʃiˈrinka]
zipper (fastener)	блискавка (ж)	[ˈbliskawka]
fastener	застібка (ж)	[ˈzastibka]
button	ґудзик (ч)	[ˈgudzik]
buttonhole	петля (ж)	[pɛtˈlʲa]
to come off (button; to fell off)	відірватися	[widirˈwatisʲa]
to sew (vi, vt)	шити	[ˈʃiti]
to embroider (vi, vt)	вишивати	[wiʃiˈwati]
embroidery	вишивка (ж)	[ˈwiʃiwka]
sewing needle	голка (ж)	[ˈɦɔlka]

| thread | нитка (ж) | ['nitka] |
| seam | шов (ч) | [ʃow] |

to get dirty (vi)	забруднитися	[zabrud'nitisʲa]
stain (mark, spot)	пляма (ж)	['plʲama]
to crease, to crumple	зім'ятися	[zi'mʲʲatisʲa]
to tear, to rip (vt)	порвати	[por'wati]
clothes moth	міль (ж)	[milʲ]

38. Personal care. Cosmetics

toothpaste	зубна паста (ж)	[zub'na 'pasta]
toothbrush	зубна щітка (ж)	[zub'na 'ɕitka]
to brush one's teeth	чистити зуби	['ʧistiti 'zubi]

razor	бритва (ж)	['britwa]
shaving cream	крем (ч) для гоління	[krɛm dlʲa ɦo'linʲa]
to shave (vi)	голитися	[ɦo'litisʲa]

| soap | мило (с) | ['milo] |
| shampoo | шампунь (ч) | [ʃam'punʲ] |

scissors	ножиці (мн)	['nɔʒiʦi]
nail file	пилочка (ж) для нігтів	['piloʧka dlʲa 'niɦtiw]
nail clippers	щипчики (мн)	['ɕipʧiki]
tweezers	пінцет (ч)	[pin'ʦɛt]

cosmetics	косметика (ж)	[kos'mɛtika]
face mask	маска (ж)	['maska]
manicure	манікюр (ч)	[mani'kʲur]
to have a manicure	робити манікюр	[ro'biti mani'kʲur]
pedicure	педикюр (ч)	[pɛdi'kʲur]

make-up bag	косметичка (ж)	[kosmɛ'tiʧka]
face powder	пудра (ж)	['pudra]
powder compact	пудрениця (ж)	['pudrɛniʦʲa]
blusher	рум'яна (мн)	[ru'mʲʲana]

perfume (bottled, spray)	парфуми (мн)	[par'fumi]
toilet water (lotion)	туалетна вода (ж)	[tua'lɛtna wo'da]
lotion	лосьйон (ч)	[lo'sjɔn]
cologne	одеколон (ч)	[odɛko'lɔn]

eyeshadow	тіні (мн) для повік	['tini dlʲa po'wik]
eyeliner	олівець (ч) для очей	[oli'wɛʦ dlʲa o'ʧɛj]
mascara	туш (ж)	[tuʃ]

lipstick	губна помада (ж)	[ɦub'na po'mada]
nail polish, enamel	лак (ч) для нігтів	[lak dlʲa 'niɦtiw]
hair spray	лак (ч) для волосся	[lak dlʲa wo'lɔssʲa]

deodorant	дезодорант (ч)	[dɛzodo'rant]
cream	крем (ч)	[krɛm]
face cream	крем (ч) для обличчя	[krɛm dlʲa ob'litʃʲa]
hand cream	крем (ч) для рук	[krɛm dlʲa ruk]
anti-wrinkle cream	крем (ч) проти зморшок	[krɛm 'proti 'zmorʃok]
day cream	денний крем (ч)	['dɛnnij krɛm]
night cream	нічний крем (ч)	[nitʃ'nij krɛm]
day (as adj)	денний	['dɛnij]
night (as adj)	нічний	[nitʃ'nij]
tampon	тампон (ч)	[tam'pɔn]
toilet paper (toilet roll)	туалетний папір (ч)	[tua'lɛtnij pa'pir]
hair dryer	фен (ч)	[fɛn]

39. Jewelry

jewelry, jewels	коштовність (ж)	[koʃ'tɔwnistʲ]
precious (e.g., ~ stone)	коштовний	[koʃ'tɔwnij]
hallmark stamp	проба (ж)	['prɔba]
ring	каблучка (ж)	[kab'luʧka]
wedding ring	обручка (ж)	[ob'ruʧka]
bracelet	браслет (ч)	[bras'lɛt]
earrings	сережки (мн)	[sɛ'rɛʒki]
necklace (~ of pearls)	намисто (с)	[na'misto]
crown	корона (ж)	[ko'rona]
bead necklace	намисто (с)	[na'misto]
diamond	діамант (ч)	[dia'mant]
emerald	смарагд (ч)	[sma'raɦd]
ruby	рубін (ч)	[ru'bin]
sapphire	сапфір (ч)	[sap'fir]
pearl	перли (мн)	['pɛrli]
amber	бурштин (ч)	[burʃ'tin]

40. Watches. Clocks

watch (wristwatch)	годинник (ч)	[ɦo'dinik]
dial	циферблат (ч)	[ʦifɛrb'lat]
hand (clock, watch)	стрілка (ж)	['strilka]
metal watch band	браслет (ч)	[bras'lɛt]
watch strap	ремінець (ч)	[rɛmi'nɛʦ]
battery	батарейка (ж)	[bata'rɛjka]
to be dead (battery)	сісти	['sisti]
to change a battery	поміняти батарейку	[pomi'nʲati bata'rɛjku]
to run fast	поспішати	[pospi'ʃati]

to run slow	відставати	[widsta'wati]
wall clock	годинник (ч) настінний	[ɦo'dinik nas'tinij]
hourglass	годинник (ч) пісочний	[ɦo'dinik pi'sɔtʃnij]
sundial	годинник (ч) сонячний	[ɦo'dinik 'sɔnʲatʃnij]
alarm clock	будильник (ч)	[bu'dilʲnik]
watchmaker	годинникар (ч)	[ɦodini'kar]
to repair (vt)	ремонтувати	[rɛmontu'wati]

Food. Nutricion

meat	м'ясо (с)	['m'jaso]
chicken	курка (ж)	['kurka]
broiler (young chicken)	курча (с)	[kur'tʃa]
duck	качка (ж)	['katʃka]
goose	гусак (ч)	[ɦu'sak]
game	дичина (ж)	[ditʃi'na]
turkey	індичка (ж)	[in'ditʃka]
pork	свинина (ж)	[swi'nina]
veal	телятина (ж)	[tɛ'l'atina]
lamb	баранина (ж)	[ba'ranina]
beef	яловичина (ж)	['jalowitʃina]
rabbit	кріль (ч)	[kril']
sausage (bologna, etc.)	ковбаса (ж)	[kowba'sa]
vienna sausage (frankfurter)	сосиска (ж)	[so'siska]
bacon	бекон (ч)	[bɛ'kɔn]
ham	шинка (ж)	['ʃinka]
gammon	окіст (ч)	['ɔkist]
pâté	паштет (ч)	[paʃ'tɛt]
liver	печінка (ж)	[pɛ'tʃinka]
ground meat	фарш (ч)	[farʃ]
tongue	язик (ч)	[ja'zik]
egg	яйце (с)	[jaj'tsɛ]
eggs	яйця (мн)	['jajts'a]
egg white	білок (ч)	[bi'lɔk]
egg yolk	жовток (ч)	[ʒow'tɔk]
fish	риба (ж)	['riba]
seafood	морепродукти (мн)	[morɛpro'dukti]
crustaceans	ракоподібні (мн)	[rakopo'dibni]
caviar	ікра (ж)	[ik'ra]
crab	краб (ч)	[krab]
shrimp	креветка (ж)	[krɛ'wɛtka]
oyster	устриця (ж)	['ustrits'a]
spiny lobster	лангуст (ч)	[lan'ɦust]
octopus	восьминіг (ч)	[wos'mi'niɦ]
squid	кальмар (ч)	[kal'j'mar]

sturgeon	осетрина (ж)	[osɛt'rina]
salmon	лосось (ч)	[lo'sɔsʲ]
halibut	палтус (ч)	['paltus]
cod	тріска (ж)	[tris'ka]
mackerel	скумбрія (ж)	['skumbriʲa]
tuna	тунець (ч)	[tu'nɛts]
eel	вугор (ч)	[wu'ɦɔr]
trout	форель (ж)	[fo'rɛlʲ]
sardine	сардина (ж)	[sar'dina]
pike	щука (ж)	['ɕuka]
herring	оселедець (ч)	[osɛ'lɛdɛts]
bread	хліб (ч)	[hlib]
cheese	сир (ч)	[sir]
sugar	цукор (ч)	['tsukor]
salt	сіль (ж)	[silʲ]
rice	рис (ч)	[ris]
pasta (macaroni, spaghetti, etc.)	макарони (мн)	[maka'rɔni]
noodles	локшина (ж)	[lokʃi'na]
butter	вершкове масло (с)	[wɛrʃ'kɔwɛ 'maslo]
vegetable oil	олія (ж) рослинна	[o'liʲa ros'lina]
sunflower oil	соняшникова олія (ж)	['sɔnʲaʃnikowa o'liʲa]
margarine	маргарин (ч)	[marɦa'rin]
olives	оливки (мн)	[o'liwki]
olive oil	олія (ж) оливкова	[o'liʲa o'liwkowa]
milk	молоко (с)	[molo'kɔ]
condensed milk	згущене молоко (с)	['zɦuɕɛnɛ molo'kɔ]
yogurt	йогурт (ч)	['jɔɦurt]
sour cream	сметана (ж)	[smɛ'tana]
cream (dairy product)	вершки (мн)	[wɛrʃ'ki]
mayonnaise	майонез (ч)	[maʲo'nɛz]
buttercream	крем (ч)	[krɛm]
groats (barley ~, etc.)	крупа (ж)	[kru'pa]
flour	борошно (с)	['bɔroʃno]
canned food	консерви (мн)	[kon'sɛrwi]
cornflakes	кукурудзяні пластівці (мн)	[kuku'rudzʲani plastiw'tsi]
honey	мед (ч)	[mɛd]
jam	джем (ч)	[dʒɛm]
chewing gum	жувальна гумка (ж)	[ʒu'walʲna 'ɦumka]

42. Drinks

water	вода (ж)	[wo'da]
drinking water	питна вода (ж)	[pit'na wo'da]
mineral water	мінеральна вода (ж)	[minɛ'ralʲna wo'da]
still (adj)	без газу	[bɛz 'ɦazu]
carbonated (adj)	газований	[ɦa'zɔwanij]
sparkling (adj)	з газом	[z 'ɦazom]
ice	лід (ч), крига (ж)	[lid], ['kriɦa]
with ice	з льодом	[z lʲodom]
non-alcoholic (adj)	безалкогольний	[bɛzalko'ɦɔlʲnij]
soft drink	безалкогольний напій (ч)	[bɛzalko'ɦɔlʲnij na'pij]
refreshing drink	прохолодний напій (ч)	[proho'lɔdnij 'napij]
lemonade	лимонад (ч)	[limo'nad]
liquors	алкогольні напої (мн)	[alko'ɦɔlʲni na'pɔji]
wine	вино (с)	[wi'nɔ]
white wine	біле вино (с)	['bilɛ wi'nɔ]
red wine	червоне вино (с)	[ʧɛr'wɔnɛ wi'nɔ]
liqueur	лікер (ч)	[li'kɛr]
champagne	шампанське (с)	[ʃam'pansʲkɛ]
vermouth	вермут (ч)	['wɛrmut]
whiskey	віскі (с)	['wiski]
vodka	горілка (ж)	[ɦo'rilka]
gin	джин (ч)	[ʤin]
cognac	коньяк (ч)	[ko'nʲak]
rum	ром (ч)	[rom]
coffee	кава (ж)	['kawa]
black coffee	чорна кава (ж)	['ʧɔrna 'kawa]
coffee with milk	кава (ж) з молоком	['kawa z molo'kɔm]
cappuccino	капучино (с)	[kapu'ʧino]
instant coffee	розчинна кава (ж)	[roz'ʧina 'kawa]
milk	молоко (с)	[molo'kɔ]
cocktail	коктейль (ч)	[kok'tɛjlʲ]
milkshake	молочний коктейль (ч)	[mo'lɔʧnij kok'tɛjlʲ]
juice	сік (ч)	[sik]
tomato juice	томатний сік (ч)	[to'matnij 'sik]
orange juice	апельсиновий сік (ч)	[apɛlʲ'sinowij sik]
freshly squeezed juice	свіжовижатий сік (ч)	[swiʒo'wiʒatij sik]
beer	пиво (с)	['piwo]
light beer	світле пиво (с)	['switlɛ 'piwo]
dark beer	темне пиво (с)	['tɛmnɛ 'piwo]

tea	чай (ч)	[tʃaj]
black tea	чорний чай (ч)	['tʃɔrnij tʃaj]
green tea	зелений чай (ч)	[zɛ'lɛnij tʃaj]

43. Vegetables

| vegetables | овочі (мн) | ['ɔwotʃi] |
| greens | зелень (ж) | ['zɛlɛnʲ] |

tomato	помідор (ч)	[pomi'dɔr]
cucumber	огірок (ч)	[ohi'rɔk]
carrot	морква (ж)	['mɔrkwa]
potato	картопля (ж)	[kar'tɔplʲa]
onion	цибуля (ж)	[tsi'bulʲa]
garlic	часник (ч)	[tʃas'nik]

cabbage	капуста (ж)	[ka'pusta]
cauliflower	кольорова капуста (ж)	[kolʲo'rowa ka'pusta]
Brussels sprouts	брюссельська капуста (ж)	[brʲu'sɛlʲsʲka ka'pusta]
broccoli	броколі (ж)	['brɔkoli]

beet	буряк (ч)	[bu'rʲak]
eggplant	баклажан (ч)	[bakla'ʒan]
zucchini	кабачок (ч)	[kaba'tʃɔk]
pumpkin	гарбуз (ч)	[har'buz]
turnip	ріпа (ж)	['ripa]

parsley	петрушка (ж)	[pɛt'ruʃka]
dill	кріп (ч)	[krip]
lettuce	салат (ч)	[sa'lat]
celery	селера (ж)	[sɛ'lɛra]
asparagus	спаржа (ж)	['sparʒa]
spinach	шпинат (ч)	[ʃpi'nat]

pea	горох (ч)	[ho'rɔh]
beans	боби (мн)	[bo'bi]
corn (maize)	кукурудза (ж)	[kuku'rudza]
kidney beans	квасоля (ж)	[kwa'sɔlʲa]

bell pepper	перець (ч)	['pɛrɛts]
radish	редиска (ж)	[rɛ'diska]
artichoke	артишок (ч)	[arti'ʃɔk]

44. Fruits. Nuts

| fruit | фрукт (ч) | [frukt] |
| apple | яблуко (с) | ['ʲabluko] |

pear	груша (ж)	['ɦruʃa]
lemon	лимон (ч)	[li'mɔn]
orange	апельсин (ч)	[apɛlʲ'sin]
strawberry (garden ~)	полуниця (ж)	[polu'nitsʲa]

mandarin	мандарин (ч)	[manda'rin]
plum	слива (ж)	['sliwa]
peach	персик (ч)	['pɛrsik]
apricot	абрикос (ч)	[abri'kɔs]
raspberry	малина (ж)	[ma'lina]
pineapple	ананас (ч)	[ana'nas]

banana	банан (ч)	[ba'nan]
watermelon	кавун (ч)	[ka'wun]
grapes	виноград (ч)	[wino'ɦrad]
cherry	вишня, черешня (ж)	['wiʃnʲa], [tʃɛ'rɛʃnʲa]
sour cherry	вишня (ж)	['wiʃnʲa]
sweet cherry	черешня (ж)	[tʃɛ'rɛʃnʲa]
melon	диня (ж)	['dinʲa]

grapefruit	грейпфрут (ч)	[ɦrɛjp'frut]
avocado	авокадо (с)	[awo'kado]
papaya	папайя (ж)	[pa'paʲa]
mango	манго (с)	['manɦo]
pomegranate	гранат (ч)	[ɦra'nat]

redcurrant	порічки (мн)	[po'ritʃki]
blackcurrant	чорна смородина (ж)	['tʃorna smo'rɔdina]
gooseberry	аґрус (ч)	['agrus]
bilberry	чорниця (ж)	[tʃor'nitsʲa]
blackberry	ожина (ж)	[o'ʒina]

raisin	родзинки (мн)	[ro'dzinki]
fig	інжир (ч)	[in'ʒir]
date	фінік (ч)	['finik]

peanut	арахіс (ч)	[a'rahis]
almond	мигдаль (ч)	[miɦ'dalʲ]
walnut	горіх (ч) волоський	[ɦo'rih wo'lɔsʲkij]
hazelnut	ліщина (ж)	[li'ɕina]
coconut	горіх (ч) кокосовий	[ɦo'rih ko'kɔsowij]
pistachios	фісташки (мн)	[fis'taʃki]

45. Bread. Candy

bakers' confectionery (pastry)	кондитерські вироби (мн)	[kon'ditɛrsʲki 'wirobi]
bread	хліб (ч)	[hlib]
cookies	печиво (с)	['pɛtʃiwo]
chocolate (n)	шоколад (ч)	[ʃoko'lad]

chocolate (as adj)	шоколадний	[ʃokoˈladnij]
candy (wrapped)	цукерка (ж)	[ʦuˈkɛrka]
cake (e.g., cupcake)	тістечко (с)	[ˈtistɛʧko]
cake (e.g., birthday ~)	торт (ч)	[tort]

| pie (e.g., apple ~) | пиріг (ч) | [piˈriɦ] |
| filling (e.g., pie ~) | начинка (ж) | [naˈʧinka] |

jam (whole fruit jam)	варення (с)	[waˈrɛnʲa]
marmalade	мармелад (ч)	[marmɛˈlad]
wafers	вафлі (мн)	[ˈwafli]
ice-cream	морозиво (с)	[moˈrɔziwo]
pudding	пудинг (ч)	[ˈpudinɦ]

46. Cooked dishes

course, dish	страва (ж)	[ˈstrawa]
cuisine	кухня (ж)	[ˈkuhnʲa]
recipe	рецепт (ч)	[rɛˈʦɛpt]
portion	порція (ж)	[ˈpɔrʦiʲa]

| salad | салат (ч) | [saˈlat] |
| soup | юшка (ж) | [ˈʲuʃka] |

clear soup (broth)	бульйон (ч)	[buˈlʲɔn]
sandwich (bread)	канапка (ж)	[kaˈnapka]
fried eggs	яєчня (ж)	[jaˈɛʃnʲa]

| hamburger (ground beef patty) | гамбургер (ч) | [ˈɦamburɦɛr] |
| beefsteak | біфштекс (ч) | [bifˈʃtɛks] |

side dish	гарнір (ч)	[ɦarˈnir]
spaghetti	спагеті (мн)	[spaˈɦɛti]
mashed potatoes	картопляне пюре (с)	[kartopˈlʲanɛ pʲuˈrɛ]
pizza	піца (ж)	[ˈpiʦa]
porridge (oatmeal, etc.)	каша (ж)	[ˈkaʃa]
omelet	омлет (ч)	[omˈlɛt]

boiled (e.g., ~ beef)	варений	[waˈrɛnij]
smoked (adj)	копчений	[kopˈʧɛnij]
fried (adj)	смажений	[ˈsmaʒɛnij]
dried (adj)	сушений	[ˈsuʃɛnij]
frozen (adj)	заморожений	[zamoˈrɔʒɛnij]
pickled (adj)	маринований	[mariˈnɔwanij]

sweet (sugary)	солодкий	[soˈlɔdkij]
salty (adj)	солоний	[soˈlɔnij]
cold (adj)	холодний	[hoˈlɔdnij]
hot (adj)	гарячий	[ɦaˈrʲaʧij]

bitter (adj)	**гіркий**	[ɦirˈkij]
tasty (adj)	**смачний**	[smatʃˈnij]

to cook in boiling water	**варити**	[waˈriti]
to cook (~ dinner, etc.)	**готувати**	[ɦotuˈwati]
to fry (vt)	**смажити**	[ˈsmaʒiti]
to heat up (food)	**розігрівати**	[roziɦriˈwati]

to salt (vt)	**солити**	[soˈliti]
to pepper (vt)	**перчити**	[pɛrˈtʃiti]
to grate (vt)	**терти**	[ˈtɛrti]
peel (n)	**шкірка** (ж)	[ˈʃkirka]
to peel (vt)	**чистити**	[ˈtʃistiti]

47. Spices

salt	**сіль** (ж)	[silʲ]
salty (adj)	**солоний**	[soˈlɔnij]
to salt (vt)	**солити**	[soˈliti]

black pepper	**чорний перець** (ч)	[ˈtʃɔrnij ˈpɛrɛts]
red pepper (milled ~)	**червоний перець** (ч)	[tʃɛrˈwɔnij ˈpɛrɛts]
mustard	**гірчиця** (ж)	[ɦirˈtʃitsʲa]
horseradish	**хрін** (ч)	[hrin]

condiment	**приправа** (ж)	[pripˈrawa]
spice	**прянощі** (мн)	[prʲaˈnɔɕi]
sauce	**соус** (ч)	[ˈsɔus]
vinegar	**оцет** (ч)	[ˈɔtsɛt]

anise	**аніс** (ч)	[ˈanis]
basil	**базилік** (ч)	[baziˈlik]
cloves	**гвоздика** (ж)	[ɦwozˈdika]
ginger	**імбир** (ч)	[imˈbir]
coriander	**коріандр** (ч)	[koriˈandr]
cinnamon	**кориця** (ж)	[koˈritsʲa]

sesame	**кунжут** (ч)	[kunˈʒut]
bay leaf	**лавровий лист** (ч)	[lawˈrɔwij list]
paprika	**паприка** (ж)	[ˈpaprika]
caraway	**кмин** (ч)	[kmin]
saffron	**шафран** (ч)	[ʃafˈran]

48. Meals

food	**їжа** (ж)	[ˈjiʒa]
to eat (vi, vt)	**їсти**	[ˈjisti]
breakfast	**сніданок** (ч)	[sniˈdanok]

to have breakfast	снідати	['snidati]
lunch	обід (ч)	[o'bid]
to have lunch	обідати	[o'bidati]
dinner	вечеря (ж)	[wɛ'ʧɛrʲa]
to have dinner	вечеряти	[wɛ'ʧɛrʲati]

appetite	апетит (ч)	[apɛ'tit]
Enjoy your meal!	Смачного!	[smaʧ'nɔɦo]

to open (~ a bottle)	відкривати	[widkri'wati]
to spill (accidentally splash liquid)	пролити	[pro'liti]
to spill out (vi)	пролитись	[pro'litisʲ]

to boil (vi)	кипіти	[ki'piti]
to boil (vt)	кип'ятити	[kipʲja'titi]
boiled (~ water)	кип'ячений	[kipʲja'ʧɛnij]
to chill, cool down (vt)	охолодити	[oholo'diti]
to chill (vi)	охолоджуватись	[oho'lɔʤuwatisʲ]

taste, flavor	смак (ч)	[smak]
aftertaste	присмак (ч)	['prismak]

to slim down (lose weight)	худнути	['hudnuti]
diet	дієта (ж)	[di'ɛla]
vitamin	вітамін (ч)	[wita'min]
calorie	калорія (ж)	[ka'lɔriʲa]
vegetarian (n)	вегетаріанець (ч)	[wɛɦɛtari'anɛʦ]
vegetarian (adj)	вегетаріанський	[wɛɦɛtari'ansʲkij]

fats (type of nutrient)	жири (мн)	[ʒi'ri]
proteins	білки (мн)	[bil'ki]
carbohydrates	вуглеводи (мн)	[wuɦlɛ'wɔdi]
slice (of lemon, ham)	скибка (ж)	['skibka]
piece (of cake, pie)	шматок (ч)	[ʃma'tɔk]
crumb (of bread, cake, etc.)	крихта (ж)	['krihta]

49. Table setting

spoon	ложка (ж)	['lɔʒka]
knife	ніж (ч)	[niʒ]
fork	виделка (ж)	[wi'dɛlka]

cup (e.g., coffee ~)	чашка (ж)	['ʧaʃka]
plate (dinner ~)	тарілка (ж)	[ta'rilka]

saucer	блюдце (с)	['blʲudʦɛ]
napkin (dinner ~)	серветка (ж)	[sɛr'wɛtka]
toothpick	зубочистка (ж)	[zubo'ʧistka]

50. Restaurant

restaurant	**ресторан** (ч)	[rɛstoˈran]
coffee house	**кав'ярня** (ж)	[kaˈwʲarnʲa]
pub, bar	**бар** (ч)	[bar]
tearoom	**чайна** (ж)	[ˈʧajna]
waiter	**офіціант** (ч)	[ofiʦiˈant]
waitress	**офіціантка** (ж)	[ofiʦiˈantka]
bartender	**бармен** (ч)	[barˈmɛn]
menu	**меню** (с)	[mɛˈnʲu]
wine list	**карта** (ж) **вин**	[ˈkarta wiⁿ]
to book a table	**забронювати столик**	[zabronʲuˈwati ˈstɔlik]
course, dish	**страва** (ж)	[ˈstrawa]
to order (in a restaurant)	**замовити**	[zaˈmɔwiti]
to make an order	**зробити замовлення**	[zroˈbiti zaˈmɔwlɛnʲa]
aperitif	**аперитив** (ч)	[apɛriˈtiw]
appetizer	**закуска** (ж)	[zaˈkuska]
dessert	**десерт** (ч)	[dɛˈsɛrt]
check	**рахунок** (ч)	[raˈhunok]
to pay the check	**оплатити рахунок**	[oplaˈtiti raˈhunok]
to give change	**дати решту**	[ˈdati ˈrɛʃtu]
tip	**чайові** (мн)	[ʧaʲoˈwi]

Family, relatives and friends

51. Personal information. Forms

name (first name)	ім'я (c)	[i'm^ja]
surname (last name)	прізвище (c)	['prizwiɕɛ]
date of birth	дата (ж) народження	['data na'rɔdʒɛnʲa]
place of birth	місце (c) народження	['mistsɛ na'rɔdʒɛnʲa]
nationality	національність (ж)	[natsio'nalʲnistʲ]
place of residence	місце (c) проживання	['mistsɛ proʒi'wanʲa]
country	країна (ж)	[kra'jina]
profession (occupation)	професія (ж)	[pro'fɛsʲa]
gender, sex	стать (ж)	[statʲ]
height	зріст (ч)	[zrist]
weight	вага (ж)	[wa'ɦa]

52. Family members. Relatives

mother	мати (ж)	['mati]
father	батько (ч)	['batʲko]
son	син (ч)	[sin]
daughter	дочка (ж)	[dotʃʲka]
younger daughter	молодша дочка (ж)	[mo'lɔdʃa dotʃʲka]
younger son	молодший син (ч)	[mo'lɔdʃij sin]
eldest daughter	старша дочка (ж)	['starʃa dotʃʲka]
eldest son	старший син (ч)	['starʃij sin]
brother	брат (ч)	[brat]
elder brother	старший брат (ч)	[star'ʃij brat]
younger brother	молодший брат (ч)	[mo'lɔdʃij brat]
sister	сестра (ж)	[sɛst'ra]
elder sister	старша сестра (ж)	[star'ʃa sɛst'ra]
younger sister	молодша сестра (ж)	[mo'lɔdʃa sɛst'ra]
cousin (masc.)	двоюрідний брат (ч)	[dwoʲu'ridnij brat]
cousin (fem.)	двоюрідна сестра (ж)	[dwoʲu'ridna sɛst'ra]
mom, mommy	мати (ж)	['mati]
dad, daddy	тато (ч)	['tato]
parents	батьки (мн)	[batʲ'ki]
child	дитина (ж)	[di'tina]
children	діти (мн)	['diti]

grandmother	бабуся (ж)	[ba'busʲa]
grandfather	дід (ч)	['did]
grandson	онук (ч)	[o'nuk]
granddaughter	онука (ж)	[o'nuka]
grandchildren	онуки (мн)	[o'nuki]

uncle	дядько (ч)	['dʲadʲko]
aunt	тітка (ж)	['titka]
nephew	племінник (ч)	[plɛ'minik]
niece	племінниця (ж)	[plɛ'minitsʲa]

mother-in-law (wife's mother)	теща (ж)	['tɛça]
father-in-law (husband's father)	свекор (ч)	['swɛkor]
son-in-law (daughter's husband)	зять (ч)	[zʲatʲ]

| stepmother | мачуха (ж) | ['matʃuha] |
| stepfather | вітчим (ч) | ['witʃim] |

infant	немовля (с)	[nɛmow'lʲa]
baby (infant)	малюк (ч)	[ma'lʲuk]
little boy, kid	малюк (ч)	[ma'lʲuk]

| wife | дружина (ж) | [dru'ʒina] |
| husband | чоловік (ч) | [tʃolo'wik] |

| spouse (husband) | чоловік (ч) | [tʃolo'wik] |
| spouse (wife) | дружина (ж) | [dru'ʒina] |

married (masc.)	одружений	[od'ruʒɛnij]
married (fem.)	заміжня	[za'miʒnʲa]
single (unmarried)	холостий	[holos'tij]
bachelor	холостяк (ч)	[holos'tʲak]
divorced (masc.)	розлучений	[roz'lutʃɛnij]

| widow | вдова (ж) | [wdo'wa] |
| widower | вдівець (ч) | [wdi'wɛts] |

| relative | родич (ч) | ['rɔditʃ] |
| close relative | близький родич (ч) | [blizʲ'kij 'rɔditʃ] |

| distant relative | далекий родич (ч) | [da'lɛkij 'rɔditʃ] |
| relatives | рідні (мн) | ['ridni] |

orphan (boy or girl)	сирота (ч)	[siro'ta]
orphan (boy)	сирота (ч)	[siro'ta]
orphan (girl)	сирота (ж)	[siro'ta]
guardian (of a minor)	опікун (ч)	[opi'kun]
to adopt (a boy)	усиновити	[usino'witi]
to adopt (a girl)	удочерити	[udotʃɛ'riti]

53. Friends. Coworkers

friend (masc.)	друг (ч)	[druɦ]
friend (fem.)	подруга (ж)	['pɔdruɦa]
friendship	дружба (ж)	['druʒba]
to be friends	дружити	[dru'ʒɨti]
buddy (masc.)	приятель (ч)	['prijatɛlʲ]
buddy (fem.)	приятелька (ж)	['prijatɛlʲka]
partner	партнер (ч)	[part'nɛr]
chief (boss)	шеф (ч)	[ʃɛf]
superior (n)	начальник (ч)	[na'ʧalʲnik]
owner, proprietor	власник	['wlasnik]
subordinate (n)	підлеглий (ч)	[pid'lɛɦlij]
colleague	колега (ч)	[ko'lɛɦa]
acquaintance (person)	знайомий (ч)	[zna'jɔmij]
fellow traveler	попутник (ч)	[po'putnik]
classmate	однокласник (ч)	[odno'klasnik]
neighbor (masc.)	сусід (ч)	[su'sid]
neighbor (fem.)	сусідка (ж)	[su'sidka]
neighbors	сусіди (мн)	[su'sɨdɨ]

54. Man. Woman

woman	жінка (ж)	['ʒinka]
girl (young woman)	дівчина (ж)	['diwʧina]
bride	наречена (ж)	[narɛ'ʧɛna]
beautiful (adj)	гарна	['ɦarna]
tall (adj)	висока	[wi'sɔka]
slender (adj)	струнка	[stru'nka]
short (adj)	невисокого зросту	[nɛwi'sɔkoɦo 'zrɔstu]
blonde (n)	блондинка (ж)	[blon'dinka]
brunette (n)	брюнетка (ж)	[brʲu'nɛtka]
ladies' (adj)	дамський	['damsʲkij]
virgin (girl)	незаймана дівчина (ж)	[nɛ'zajmana 'diwʧina]
pregnant (adj)	вагітна	[wa'ɦitna]
man (adult male)	чоловік (ч)	[ʧolo'wik]
blond (n)	блондин (ч)	[blon'din]
brunet (n)	брюнет (ч)	[brʲu'nɛt]
tall (adj)	високий	[wi'sɔkij]
short (adj)	невисокого зросту	[nɛwi'sɔkoɦo 'zrɔstu]
rude (rough)	брутальний	[bru'talʲnij]

stocky (adj)	кремезний	[krɛ'mɛznij]
robust (adj)	міцний	[mits'nij]
strong (adj)	сильний	['silʲnij]
strength	сила (ж)	['sila]

stout, fat (adj)	повний	['pɔwnij]
swarthy (adj)	смаглявий	[smaɦ'lʲawij]
slender (well-built)	стрункий	[stru'nkij]
elegant (adj)	елегантний	[ɛlɛ'ɦantnij]

55. Age

age	вік (ч)	[wik]
youth (young age)	юність (ж)	['ʲunistʲ]
young (adj)	молодий	[molo'dij]

| younger (adj) | молодший | [mo'lɔdʃij] |
| older (adj) | старший | ['starʃij] |

young man	юнак (ч)	[ʲu'nak]
teenager	підліток (ч)	['pidlitok]
guy, fellow	хлопець (ч)	['hlɔpɛʦ]

| old man | старий (ч) | [sta'rij] |
| old woman | стара жінка (ж) | [sta'ra 'ʒinka] |

adult (adj)	дорослий	[do'rɔslij]
middle-aged (adj)	середніх років	[sɛ'rɛdnih ro'kiw]
elderly (adj)	похилий	[po'hilij]
old (adj)	старий	[sta'rij]

retirement	пенсія (ж)	['pɛnsiʲa]
to retire (from a job)	вийти на пенсію	['wijti na 'pɛnsiʲu]
retiree	пенсіонер (ч)	[pɛnsio'nɛr]

56. Children

child	дитина (ж)	[di'tina]
children	діти (мн)	['diti]
twins	близнюки (мн)	[bliznʲu'ki]

cradle	колиска (ж)	[ko'liska]
rattle	брязкальце (с)	['brʲazkalʲʦɛ]
diaper	підгузок (ч)	[pid'ɦuzok]

pacifier	соска (ж)	['sɔska]
baby carriage	коляска (ж)	[ko'lʲaska]
kindergarten, preschool	дитячий садок (ч)	[di'tʲatʃij sa'dɔk]

babysitter	**няня** (ж)	['nʲanʲa]
childhood	**дитинство** (с)	[dɨ'tinstwo]
doll	**лялька** (ж)	['lʲalʲka]
toy	**іграшка** (ж)	['iɦraʃka]
construction set (toy)	**конструктор** (ч)	[kon'struktor]

well-bred (adj)	**вихований**	['wixowanɨj]
ill-bred (adj)	**невихований**	[nɛ'wixowanɨj]
spoiled (adj)	**розбещений**	[roz'bɛɕɛnɨj]

to be naughty	**пустувати**	[pustu'wati]
mischievous (adj)	**пустотливий**	[pustot'liwɨj]
mischievousness	**пустощі** (мн)	['pustoɕi]
mischievous child	**пустун** (ч)	[pus'tun]

obedient (adj)	**слухняний**	[sluh'nʲanɨj]
disobedient (adj)	**неслухняний**	[nɛsluh'nʲanɨj]

docile (adj)	**розумний**	[ro'zumnɨj]
clever (smart)	**розумний**	[ro'zumnɨj]
child prodigy	**вундеркінд** (ч)	[wundɛr'kind]

57. Married couples. Family life

to kiss (vt)	**цілувати**	[tsilu'wati]
to kiss (vi)	**цілуватися**	[tsilu'watisʲa]
family (n)	**сім'я** (ж)	[si'mʲa]
family (as adj)	**сімейний**	[si'mɛjnɨj]
couple	**пара** (ж)	['para]
marriage (state)	**шлюб** (ч)	[ʃlʲub]
hearth (home)	**домашнє вогнище** (с)	[do'maʃnɛ 'woɦniɕɛ]
dynasty	**династія** (ж)	[dɨ'nastiʲa]

date	**побачення** (с)	[po'batʃɛnʲa]
kiss	**поцілунок** (ч)	[potsi'lunok]

love (for sb)	**кохання** (с)	[ko'hanʲa]
to love (sb)	**кохати**	[ko'hati]
beloved	**кохана**	[ko'hana]

tenderness	**ніжність** (ж)	['niʒnistʲ]
tender (affectionate)	**ніжний**	['niʒnɨj]
faithfulness	**вірність** (ж)	['wirnistʲ]
faithful (adj)	**вірний**	['wirnɨj]
care (attention)	**турбота** (ж)	[tur'bota]
caring (~ father)	**турботливий**	[tur'botliwɨj]
newlyweds	**молодята** (мн)	[molo'dʲata]
honeymoon	**медовий місяць** (ч)	[mɛ'dowɨj 'misʲatsʲ]
to get married (ab. woman)	**вийти заміж**	['wɨjti 'zamiʒ]

to get married (ab. man)	одружуватися (c)	[od'ruʒuwatisʲa]
wedding	весілля (c)	[wɛ'silʲa]
golden wedding	золоте весілля (c)	[zolo'tɛ wɛ'silʲa]
anniversary	річниця (ж)	[ritʃ'nitsʲa]

| lover (romantic partner) | коханець (ч) | [ko'hanɛts] |
| mistress (female lover) | коханка (ж) | [ko'hanka] |

| adultery | зрада (ж) | ['zrada] |
| to cheat on ... (commit adultery) | зрадити | ['zraditi] |

jealous (adj)	ревнивий	[rɛw'niwij]
to be jealous	ревнувати	[rɛwnu'wati]
divorce	розлучення (c)	[roz'lutʃɛnʲa]
to divorce (vi)	розлучитися	[rozlu'tʃitisʲa]

to quarrel (vi)	сваритися	[swa'ritisʲa]
to be reconciled (after an argument)	миритися	[mi'ritisʲa]
together (adv)	разом	['razom]
sex	секс (ч)	[sɛks]

happiness	щастя (c)	['ɕastʲa]
happy (adj)	щасливий	[ɕas'liwij]
misfortune (accident)	нещастя (c)	[nɛ'ɕastʲa]
unhappy (adj)	нещасний	[nɛ'ɕasnij]

Character. Feelings. Emotions

58. Feelings. Emotions

feeling (emotion)	почуття (с)	[poʧut'tʲa]
feelings	почуття (мн)	[poʧut'tʲa]
to feel (vt)	відчувати	[widʧu'wati]
hunger	голод (ч)	['hɔlod]
to be hungry	хотіти їсти	[ho'titi 'jisti]
thirst	спрага (ж)	['spraɦa]
to be thirsty	хотіти пити	[ho'titi 'piti]
sleepiness	сонливість (ж)	[son'liwistʲ]
to feel sleepy	хотіти спати	[ho'titi 'spati]
tiredness	втома (ж)	['wtɔma]
tired (adj)	втомлений	['wtɔmlɛnij]
to get tired	втомитися	[wto'mitisʲa]
mood (humor)	настрій (ч)	['nastrij]
boredom	нудьга (ж)	[nudʲ'ɦa]
to be bored	нудьгувати	[nudʲɦu'wati]
seclusion	самота (ж)	[samo'ta]
to seclude oneself	усамітнюватися	[usa'mitnʲuwatisʲa]
to worry (make anxious)	хвилювати	[hwilʲu'wati]
to be worried	хвилюватися	[hwilʲu'watisʲa]
worry (n)	хвилювання (с)	[hwilʲu'wanʲa]
anxiety	занепокоєння (с)	[zanɛpo'kɔɛnʲa]
preoccupied (adj)	занепокоєний	[zanɛpo'kɔɛnij]
to be nervous	нервуватися	[nɛrwu'watisʲa]
to panic (vi)	панікувати	[paniku'wati]
hope	надія (ж)	[na'diʲa]
to hope (vi, vt)	сподіватися	[spodi'watisʲa]
certainty	упевненість (ж)	[u'pɛwnɛnistʲ]
certain, sure (adj)	упевнений	[u'pɛwnɛnij]
uncertainty	невпевненість (ж)	[nɛw'pɛwnɛnistʲ]
uncertain (adj)	невпевнений	[nɛw'pɛwnɛnij]
drunk (adj)	п'яний	['pʲanij]
sober (adj)	тверезий	[twɛ'rɛzij]
weak (adj)	слабкий	[slab'kij]
happy (adj)	щасливий	[ɕas'liwij]
to scare (vt)	налякати	[nalʲa'kati]

| fury (madness) | шаленство (с) | [ʃaˈlɛnstwo] |
| rage (fury) | лють (ж) | [lʲutʲ] |

depression	депресія (ж)	[dɛˈprɛsʲia]
discomfort (unease)	дискомфорт (ч)	[diskomˈfɔrt]
comfort	комфорт (ч)	[komˈfɔrt]
to regret (be sorry)	жалкувати	[ʒalkuˈwati]
regret	жаль (ч)	[ʒalʲ]
bad luck	невезіння (с)	[nɛwɛˈzʲinʲa]
sadness	прикрість (ж)	[ˈprikristʲ]

shame (remorse)	сором (ч)	[ˈsɔrom]
gladness	веселість (ж)	[wɛˈsɛlistʲ]
enthusiasm, zeal	ентузіазм (ч)	[ɛntuziˈazm]
enthusiast	ентузіаст (ч)	[ɛntuziˈast]
to show enthusiasm	проявити ентузіазм	[projaˈwiti ɛntuziˈazm]

59. Character. Personality

character	характер (ч)	[haˈraktɛr]
character flaw	вада (ж)	[ˈwada]
mind, reason	ум (ч), розум (ч)	[um], [ˈrɔzum]
mind	ум (ч)	[um]
reason	розум (ч)	[ˈrɔzum]

conscience	совість (ж)	[ˈsɔwistʲ]
habit (custom)	звичка (ж)	[ˈzwiʧka]
ability (talent)	здібність (ж)	[ˈzdibnistʲ]
can (e.g., ~ swim)	уміти	[uˈmiti]

patient (adj)	терплячий	[tɛrpˈlʲaʧij]
impatient (adj)	нетерплячий	[nɛtɛrpˈlʲaʧij]
curious (inquisitive)	цікавий	[ʦiˈkawij]
curiosity	цікавість (ж)	[ʦiˈkawistʲ]

modesty	скромність (ж)	[ˈskrɔmnistʲ]
modest (adj)	скромний	[ˈskrɔmnij]
immodest (adj)	нескромний	[nɛˈskrɔmnij]

laziness	лінь (ж)	[linʲ]
lazy (adj)	ледачий	[lɛˈdaʧij]
lazy person (masc.)	ледар (ч)	[ˈlɛdar]

cunning (n)	хитрість (ж)	[ˈhitristʲ]
cunning (as adj)	хитрий	[ˈhitrij]
distrust	недовіра (ж)	[nɛdoˈwira]
distrustful (adj)	недовірливий	[nɛdoˈwirliwij]

| generosity | щедрість (ж) | [ˈɕedristʲ] |
| generous (adj) | щедрий | [ˈɕedrij] |

talented (adj)	талановитий	[talano'witij]
talent	талант (ч)	[ta'lant]
courageous (adj)	сміливий	[smi'liwij]
courage	сміливість (ж)	[smi'liwistʲ]
honest (adj)	чесний	['ʧɛsnij]
honesty	чесність (ж)	['ʧɛsnistʲ]
careful (cautious)	обережний	[obɛ'rɛʒnij]
brave (courageous)	відважний	[wid'waʒnij]
serious (adj)	серйозний	[sɛ'rʲɔznij]
strict (severe, stern)	суворий	[su'wɔrij]
decisive (adj)	рішучий	[ri'ʃuʧij]
indecisive (adj)	нерішучий	[nɛri'ʃuʧij]
shy, timid (adj)	сором'язливий	[soro'mʲazliwij]
shyness, timidity	сором'язливість (ж)	[soro'mʲazliwistʲ]
confidence (trust)	довіра (ж)	[do'wira]
to believe (trust)	вірити	['wiriti]
trusting (credulous)	довірливий	[do'wirliwij]
sincerely (adv)	щиро	['ɕiro]
sincere (adj)	щирий	['ɕirij]
sincerity	щирість (ж)	['ɕiristʲ]
open (person)	відкритий	[wid'kritij]
calm (adj)	тихий	['tihij]
frank (sincere)	відвертий	[wid'wɛrtij]
naïve (adj)	наївний	[na'jiwnij]
absent-minded (adj)	неуважний	[nɛu'waʒnij]
funny (odd)	кумедний	[ku'mɛdnij]
greed, stinginess	жадібність (ж)	['ʒadibnistʲ]
greedy, stingy (adj)	жадібний	['ʒadibnij]
stingy (adj)	скупий	[sku'pij]
evil (adj)	злий	['zɫij]
stubborn (adj)	впертий	['wpɛrtij]
unpleasant (adj)	неприємний	[nɛpri'ɛmnij]
selfish person (masc.)	егоїст (ч)	[ɛɦo'jist]
selfish (adj)	егоїстичний	[ɛɦojis'tiʧnij]
coward	боягуз (ч)	[boja'ɦuz]
cowardly (adj)	боягузливий	[boja'ɦuzliwij]

60. Sleep. Dreams

to sleep (vi)	спати	['spati]
sleep, sleeping	сон (ч)	[son]
dream	сон (ч)	[son]

| to dream (in sleep) | бачити сни | ['batʃiti sni] |
| sleepy (adj) | сонний | ['sɔnij] |

bed	ліжко (с)	['liʒko]
mattress	матрац (ч)	[mat'rats]
blanket (comforter)	ковдра (ж)	['kɔwdra]
pillow	подушка (ж)	[po'duʃka]
sheet	простирадло (с)	[prosti'radlo]

insomnia	безсоння (с)	[bɛz'sɔnʲa]
sleepless (adj)	безсонний	[bɛz'sɔnij]
sleeping pill	снодійне (с)	[sno'dijnɛ]
to take a sleeping pill	прийняти снодійне	[prij'nʲati sno'dijnɛ]

to feel sleepy	хотіти спати	[ho'titi 'spati]
to yawn (vi)	позіхати	[pozi'hati]
to go to bed	йти спати	[jti 'spati]
to make up the bed	стелити ліжко	[stɛ'liti 'liʒko]
to fall asleep	заснути	[zas'nuti]

nightmare	страхіття (с)	[stra'hitʲa]
snore, snoring	хропіння (с)	[hro'pinʲa]
to snore (vi)	хропіти	[hro'piti]

alarm clock	будильник (ч)	[bu'dilʲnik]
to wake (vt)	розбудити	[rozbu'diti]
to wake up	прокидатися	[proki'datisʲa]
to get up (vi)	вставати	[wsta'wati]
to wash up (clean face)	умитися	[u'mitisʲa]

61. Humour. Laughter. Gladness

humor (wit, fun)	гумор (ч)	['ɦumor]
sense of humor	почуття (с) гумору	[potʃu'tʲa 'ɦumoru]
to enjoy oneself	веселитися	[wɛsɛ'litisʲa]
cheerful (merry)	веселий	[wɛ'sɛlij]
merriment (gaiety)	веселощі (мн)	[wɛ'sɛloɕi]

smile	посмішка (ж)	['pɔsmiʃka]
to smile (vi)	посміхатися	[posmi'hatisʲa]
to start laughing	засміятися	[zasmiʲatisʲa]
to laugh (vi)	сміятися	[smiʲatisʲa]
laugh, laughter	сміх (ч)	[smih]

anecdote	анекдот (ч)	[anɛk'dɔt]
funny (anecdote, etc.)	смішний	[smiʃ'nij]
funny (odd)	кумедний	[ku'mɛdnij]

| to joke (vi) | жартувати | [ʒartu'wati] |
| joke (verbal) | жарт (ч) | [ʒart] |

joy (emotion)	радість (ж)	['radistʲ]
to rejoice (vi)	радіти	[ra'diti]
joyful (adj)	радісний	['radisnij]

62. Discussion, conversation. Part 1

| communication | спілкування (с) | [spilku'wanʲa] |
| to communicate | спілкуватися | [spilku'watisʲa] |

conversation	розмова (ж)	[roz'mɔwa]
dialog	діалог (ч)	[dia'lɔɦ]
discussion (discourse)	дискусія (ж)	[dis'kusiʲa]
dispute (debate)	суперечка (ж)	[supɛ'rɛtʃka]
to dispute, to debate	сперечатися	[spɛrɛ'tʃatisʲa]

interlocutor	співрозмовник (ч)	[spiwroz'mɔwnik]
topic (theme)	тема (ж)	['tɛma]
point of view	точка (ж) зору	['tɔtʃka 'zɔru]
opinion (point of view)	думка (ж)	['dumka]
speech (talk)	промова (ж)	[pro'mɔwa]

discussion (of a report, etc.)	обговорення (с)	[obɦo'wɔrɛnʲa]
to discuss (vt)	обговорювати	[obɦo'wɔrʲuwati]
talk (conversation)	бесіда (ж)	['bɛsida]
to talk (to chat)	бесідувати	[bɛ'siduwati]
meeting (encounter)	зустріч (ж)	['zustritʃ]
to meet (vi, vt)	зустрічатися	[zustri'tʃatisʲa]

proverb	прислів'я (с)	[pris'liwʲʲa]
saying	приказка (ж)	['prikazka]
riddle (poser)	загадка (ж)	['zaɦadka]
to pose a riddle	загадувати загадку	[za'ɦaduwati 'zaɦadku]
password	пароль (ч)	[pa'rɔlʲ]
secret	секрет (ч)	[sɛk'rɛt]

oath (vow)	клятва (ж)	['klʲatwa]
to swear (~ an oath)	клястися	['klʲastisʲa]
promise	обіцянка (ж)	[obi'tsʲanka]
to promise (vt)	обіцяти	[obi'tsʲati]

advice (counsel)	порада (ж)	[po'rada]
to advise (vt)	радити	['raditi]
to follow one's advice	дотримуватись поради	[do'trimuwatisʲ po'radi]
to listen to ... (obey)	слухатись	['sluhatisʲ]

news	новина (ж)	[nowi'na]
sensation (news)	сенсація (ж)	[sɛn'satsiʲa]
information (report)	відомості (мн)	[wi'dɔmosti]
conclusion (decision)	висновок (ч)	['wisnowok]

voice	голос (ч)	['hɔlos]
compliment	комплімент (ч)	[kompli'mɛnt]
kind (nice)	люб'язний	[lʲu'bʲaznij]

word	слово (с)	['slɔwo]
phrase	фраза (ж)	['fraza]
answer	відповідь (ж)	['widpowidʲ]

| truth | правда (ж) | ['prawda] |
| lie | брехня (ж) | [brɛh'nʲa] |

thought	думка (ж)	['dumka]
idea (inspiration)	думка (ж)	['dumka]
fantasy	фантазія (ж)	[fan'taziʲa]

63. Discussion, conversation. Part 2

respected (adj)	шановний	[ʃa'nɔwnij]
to respect (vt)	поважати	[powa'ʒati]
respect	повага (ж)	[po'waɦa]
Dear ... (letter)	Шановний...	[ʃa'nɔwnij]

to introduce (sb to sb)	познайомити	[pozna'jɔmiti]
to make acquaintance	познайомитися	[pozna'jɔmitisʲa]
intention	намір (ч)	['namir]
to intend (have in mind)	мати наміри	['mati 'namiri]
wish	побажання (с)	[poba'ʒanʲa]
to wish (~ good luck)	побажати	[poba'ʒati]

surprise (astonishment)	здивування (с)	[zdiwu'wanʲa]
to surprise (amaze)	дивувати	[diwu'wati]
to be surprised	дивуватись	[diwu'watisʲ]

to give (vt)	дати	['dati]
to take (get hold of)	взяти	['wzʲati]
to give back	повернути	[powɛr'nuti]
to return (give back)	віддати	[wid'dati]

to apologize (vi)	вибачатися	[wiba'tʃatisʲa]
apology	вибачення (с)	['wibatʃɛnʲa]
to forgive (vt)	вибачати	[wiba'tʃati]

to talk (speak)	розмовляти	[rozmow'lʲati]
to listen (vi)	слухати	['sluhati]
to hear out	вислухати	['wisluhati]
to understand (vt)	зрозуміти	[zrozu'miti]

to show (to display)	показати	[poka'zati]
to look at ...	дивитися	[di'witisʲa]
to call (yell for sb)	покликати	[pok'likati]

to distract (disturb)	турбувати	[turbu'wati]
to disturb (vt)	заважати	[zawa'ʒati]
to pass (to move an item to someone)	передати	[pɛrɛ'dati]
demand (request)	прохання (с)	[pro'hanʲa]
to request (ask)	просити	[pro'siti]
demand (firm request)	вимога (ж)	[wi'mɔha]
to demand (request firmly)	вимагати	[wima'hati]
to tease (call names)	дражнити	[draʒ'niti]
to mock (make fun of)	насміхатися	[nasmi'hatisʲa]
mockery, derision	насмішка (ж)	[na'smiʃka]
nickname	прізвисько (с)	['prizwisʲko]
insinuation	натяк (ч)	['natʲak]
to insinuate (imply)	натякати	[natʲa'kati]
to mean (vt)	мати на увазі	['mati na u'wazi]
description	опис (ч)	['ɔpis]
to describe (vt)	описати	[opi'sati]
praise (compliments)	похвала (ж)	[pohwa'la]
to praise (vt)	хвалити	[hwa'liti]
disappointment	розчарування (с)	[roztʃaru'wanʲa]
to disappoint (vt)	розчарувати	[roztʃaru'wati]
to be disappointed	розчаруватися	[roztʃaru'watisʲa]
supposition	припущення (с)	[pri'puɕɛnʲa]
to suppose (assume)	припускати	[pripus'kati]
warning (caution)	застереження (с)	[zastɛ'rɛʒɛnʲa]
to warn (vt)	застерегти	[zastɛrɛh'ti]

64. Discussion, conversation. Part 3

to talk into (convince)	умовити	[u'mɔwiti]
to calm down (vt)	заспокоювати	[zaspo'kɔʲuwati]
silence (~ is golden)	мовчання (с)	[mow'tʃanʲa]
to be silent (not speaking)	мовчати	[mow'tʃati]
to whisper (vi, vt)	шепнути	[ʃɛp'nuti]
whisper	шепіт (ч)	['ʃɛpit]
frankly, sincerely (adv)	відверто	[wid'wɛrto]
in my opinion ...	на мою думку...	[na mo'ʲu 'dumku]
detail (particulars in a story)	деталь (ж)	[dɛ'talʲ]
detailed (adj)	детальний	[dɛ'talʲnij]
in detail (adv)	детально	[dɛ'talʲno]

| hint, clue | підказка (ж) | [pid'kazka] |
| to give a hint | підказати | [pidka'zati] |

look (glance)	погляд (ч)	['pɔɦlʲad]
to have a look	поглянути	[poɦ'lʲanuti]
fixed (look)	нерухомий	[nɛru'ɦɔmij]
to blink (vi)	кліпати	['klipati]
to wink (vi)	підморгнути	[pidmorɦ'nuti]
to nod (in assent)	кивнути	[kiw'nuti]

sigh	зітхання (c)	[zit'hanʲa]
to sigh (vi)	зітхнути	[zith'nuti]
to shudder (vi)	здригатися	[zdri'ɦatisʲa]
gesture	жест (ч)	[ʒɛst]
to touch (one's arm, etc.)	доторкнутися	[dotor'knutisʲa]
to seize (e.g., to grab, ~ by the arm)	хапати	[ha'pati]
to tap (on the shoulder)	плескати	[plɛs'kati]

Look out!	Обережно!	[obɛ'rɛʒno]
Really?	Невже?	[nɛw'ʒɛ]
Are you sure?	Ти впевнений?	[tiⁱ 'wpɛwnɛnij]
Good luck!	Хай щастить!	[haj ɕas'titʲ]
I see!	Зрозуміло!	[zrozu'milo]
It's a pity!	Шкода!	['ʃkɔda]

65. Agreement. Refusal

consent	згода (ж)	['zɦɔda]
to consent (vi)	погоджуватися	[po'ɦɔʤuwatisʲa]
approval	схвалення (c)	[sh'walɛnʲa]
to approve (vt)	схвалити	[shwa'liti]
refusal	відмова (ж)	[wid'mɔwa]
to refuse (vi, vt)	відмовлятися	[widmow'lʲatisʲa]

Great!	Чудово!	[tʃu'dɔwo]
All right!	Добре!	['dɔbrɛ]
Okay! (I agree)	Згода!	['zɦɔda]

forbidden (adj)	заборонений	[zabo'rɔnɛnij]
it's forbidden	не можна	[nɛ 'mɔʒna]
it's impossible	неможливо	[nɛmoʒ'liwo]
incorrect (adj)	помилковий	[pomilʲ'kɔwij]

to reject (~ a demand)	відхилити	[widhi'liti]
to support (cause, idea)	підтримати	[pid'trimati]
to accept (~ an apology)	прийняти	[prij'nʲati]

| to confirm (vt) | підтвердити | [pid'twɛrditi] |
| confirmation | підтвердження (c) | [pid'twɛrdʒɛnʲa] |

T&P Books. Ukrainian vocabulary for English speakers - 7000 words

permission	дозвіл (ч)	['dɔzwil]
to permit (vt)	дозволити	[doz'wɔliti]
decision	рішення (с)	['riʃɛnʲa]
to say nothing (hold one's tongue)	промовчати	[promow'tʃati]

condition (term)	умова (ж)	[u'mɔwa]
excuse (pretext)	відмовка (ж)	[wid'mɔwka]
praise (compliments)	похвала (ж)	[pohwa'la]
to praise (vt)	хвалити	[hwa'liti]

66. Success. Good luck. Failure

success	успіх (ч)	['uspih]
successfully (adv)	успішно	[us'piʃno]
successful (adj)	успішний	[us'piʃnij]

luck (good luck)	везіння (с)	[wɛ'zinʲa]
Good luck!	Хай щастить!	[haj ɕas'titʲ]
lucky (e.g., ~ day)	вдалий	['wdalij]
lucky (fortunate)	везучий	[wɛ'zutʃij]

failure	невдача (ж)	[nɛw'datʃa]
misfortune	невдача (ж)	[nɛw'datʃa]
bad luck	невезіння (с)	[nɛwɛ'zinʲa]
unsuccessful (adj)	невдалий	[nɛw'dalij]
catastrophe	катастрофа (ж)	[kata'strɔfa]

pride	гордість (ж)	['hɔrdistʲ]
proud (adj)	гордовитий	[hordo'witij]
to be proud	гордитися	[hor'ditisʲa]

winner	переможець (ч)	[pɛrɛ'mɔʒɛts]
to win (vi)	перемогти	[pɛrɛmoh'ti]
to lose (not win)	програти	[proh'rati]
try	спроба (ж)	['sprɔba]
to try (vi)	намагатися	[nama'hatisʲa]
chance (opportunity)	шанс (ч)	[ʃans]

67. Quarrels. Negative emotions

shout (scream)	крик (ч)	[krik]
to shout (vi)	кричати	[kri'tʃati]
to start to cry out	закричати	[zakri'tʃati]

quarrel	сварка (ж)	['swarka]
to quarrel (vi)	сваритися	[swa'ritisʲa]
fight (argue, squabble)	скандал (ч)	[skan'dal]

to make a scene	сваритися	[swa'ritisʲa]
conflict	конфлікт (ч)	[kon'flikt]
misunderstanding	непорозуміння (с)	[nɛporozu'minʲa]

insult	приниження (с)	[pri'niʒɛnʲa]
to insult (vt)	принизити	[pri'niziti]
insulted (adj)	принижений	[pri'niʒɛnij]
resentment	образа (ж)	[ob'raza]
to offend (vt)	образити	[ob'raziti]
to take offense	образитись	[ob'razitisʲ]

indignation	обурення (с)	[o'burɛnʲa]
to be indignant	обурюватися	[o'burʲuwatisʲa]
complaint	скарга (ж)	['skarɦa]
to complain (vi, vt)	скаржитися	['skarʒitisʲa]

apology	вибачення (с)	['wibatʃɛnʲa]
to apologize (vi)	вибачатися	[wiba'tʃatisʲa]
to beg pardon	просити вибачення	[pro'siti 'wibatʃɛnʲa]

criticism	критика (ж)	['kritika]
to criticize (vt)	критикувати	[kritiku'wati]
accusation (charge)	обвинувачення (с)	[obwinu'watʃɛnʲa]
to accuse (vt)	звинувачувати	[zwinu'watʃuwati]

revenge	помста (ж)	['pomsta]
to avenge (get revenge)	мстити	['mstiti]
to pay back	помститися	[poms'titisʲa]

disdain	зневага (ж)	[znɛ'waɦa]
to despise (vt)	зневажати	[znɛwa'ʒati]
hatred, hate	ненависть (ж)	[nɛ'nawistʲ]
to hate (vt)	ненавидіти	[nɛna'widiti]

nervous (adj)	нервовий	[nɛr'wowij]
to be nervous	нервувати	[nɛrwu'wati]
angry (mad)	сердитий	[sɛr'ditij]
to make angry	розсердити	[roz'sɛrditi]

humiliation	приниження (с)	[pri'niʒɛnʲa]
to humiliate (vt)	принижувати	[pri'niʒuwati]
to humiliate oneself	принижуватись	[pri'niʒuwatisʲ]

| shock | шок (ч) | [ʃok] |
| to shock (vt) | шокувати | [ʃoku'wati] |

| trouble (e.g., serious ~) | неприємність (ж) | [nɛpri'ɛmnistʲ] |
| unpleasant (adj) | неприємний | [nɛpri'ɛmnij] |

fear (dread)	страх (ч)	[strah]
terrible (storm, heat)	страшний	['straʃnij]
scary (e.g., ~ story)	страшний	['straʃnij]

horror	жах (ч)	[ʒah]
awful, horrible	жахливий	[ʒah'liwij]
to begin to tremble	почати тремтіти	[po'ʧatɨ trɛm'titi]
to cry (weep)	плакати	['plakati]
to start crying	заплакати	[za'plakati]
tear	сльоза (ж)	[slʲo'za]
fault	провина (ж)	[pro'wina]
guilt (feeling)	провина (ж)	[pro'wina]
dishonor (disgrace)	ганьба (ж)	[hanʲ'ba]
protest	протест (ч)	[pro'tɛst]
stress	стрес (ч)	['strɛs]
to disturb (vt)	заважати	[zawa'ʒati]
to be furious	лютувати	[lʲutu'wati]
mad, angry (adj)	злий	['zlij]
to end (~ a relationship)	припиняти	[pripi'nʲati]
to swear (curse)	лаятися	['laʲatisʲa]
to scare (vi; get scared)	лякатися	[lʲa'katisʲa]
to hit (strike with hand)	ударити	[u'dariti]
to fight (street fight, etc.)	битися	['bitisʲa]
to settle (a conflict)	урегулювати	[urɛhulʲu'wati]
discontented (adj)	незадоволений	[nɛzado'wolɛnij]
furious (adj)	розлючений	[roz'lʲuʧɛnij]
It's not good!	Це недобре!	[ʦɛ nɛ'dɔbrɛ]
It's bad!	Це погано!	[ʦɛ po'ɦano]

Medicine

sickness	хвороба (ж)	[hwo'rɔba]
to be sick	хворіти	[hwo'riti]
health	здоров'я (с)	[zdo'rɔwʲa]

runny nose (dripping congestion)	нежить (ч)	['nɛʒitʲ]
tonsillitis	ангіна (ж)	[an'ɦina]
cold (illness)	застуда (ж)	[za'studa]
to catch a cold	застудитися	[zastu'ditisʲa]

bronchitis	бронхіт (ч)	[bron'hit]
pneumonia	запалення (с) легенів	[za'palɛnja lɛ'ɦɛniw]
flu, influenza	грип (ч)	[ɦrip]

nearsighted (adj)	короткозорий	[korotko'zɔrij]
farsighted (adj)	далекозорий	[dalɛko'zɔrij]
strabismus (crossed eyes)	косоокість (ж)	[koso'ɔkistʲ]
cross-eyed (adj)	косоокий	[koso'ɔkij]
cataract	катаракта (ж)	[kata'rakta]
glaucoma	глаукома (ж)	[ɦlau'kɔma]

stroke	інсульт (ч)	[in'sulʲt]
heart attack	інфаркт (ч)	[in'farkt]
myocardial infarction	інфаркт (ч) міокарду	[in'farkt mio'kardu]
paralysis	параліч (ч)	[para'litʃ]
to paralyze (vt)	паралізувати	[paralizu'wati]

allergy	алергія (ж)	[alɛr'ɦiʲa]
asthma	астма (ж)	['astma]
diabetes	діабет (ч)	[dia'bɛt]

| toothache | зубний біль (ч) | [zub'nij bilʲ] |
| caries | карієс (ч) | ['kariɛs] |

diarrhea	діарея (ж)	[dia'rɛʲa]
constipation	запор (ч)	[za'pɔr]
stomach upset	розлад (ч) шлунку	['rɔzlad 'ʃlunku]
food poisoning	отруєння (с)	[ot'ruɛnʲa]
to get food poisoning	отруїтись	[otru'jitisʲ]

| arthritis | артрит (ч) | [art'rit] |
| rickets | рахіт (ч) | [ra'hit] |

| rheumatism | ревматизм (ч) | [rɛwma'tizm] |
| atherosclerosis | атеросклероз (ч) | [atɛrosklɛ'rɔz] |

gastritis	гастрит (ч)	[ɦast'rit]
appendicitis	апендицит (ч)	[apɛndi'tsit]
cholecystitis	холецистит (ч)	[holɛtsis'tit]
ulcer	виразка (ж)	['wirazka]

measles	кір (ч)	[kir]
rubella (German measles)	краснуха (ж)	[kras'nuɦa]
jaundice	жовтуха (ж)	[ʒow'tuɦa]
hepatitis	гепатит (ч)	[ɦɛpa'tit]

schizophrenia	шизофренія (ж)	[ʃizofrɛ'niʲa]
rabies (hydrophobia)	сказ (ч)	[skaz]
neurosis	невроз (ч)	[nɛw'rɔz]
concussion	струс (ч) мозку	['strus 'mɔzku]

cancer	рак (ч)	[rak]
sclerosis	склероз (ч)	[sklɛ'rɔz]
multiple sclerosis	розсіяний склероз (ч)	[roz'siʲanij sklɛ'rɔz]

alcoholism	алкоголізм (ч)	[alkoɦo'lizm]
alcoholic (n)	алкоголік (ч)	[alko'ɦɔlik]
syphilis	сифіліс (ч)	['sifilis]
AIDS	СНІД (ч)	[snid]

tumor	пухлина (ж)	[puɦ'lina]
malignant (adj)	злоякісна	[zlo'ʲakisna]
benign (adj)	доброякісна	[dobro'ʲakisna]

fever	гарячка (ж)	[ɦa'rʲatʃka]
malaria	малярія (ж)	[malʲa'riʲa]
gangrene	гангрена (ж)	[ɦan'ɦrɛna]
seasickness	морська хвороба (ж)	[morsʲ'ka hwo'rɔba]
epilepsy	епілепсія (ж)	[ɛpi'lɛpsiʲa]

epidemic	епідемія (ж)	[ɛpi'dɛmiʲa]
typhus	тиф (ч)	[tif]
tuberculosis	туберкульоз (ч)	[tubɛrku'lʲoz]
cholera	холера (ж)	[ho'lɛra]
plague (bubonic ~)	чума (ж)	[tʃu'ma]

69. Symptoms. Treatments. Part 1

symptom	симптом (ч)	[simp'tɔm]
temperature	температура (ж)	[tɛmpɛra'tura]
high temperature (fever)	висока температура (ж)	[wi'sɔka tɛmpɛra'tura]
pulse (heartbeat)	пульс (ч)	[pulʲs]
dizziness (vertigo)	запаморочення (с)	[za'pamorotʃɛnʲa]

hot (adj)	гарячий	[ɦaˈrʲatʃij]
shivering	озноб (ч)	[ozˈnɔb]
pale (e.g., ~ face)	блідий	[bliˈdij]

cough	кашель (ч)	[ˈkaʃɛlʲ]
to cough (vi)	кашляти	[ˈkaʃlʲati]
to sneeze (vi)	чхати	[ˈtʃhati]
faint	непритомність (ж)	[nɛpriˈtɔmnistʲ]
to faint (vi)	знепритомніти	[znɛpriˈtɔmniti]

bruise (hematoma)	синець (ч)	[siˈnɛts]
bump (lump)	гуля (ж)	[ˈɦulʲa]
to bang (bump or hit)	удатись	[uˈdaritisʲ]
contusion (bruise)	забите місце (с)	[zaˈbitɛ ˈmistsɛ]
to get a bruise	забитися	[zaˈbitisʲa]

to limp (vi)	кульгати	[kulʲˈɦati]
dislocation	вивих (ч)	[ˈwiwiɦ]
to dislocate (vt)	вивихнути	[ˈwiwiɦnuti]
fracture	перелом (ч)	[pɛrɛˈlɔm]
to have a fracture	отримати перелом	[otˈrimati pɛrɛˈlom]

cut (e.g., paper ~)	поріз (ч)	[poˈriz]
to cut oneself	порізатися	[poˈrizatisʲa]
bleeding	кровотеча (ж)	[krowoˈtɛtʃa]

| burn (injury) | опік (ч) | [ˈɔpik] |
| to get burned | обпектися | [obpɛkˈtisʲa] |

to prick (vt)	уколоти	[ukoˈlɔti]
to prick oneself	уколотися	[ukoˈlɔtisʲa]
to injure (vt)	пошкодити	[poʃˈkɔditi]
injury	ушкодження (с)	[uʃˈkɔdʒɛnʲa]
wound	рана (ж)	[ˈrana]
trauma	травма (ж)	[ˈtrawma]

to be delirious	марити	[ˈmariti]
to stutter (vi)	заїкатися	[zajiˈkatisʲa]
sunstroke	сонячний удар (ч)	[ˈsɔnʲatʃnij uˈdar]

70. Symptoms. Treatments. Part 2

| pain, ache | біль (ч) | [bilʲ] |
| splinter (sliver) | скалка (ж) | [ˈskalka] |

sweat (perspiration)	піт (ч)	[pit]
to sweat (perspire)	спітніти	[spitˈniti]
vomiting	блювота (ж)	[blʲuˈwota]
convulsions	судома (ж)	[suˈdɔma]
pregnant (adj)	вагітна	[waˈɦitna]

to be born	народитися	[naroˈditisʲa]
delivery, labor	пологи (мн)	[poˈlɔɦi]
to deliver (~ a baby)	народжувати	[naˈrɔdʒuwati]
abortion	аборт (ч)	[aˈbɔrt]

breathing, respiration	дихання (с)	[ˈdihanʲa]
in-breath (inhalation)	вдих (ч)	[wdih]
out-breath (exhalation)	видих (ч)	[ˈwidih]
to exhale (breathe out)	видихнути	[ˈwidihnuti]
to inhale (vi)	зробити вдих	[zroˈbiti wdih]

disabled person	інвалід (ч)	[inwaˈlid]
cripple	каліка (ч)	[kaˈlika]
drug addict	наркоман (ч)	[narkoˈman]

deaf (adj)	глухий	[ɦluˈhij]
mute (adj)	німий	[niˈmij]
deaf mute (adj)	глухонімий	[ɦluhoniˈmij]

mad, insane (adj)	божевільний	[bɔʒɛˈwilʲnij]
madman	божевільний (ч)	[bɔʒɛˈwilʲnij]
(demented person)		
madwoman	божевільна (ж)	[bɔʒɛˈwilʲna]
to go insane	збожеволіти	[zbɔʒɛˈwɔliti]

gene	ген (ч)	[ɦɛn]
immunity	імунітет (ч)	[imuniˈtɛt]
hereditary (adj)	спадковий	[spadˈkɔwij]
congenital (adj)	вроджений	[ˈwrɔdʒɛnij]

virus	вірус (ч)	[ˈwirus]
microbe	мікроб (ч)	[mikˈrɔb]
bacterium	бактерія (ж)	[bakˈtɛriʲa]
infection	інфекція (ж)	[inˈfɛktsiʲa]

71. Symptoms. Treatments. Part 3

| hospital | лікарня (ж) | [liˈkarnʲa] |
| patient | пацієнт (ч) | [patsiˈɛnt] |

diagnosis	діагноз (ч)	[diˈaɦnoz]
cure	лікування (с)	[likuˈwanʲa]
medical treatment	лікування (с)	[likuˈwanʲa]
to get treatment	лікуватися	[likuˈwatisʲa]
to treat (~ a patient)	лікувати	[likuˈwati]
to nurse (look after)	доглядати	[doɦlʲaˈdati]
care (nursing ~)	догляд (ч)	[ˈdɔɦlʲad]

| operation, surgery | операція (ж) | [opɛˈratsiʲa] |
| to bandage (~ a wound) | перев'язати | [pɛrɛwʲˈaˈzati] |

bandaging	перев'язка (ж)	[pɛrɛ'wʲazka]
vaccination	щеплення (с)	['ɕɛplɛnʲa]
to vaccinate (vt)	робити щеплення	[ro'bitɨ 'ɕɛplɛnʲa]
injection, shot	ін'єкція (ж)	[i'nʲɛktsiʲa]
to give an injection	робити укол	[ro'bitɨ u'kɔl]

attack	напад	['napad]
amputation	ампутація (ж)	[ampu'tatsiʲa]
to amputate (vt)	ампутувати	[amputu'watɨ]
coma	кома (ж)	['kɔma]
to be in a coma	бути в комі	['butɨ w 'kɔmi]
intensive care	реанімація (ж)	[rɛani'matsiʲa]

to recover (e.g., ~ from flu)	видужувати	[wi'duʒuwatɨ]
condition (patient's ~)	стан (ч)	['stan]
consciousness	свідомість (ж)	[swi'dɔmistʲ]
memory (ability to recall)	пам'ять (ж)	['pamʲatʲ]

to pull out (extract, ~ a tooth)	видалити	['widalitɨ]
filling	пломба (ж)	['plɔmba]
to fill (~ a dental cavity)	пломбувати	[plombu'watɨ]

hypnosis	гіпноз (ч)	[ɦip'nɔz]
to hypnotize (vt)	гіпнотизувати	[ɦipnotizu'watɨ]

72. Doctors

doctor	лікар (ч)	['likar]
nurse	медсестра (ж)	[mɛdsɛst'ra]
personal doctor	особистий лікар (ч)	[oso'bistij 'likar]

dentist	стоматолог (ч)	[stoma'tɔloɦ]
eye doctor	окуліст (ч)	[oku'list]
internist	терапевт (ч)	[tɛra'pɛwt]
surgeon	хірург (ч)	[hi'rurɦ]

psychiatrist	психіатр (ч)	[psihi'atr]
pediatrician	педіатр (ч)	[pɛdi'atr]
psychologist	психолог (ч)	[psi'hɔloɦ]
gynecologist	гінеколог (ч)	[ɦinɛ'kɔloɦ]
cardiologist	кардіолог (ч)	[kardi'ɔloɦ]

73. Medicine. Drugs. Accessories

medicine, drug	ліки (мн)	['liki]
remedy	засіб (ч)	['zasib]
to prescribe (vt)	прописати	[propi'sati]

prescription	рецепт (ч)	[rɛ'tsɛpt]
tablet, pill	пігулка (ж)	[pi'ɦulka]
ointment	мазь (ж)	[mazʲ]
ampule	ампула (ж)	['ampula]
mixture, solution	мікстура (ж)	[miks'tura]
syrup	сироп (ч)	[si'rɔp]
capsule	пігулка (ж)	[pi'ɦulka]
powder	порошок (ч)	[poro'ʃɔk]

gauze bandage	бинт (ч)	[bint]
cotton wool	вата (ж)	['wata]
iodine	йод (ч)	[ˈiod]

Band-Aid	лейкопластир (ч)	[lɛjko'plastir]
eyedropper	піпетка (ж)	[pi'pɛtka]
thermometer	градусник (ч)	['ɦradusnik]
syringe	шприц (ч)	[ʃprits]

| wheelchair | інвалідне крісло (с) | [inwa'lidnɛ 'krislo] |
| crutches | милиці (мн) | ['militsi] |

painkiller	знеболювальне (с)	[znɛ'bolʲuwalʲnɛ]
laxative	проносне (с)	[pronos'nɛ]
alcohol (rubbing ~)	спирт (ч)	[spirt]
medicinal herbs	лікарська трава (ж)	['likarsʲka tra'wa]
herbal (~ tea)	трав'яний	[trawˀʲa'nij]

74. Smoking. Tobacco products

tobacco	тютюн (ч)	[tʲu'tʲun]
cigarette	цигарка (ж)	[tsi'ɦarka]
cigar	сигара (ж)	[si'ɦara]
pipe	люлька (ж)	['lʲulʲka]
pack (of cigarettes)	пачка (ж)	['patʃka]

matches	сірники (мн)	[sirni'ki]
matchbox	сірникова коробка (ж)	[sirni'kɔwa ko'rɔbka]
lighter	запальничка (ж)	[zapalʲ'nitʃka]
ashtray	попільниця (ж)	[popilʲ'nitsʲa]
cigarette case	портсигар (ч)	[portsi'ɦar]
cigarette holder	мундштук (ч)	[mund'ʃtuk]
filter (cigarette tip)	фільтр (ч)	['filʲtr]

to smoke (vi, vt)	палити	[pa'liti]
to light a cigarette	запалити	[zapa'liti]
smoking	паління (с)	[pa'linʲa]
smoker	курець (ч)	[ku'rɛts]
stub, butt (cigarette ~)	недопалок (ч)	[nɛdo'palok]
smoke, fumes	дим (ч)	[dim]
ash	попіл (ч)	['pɔpil]

HUMAN HABITAT

City

city, town	місто (с)	['misto]
capital city	столиця (ж)	[stoˈliʦⁱa]
village	село (с)	[sɛˈlɔ]

city map	план (ч) міста	[plan ˈmista]
downtown	центр (ч) міста	[ʦɛntr ˈmista]
suburb	передмістя (с)	[pɛrɛdˈmistⁱa]
suburban (adj)	приміський	[primisⁱˈkij]

outskirts	околиця (ж)	[oˈkɔliʦⁱa]
environs (suburbs)	околиці (мн)	[oˈkɔliʦi]
city block	квартал (ч)	[kwarˈtal]
residential block (area)	житловий квартал (ч)	[ʒitloˈwij kwarˈtal]

traffic	вуличний рух (ч)	[ˈwuliʧnij ruh]
traffic lights	світлофор (ч)	[switloˈfɔr]
public transportation	міський транспорт (ч)	[misⁱˈkij ˈtransport]
intersection	перехрестя (с)	[pɛrɛhˈrɛstⁱa]

crosswalk	пішохідний перехід (ч)	[piʃoˈhidnij pɛrɛˈhid]
pedestrian underpass	підземний перехід (ч)	[piˈdzɛmnij pɛrɛˈhid]
to cross (~ the street)	переходити	[pɛrɛˈhɔditi]
pedestrian	пішохід (ч)	[piʃoˈhid]
sidewalk	тротуар (ч)	[trotuˈar]

bridge	міст (ч)	[mist]
embankment (river walk)	набережна (ж)	[ˈnabɛrɛʒna]
fountain	фонтан (ч)	[fonˈtan]

allée (garden walkway)	алея (ж)	[aˈlɛⁱa]
park	парк (ч)	[park]
boulevard	бульвар (ч)	[bulⁱˈwar]
square	площа (ж)	[ˈplɔʧa]
avenue (wide street)	проспект (ч)	[prosˈpɛkt]
street	вулиця (ж)	[ˈwuliʦⁱa]
side street	провулок (ч)	[proˈwulok]
dead end	глухий кут (ч)	[ɦluˈhij kut]
house	будинок (ч)	[buˈdinok]
building	споруда (ж)	[spoˈruda]

skyscraper	хмарочос (ч)	[hmaro'tʃɔs]
facade	фасад (ч)	[fa'sad]
roof	дах (ч)	[dah]
window	вікно (с)	[wik'nɔ]
arch	арка (ж)	['arka]
column	колона (ж)	[ko'lɔna]
corner	ріг (ч)	[riĥ]

store window	вітрина (ж)	[wi'trina]
signboard (store sign, etc.)	вивіска (ж)	['wiwiska]
poster (e.g., playbill)	афіша (ж)	[a'fiʃa]
advertising poster	рекламний плакат (ч)	[rɛk'lamnij pla'kat]
billboard	рекламний щит (ч)	[rɛk'lamnij ɕit]

garbage, trash	сміття (с)	[smit'tʲa]
trash can (public ~)	урна (ж)	['urna]
to litter (vi)	смітити	[smi'titi]
garbage dump	смітник (ч)	[smit'nik]

phone booth	телефонна будка (ж)	[tɛlɛ'fɔna 'budka]
lamppost	ліхтарний стовп (ч)	[lih'tarnij stowp]
bench (park ~)	лавка (ж)	['lawka]

police officer	поліцейський (ч)	[poli'tsɛjsʲkij]
police	поліція (ж)	[po'litsiʲa]
beggar	жебрак (ч)	[ʒɛb'rak]
homeless (n)	безпритульний (ч)	[bɛzpri'tulʲnij]

76. Urban institutions

store	магазин (ч)	[maĥa'zin]
drugstore, pharmacy	аптека (ж)	[ap'tɛka]
eyeglass store	оптика (ж)	['ɔptika]
shopping mall	торгівельний центр (ч)	[torĥi'wɛlʲnij 'tsɛntr]
supermarket	супермаркет (ч)	[supɛr'markɛt]

bakery	пекарня (ж)	[pɛ'karnʲa]
baker	пекар (ч)	['pɛkar]
pastry shop	кондитерська (ж)	[kon'ditɛrsʲka]
grocery store	бакалія (ж)	[baka'liʲa]
butcher shop	м'ясний магазин (ч)	[mʲʲas'nij maĥa'zin]

| produce store | овочевий магазин (ч) | [owo'tʃɛwij maĥa'zin] |
| market | ринок (ч) | ['rinok] |

coffee house	кав'ярня (ж)	[ka'wʲʲarnʲa]
restaurant	ресторан (ч)	[rɛsto'ran]
pub, bar	пивна (ж)	[piw'na]
pizzeria	піцерія (ж)	[pitsɛ'riʲa]
hair salon	перукарня (ж)	[pɛru'karnʲa]

post office	пошта (ж)	['pɔʃta]
dry cleaners	хімчистка (ж)	[him'tʃistka]
photo studio	фотоательє (с)	[fotoatɛ'ljɛ]

shoe store	взуттєвий магазин (ч)	[wzut'tɛwij maɦa'zin]
bookstore	книгарня (ж)	[kni'ɦarnʲa]
sporting goods store	спортивний магазин (ч)	[spor'tiwnij maɦa'zin]

clothes repair shop	ремонт (ч) одягу	[rɛ'mɔnt 'ɔdʲaɦu]
formal wear rental	прокат (ч) одягу	[pro'kat 'ɔdʲaɦu]
video rental store	прокат (ч) фільмів	[pro'kat 'filʲmiw]

circus	цирк (ч)	[tsirk]
zoo	зоопарк (ч)	[zoo'park]
movie theater	кінотеатр (ч)	[kinotɛ'atr]
museum	музей (ч)	[mu'zɛj]
library	бібліотека (ж)	[biblio'tɛka]

| theater | театр (ч) | [tɛ'atr] |
| opera (opera house) | опера (ж) | ['ɔpɛra] |

| nightclub | нічний клуб (ч) | [nitʃ'nij klub] |
| casino | казино (с) | [kazi'nɔ] |

mosque	мечеть (ж)	[mɛ'tʃɛtʲ]
synagogue	синагога (ж)	[sina'ɦoɦa]
cathedral	собор (ч)	[so'bɔr]

| temple | храм (ч) | [hram] |
| church | церква (ж) | ['tsɛrkwa] |

college	інститут (ч)	[insti'tut]
university	університет (ч)	[uniwɛrsi'tɛt]
school	школа (ж)	['ʃkɔla]

| prefecture | префектура (ж) | [prɛfɛk'tura] |
| city hall | мерія (ж) | ['mɛriʲa] |

| hotel | готель (ч) | [ɦo'tɛlʲ] |
| bank | банк (ч) | [bank] |

| embassy | посольство (с) | [po'sɔlʲstwo] |
| travel agency | турагентство (с) | [tura'ɦɛntstwo] |

| information office | довідкове бюро (с) | [dowid'kɔwɛ bʲu'rɔ] |
| currency exchange | обмінний пункт (ч) | [ob'minij punkt] |

| subway | метро (с) | [mɛt'rɔ] |
| hospital | лікарня (ж) | [li'karnʲa] |

| gas station | автозаправка (ж) | [awtoza'prawka] |
| parking lot | автостоянка (ж) | [awtosto'ʲanka] |

77. Urban transportation

bus	автобус (ч)	[aw'tɔbus]
streetcar	трамвай (ч)	[tram'waj]
trolley bus	тролейбус (ч)	[tro'lɛjbus]
route (bus ~)	маршрут (ч)	[marʃ'rut]
number (e.g., bus ~)	номер (ч)	['nɔmɛr]
to go by …	їхати на…	['jihati na]
to get on (~ the bus)	сісти	['sisti]
to get off …	вийти	['wijti]
stop (e.g., bus ~)	зупинка (ж)	[zu'pinka]
next stop	наступна зупинка (ж)	[na'stupna zu'pinka]
terminus	кінцева зупинка (ж)	[kin'ʦɛwa zu'pinka]
schedule	розклад (ч)	['rɔzklad]
to wait (vt)	чекати	[ʧɛ'kati]
ticket	квиток (ч)	[kwi'tɔk]
fare	вартість (ж) квитка	['wartistʲ kwit'ka]
cashier (ticket seller)	касир (ч)	[ka'sir]
ticket inspection	контроль (ч)	[kon'trɔlʲ]
ticket inspector	контролер (ч)	[kontro'lɛr]
to be late (for …)	запізнюватися	[za'piznʲuwatisʲa]
to miss (~ the train, etc.)	спізнитися	[spiz'nitisʲa]
to be in a hurry	поспішати	[pospi'ʃati]
taxi, cab	таксі (с)	[tak'si]
taxi driver	таксист (ч)	[tak'sist]
by taxi	на таксі	[na tak'si]
taxi stand	стоянка таксі	[stoʲanka tak'si]
to call a taxi	викликати таксі	['wiklikati tak'si]
to take a taxi	взяти таксі	['wzʲati tak'si]
traffic	вуличний рух (ч)	['wuliʧnij ruh]
traffic jam	затор (ч)	[za'tɔr]
rush hour	години (мн) пік	[ɦo'dini pik]
to park (vi)	паркуватися	[parku'watisʲa]
to park (vt)	паркувати	[parku'wati]
parking lot	стоянка (ж)	[stoʲanka]
subway	метро (с)	[mɛt'rɔ]
station	станція (ж)	['stanʦiʲa]
to take the subway	їхати в метро	['jihati w mɛt'rɔ]
train	поїзд (ч)	['pɔjizd]
train station	вокзал (ч)	[wok'zal]

78. Sightseeing

monument	пам'ятник (ч)	['pamʲatnik]
fortress	фортеця (ж)	[for'tɛtsʲa]
palace	палац (ч)	[pa'lats]
castle	замок (ч)	['zamok]
tower	вежа (ж)	['wɛʒa]
mausoleum	мавзолей (ч)	[mawzo'lɛj]
architecture	архітектура (ж)	[arhitɛk'tura]
medieval (adj)	середньовічний	[sɛrɛdnʲo'witʃnij]
ancient (adj)	старовинний	[staro'winij]
national (adj)	національний	[natsio'nalʲnij]
famous (~ monument, etc.)	відомий	[wi'dɔmij]
tourist	турист (ч)	[tu'rist]
guide (person)	гід (ч)	[ɦid]
excursion, sightseeing tour	екскурсія (ж)	[ɛks'kursiʲa]
to show (vt)	показувати	[po'kazuwati]
to tell (vt)	розповідати	[rozpowi'dati]
to find (vt)	знайти	[znaj'ti]
to get lost (lose one's way)	загубитися	[zaɦu'bitisʲa]
map (e.g., subway ~)	схема (ж)	['sxɛma]
map (e.g., city ~)	план (ч)	[plan]
souvenir, gift	сувенір (ч)	[suwɛ'nir]
gift shop	магазин (ч) сувенірів	[maɦa'zin suwɛ'niriw]
to take pictures	фотографувати	[fotoɦrafu'wati]
to have one's picture taken	фотографуватися	[fotoɦrafu'watisʲa]

79. Shopping

to buy (purchase)	купляти	[kup'lʲati]
purchase	покупка (ж)	[po'kupka]
to go shopping	робити покупки	[ro'biti po'kupki]
shopping	шопінг (ч)	['ʃopinɦ]
to be open (ab. store)	працювати	[pratsʲu'wati]
to be closed	зачинитися	[zatʃi'nitisʲa]
footwear, shoes	взуття (с)	[wzut'tʲa]
clothes, clothing	одяг (ч)	['ɔdʲaɦ]
cosmetics	косметика (ж)	[kos'mɛtika]
food products	продукти (мн)	[pro'dukti]
gift, present	подарунок (ч)	[poda'runok]
salesman	продавець (ч)	[proda'wɛts]
saleswoman	продавщиця (ж)	[prodaw'çitsʲa]

check out, cash desk	каса (ж)	['kasa]
mirror	дзеркало (с)	['dzɛrkalo]
counter (store ~)	прилавок (ч)	[pri'lawok]
fitting room	примірочна (ж)	[pri'mirotʃna]

to try on	приміряти	[pri'mirʲati]
to fit (ab. dress, etc.)	пасувати	[pasu'wati]
to like (I like …)	подобатися	[po'dobatisʲa]

price	ціна (ж)	[ʦi'na]
price tag	цінник (ч)	['ʦinik]
to cost (vt)	коштувати	['kɔʃtuwati]
How much?	Скільки?	['skilʲki]
discount	знижка (ж)	['zniʒka]

inexpensive (adj)	недорогий	[nɛdoro'hij]
cheap (adj)	дешевий	[dɛ'ʃɛwij]
expensive (adj)	дорогий	[doro'hij]
It's expensive	Це дорого.	[ʦɛ 'dɔroɦo]

rental (n)	прокат (ч)	[pro'kat]
to rent (~ a tuxedo)	взяти напрокат	['wzʲati napro'kat]
credit (trade credit)	кредит (ч)	[krɛ'dit]
on credit (adv)	в кредит	[w krɛ'dit]

80. Money

money	гроші (мн)	['ɦrɔʃi]
currency exchange	обмін (ч)	['ɔbmin]
exchange rate	курс (ч)	[kurs]
ATM	банкомат (ч)	[banko'mat]
coin	монета (ж)	[mo'nɛta]

| dollar | долар (ч) | ['dɔlar] |
| euro | євро (с) | ['ɛwro] |

lira	італійська ліра (ж)	[ita'lijsʲka 'lira]
Deutschmark	марка (ж)	['marka]
franc	франк (ч)	['frank]
pound sterling	фунт (ч)	['funt]
yen	єна (ж)	['ɛna]

debt	борг (ч)	['bɔrɦ]
debtor	боржник (ч)	[borʒ'nik]
to lend (money)	позичити	[po'zitʃiti]
to borrow (vi, vt)	взяти в борг	['wzʲati w bɔrɦ]

bank	банк (ч)	[bank]
account	рахунок (ч)	[ra'hunok]
to deposit (vt)	покласти	[pok'lasti]

| to deposit into the account | покласти на рахунок | [pok'lasti na ra'hunok] |
| to withdraw (vt) | зняти з рахунку | ['znʲati z ra'hunku] |

credit card	кредитна картка (ж)	[krɛ'ditna 'kartka]
cash	готівка (ж)	[ɦo'tiwka]
check	чек (ч)	[tʃɛk]
to write a check	виписати чек	['wipisati 'tʃɛk]
checkbook	чекова книжка (ж)	['tʃɛkowa 'kniʒka]

wallet	портмоне (с)	[portmo'nɛ]
change purse	гаманець (ч)	[ɦama'nɛts]
safe	сейф (ч)	[sɛjf]

heir	спадкоємець (ч)	[spadko'ɛmɛts]
inheritance	спадщина (ж)	['spadɕina]
fortune (wealth)	статок (ч)	['statok]

lease	оренда (ж)	[o'rɛnda]
rent (money)	квартирна плата (ж)	[kwar'tirna 'plata]
to rent (sth from sb)	зняти	['znʲati]

price	ціна (ж)	[tsi'na]
cost	вартість (ж)	['wartistʲ]
sum	сума (ж)	['suma]

to spend (vt)	витрачати	[witra'tʃati]
expenses	витрати (мн)	['witrati]
to economize (vi, vt)	економити	[ɛko'nɔmiti]
economical	економний	[ɛko'nɔmnij]

to pay (vi, vt)	платити	[pla'titi]
payment	оплата (ж)	[op'lata]
change (give the ~)	решта (ж)	['rɛʃta]

tax	податок (ч)	[po'datok]
fine	штраф (ч)	[ʃtraf]
to fine (vt)	штрафувати	[ʃtrafu'wati]

81. Post. Postal service

post office	пошта (ж)	['pɔʃta]
mail (letters, etc.)	пошта (ж)	['pɔʃta]
mailman	листоноша (ч)	[listo'nɔʃa]
opening hours	години (мн) роботи	[ɦo'dini ro'bɔti]

| letter | лист (ч) | [list] |
| registered letter | рекомендований лист (ч) | [rɛkomɛn'dɔwanij list] |

| postcard | листівка (ж) | [lis'tiwka] |
| telegram | телеграма (ж) | [tɛlɛ'ɦrama] |

| package (parcel) | посилка (ж) | [po'siɫka] |
| money transfer | грошовий переказ (ч) | [ɦroʃo'wij pɛ'rɛkaz] |

to receive (vt)	отримати	[ot'rimati]
to send (vt)	відправити	[wid'prawiti]
sending	відправлення (с)	[wid'prawlɛnʲa]

address	адреса (ж)	[ad'rɛsa]
ZIP code	індекс (ч)	['indɛks]
sender	відправник (ч)	[wid'prawnik]
receiver	одержувач (ч)	[o'dɛrʒuwatʃ]

| name (first name) | ім'я (с) | [i'mʲa] |
| surname (last name) | прізвище (с) | ['prizwiɕɛ] |

postage rate	тариф (ч)	[ta'rif]
standard (adj)	звичайний	[zwɨ'tʃajnij]
economical (adj)	економічний	[ɛkono'mitʃnij]

weight	вага (ж)	[wa'ɦa]
to weigh (~ letters)	зважувати	['zwaʒuwati]
envelope	конверт (ч)	[kon'wɛrt]
postage stamp	марка (ж)	['marka]
to stamp an envelope	приклеювати марку	[prik'lɛʲuwati 'marku]

Dwelling. House. Home

82. House. Dwelling

house	будинок (ч)	[bu'dinok]
at home (adv)	вдома	['wdɔma]
yard	двір (ч)	[dwir]
fence (iron ~)	огорожа (ж)	[oɦo'rɔʒa]
brick (n)	цегла (ж)	['tsɛɦla]
brick (as adj)	цегляний	[tsɛɦlʲa'nij]
stone (n)	камінь (ч)	['kaminʲ]
stone (as adj)	кам'яний	[kamʲʲa'nij]
concrete (n)	бетон (ч)	[bɛ'tɔn]
concrete (as adj)	бетонний	[bɛ'tɔnij]
new (new-built)	новий	[no'wij]
old (adj)	старий	[sta'rij]
ramshackle	обвітшалий	[obwit'ʃalij]
modern (adj)	сучасний	[su'tʃasnij]
multistory (adj)	багатоповерховий	[ba'ɦato powɛr'ɦowij]
tall (~ building)	високий	[wi'sɔkij]
floor, story	поверх (ч)	['pɔwɛrh]
single-story (adj)	одноповерховий	[odnopowɛr'ɦowij]
1st floor	нижній поверх (ч)	['niʒnij 'pɔwɛrh]
top floor	верхній поверх (ч)	['wɛrhnij 'pɔwɛrh]
roof	дах (ч)	[dah]
chimney	труба (ж)	[tru'ba]
roof tiles	черепиця (ж)	[tʃɛrɛ'pitsʲa]
tiled (adj)	черепичний	[tʃɛrɛ'pitʃnij]
attic (storage place)	горище (c)	[ɦo'riɕɛ]
window	вікно (c)	[wik'nɔ]
glass	скло (c)	['sklo]
window ledge	підвіконня (c)	[pidwi'konʲa]
shutters	віконниці (мн)	[wi'kɔnitsi]
wall	стіна (ж)	[sti'na]
balcony	балкон (ч)	[bal'kɔn]
downspout	ринва (ж)	['rinwa]
upstairs (to be ~)	нагорі	[naɦo'ri]
to go upstairs	підніматися	[pidni'matisʲa]

| to come down (the stairs) | спускатися | [spus'katisʲa] |
| to move (relocate to new premises) | переїздити | [pɛrɛjiz'diti] |

83. House. Entrance. Elevator

entrance	під'їзд (ч)	[pidˀjizd]
stairs (stairway)	сходи (мн)	['shɔdi]
steps	сходинки (мн)	['shɔdinki]
banister	поруччя (мн)	[po'ruʧʲa]
lobby (hotel ~)	хол (ч)	[hol]
mailbox	поштова скринька (ж)	[poʃ'tɔwa sk'rinʲka]
garbage can	бак (ч) для сміття	[bak dlʲa smit'tʲa]
trash chute	сміттєпровід (ч)	[smittɛ'prɔwid]
elevator	ліфт (ч)	[lift]
freight elevator	вантажний ліфт (ч)	[wan'taʒnij lift]
elevator cage	кабіна (ж)	[ka'bina]
to take the elevator	їхати в ліфті	['jihati w 'lifti]
apartment	квартира (ж)	[kwar'tira]
residents (~ of a building)	мешканці (мн)	['mɛʃkanʦi]
neighbor (masc.)	сусід (ч)	[su'sid]
neighbor (fem.)	сусідка (ж)	[su'sidka]
neighbors	сусіди (мн)	[su'sidi]

84. House. Doors. Locks

door	двері (мн)	['dwɛri]
gate (vehicle ~)	брама (ж)	['brama]
handle, doorknob	ручка (ж)	['ruʧka]
to unlock (unbolt)	відкрити	[wid'kriti]
to open (vt)	відкривати	[widkri'wati]
to close (vt)	закривати	[zakri'wati]
key	ключ (ч)	[klʲuʧ]
bunch (~ of keys)	в'язка (ж)	['wʲazka]
to creak (door, etc.)	скрипіти	[skri'piti]
creak	скрипіння (с)	[skri'pinʲa]
hinge (door ~)	петля (ж)	[pɛt'lʲa]
doormat	килимок (ч)	[kili'mɔk]
door lock	замок (ч)	[za'mɔk]
keyhole	замкова щілина (ж)	[zam'kowa ɕi'lina]
crossbar (sliding bar)	засув (ч)	['zasuw]
door latch	засувка (ж)	['zasuwka]
padlock	навісний замок (ч)	[nawis'nij za'mɔk]

to ring (~ the door bell)	дзвонити	[dʒwo'niti]
ringing (sound)	дзвінок (ч)	[dʒwi'nɔk]
doorbell	дзвінок (ч)	[dʒwi'nɔk]
doorbell button	кнопка (ж)	['knɔpka]
knock (at the door)	стукіт (ч)	['stukit]
to knock (vi)	стукати	['stukati]

code	код (ч)	[kod]
combination lock	кодовий замок (ч)	['kɔdowij za'mɔk]
intercom	домофон (ч)	[domo'fɔn]
number (on the door)	номер (ч)	['nɔmɛr]
doorplate	табличка (ж)	[tab'litʃka]
peephole	вічко (с)	['witʃko]

85. Country house

village	село (с)	[sɛ'lɔ]
vegetable garden	город (ч)	[ɦo'rɔd]
fence	паркан (ч)	[par'kan]
picket fence	тин (ч)	[tin]
wicket gate	хвіртка (ж)	['hwirtka]

granary	комора (ж)	[ko'mɔra]
root cellar	льох (ч)	[lʲoh]
shed (garden ~)	сарай (ч)	[sa'raj]
water well	криниця (ж)	[kri'nitsʲa]

stove (wood-fired ~)	піч (ж)	[pitʃ]
to stoke the stove	розпалювати піч	[roz'palʲuwati pitʃ]
firewood	дрова (мн)	['drɔwa]
log (firewood)	поліно (с)	[po'lino]

veranda	веранда (ж)	[wɛ'randa]
deck (terrace)	тераса (ж)	[tɛ'rasa]
stoop (front steps)	ґанок (ч)	['ɦanok]
swing (hanging seat)	гойдалка (ж)	['ɦɔjdalka]

86. Castle. Palace

castle	замок (ч)	['zamok]
palace	палац (ч)	[pa'laʦ]
fortress	фортеця (ж)	[for'tɛtsʲa]

wall (castle wall)	стіна (ж)	[sti'na]
tower	вежа (ж)	['wɛʒa]
keep, donjon	головна вежа (ж)	[ɦolow'na 'wɛʒa]
portcullis	підйомна брама (ж)	[pid'jɔmna 'brama]
underground passage	підземний хід (ч)	[pi'dzɛmnij hid]

moat	рів (ч)	[riw]
chain	ланцюг (ч)	[lanˈʦʲuɦ]
arrow loop	бійниця (ж)	[bijˈniʦʲa]

magnificent (adj)	пишний	[ˈpiʃnij]
majestic (adj)	величний	[wɛˈlitʃnij]
impregnable (adj)	неприступний	[nɛpriˈstupnij]
medieval (adj)	середньовічний	[sɛrɛdnʲoˈwitʃnij]

87. Apartment

apartment	квартира (ж)	[kwarˈtira]
room	кімната (ж)	[kimˈnata]
bedroom	спальня (ж)	[ˈspalʲnʲa]
dining room	їдальня (ж)	[ˈjidalʲnʲa]
living room	вітальня (ж)	[wiˈtalʲnʲa]
study (home office)	кабінет (ч)	[kabiˈnɛt]

entry room	передпокій (ч)	[pɛrɛdˈpɔkij]
bathroom	ванна кімната (ж)	[ˈwana kimˈnata]
half bath	туалет (ч)	[tuaˈlɛt]

ceiling	стеля (ж)	[ˈstɛlʲa]
floor	підлога (ж)	[pidˈlɔɦa]
corner	куток (ч)	[kuˈtɔk]

88. Apartment. Cleaning

to clean (vi, vt)	прибирати	[pribiˈrati]
to put away (to stow)	прибирати	[pribiˈrati]
dust	пил (ч)	[pil]
dusty (adj)	курний	[kurˈnij]
to dust (vt)	витирати пил	[witiˈrati pil]

| vacuum cleaner | пилосос (ч) | [piɫoˈsɔs] |
| to vacuum (vt) | пилососити | [piɫoˈsɔsiti] |

| to sweep (vi, vt) | підмітати | [pidmiˈtati] |
| sweepings | сміття (с) | [smitˈtʲa] |

| order | лад (ч) | [lad] |
| disorder, mess | безлад (ч) | [ˈbɛzlad] |

| mop | швабра (ж) | [ˈʃwabra] |
| dust cloth | ганчірка (ж) | [ɦanˈtʃirka] |

| short broom | віник (ч) | [ˈwinik] |
| dustpan | совок (ч) для сміття | [soˈwɔk dlʲa smitˈtʲa] |

89. Furniture. Interior

furniture	меблі (мн)	['mɛbli]
table	стіл (ч)	[stil]
chair	стілець (ч)	[sti'lɛts]
bed	ліжко (с)	['liʒko]
couch, sofa	диван (ч)	[di'wan]
armchair	крісло (с)	['krislo]

| bookcase | шафа (ж) | ['ʃafa] |
| shelf | полиця (ж) | [po'litsʲa] |

wardrobe	шафа (ж)	['ʃafa]
coat rack (wall-mounted ~)	вішалка (ж)	['wiʃalka]
coat stand	вішак (ч)	[wi'ʃak]

| bureau, dresser | комод (ч) | [ko'mɔd] |
| coffee table | журнальний столик (ч) | [ʒur'nalʲnij 'stɔlik] |

mirror	дзеркало (с)	['dzɛrkalo]
carpet	килим (ч)	['kilim]
rug, small carpet	килимок (ч)	[kili'mɔk]

fireplace	камін (ч)	[ka'min]
candle	свічка (ж)	['switʃka]
candlestick	свічник (ч)	[switʃ'nik]

drapes	штори (мн)	['ʃtɔri]
wallpaper	шпалери (мн)	[ʃpa'lɛri]
blinds (jalousie)	жалюзі (мн)	['ʒalʲuzi]

table lamp	настільна лампа (ж)	[na'stilʲna 'lampa]
wall lamp (sconce)	світильник (ч)	[swi'tilʲnik]
floor lamp	торшер (ч)	[tor'ʃɛr]
chandelier	люстра (ж)	['lʲustra]

leg (of a chair, table)	ніжка (ж)	['niʒka]
armrest	підлокітник (ч)	[pidlo'kitnik]
back (backrest)	спинка (ж)	['spinka]
drawer	шухляда (ж)	[ʃuh'lʲada]

90. Bedding

bedclothes	білизна (ж)	[bi'lizna]
pillow	подушка (ж)	[po'duʃka]
pillowcase	наволочка (ж)	['nawolotʃka]
duvet, comforter	ковдра (ж)	['kɔwdra]
sheet	простирадло (с)	[prosti'radlo]
bedspread	покривало (с)	[pokri'walo]

91. Kitchen

kitchen	кухня (ж)	['kuhnʲa]
gas	газ (ч)	[ɦaz]
gas stove (range)	плита (ж) газова	[pliˈta 'ɦazowa]
electric stove	плита (ж) електрична	[pliˈta ɛlɛktˈritʃna]
oven	духовка (ж)	[du'ɦowka]
microwave oven	мікрохвильова піч (ж)	[mikrohwilʲo'wa pitʃ]
refrigerator	холодильник (ч)	[holoˈdilʲnik]
freezer	морозильник (ч)	[moro'zilʲnik]
dishwasher	посудомийна машина (ж)	[posudo'mijna ma'ʃina]
meat grinder	м'ясорубка (ж)	[mʲʲaso'rubka]
juicer	соковижималка (ж)	[sokowiʒi'malka]
toaster	тостер (ч)	['tɔstɛr]
mixer	міксер (ч)	['miksɛr]
coffee machine	кавоварка (ж)	[kawo'warka]
coffee pot	кавник (ч)	[kaw'nik]
coffee grinder	кавомолка (ж)	[kawo'mɔlka]
kettle	чайник (ч)	['tʃajnik]
teapot	заварник (ч)	[za'warnik]
lid	кришка (ж)	['kriʃka]
tea strainer	ситечко (с)	['sitɛtʃko]
spoon	ложка (ж)	['lɔʒka]
teaspoon	чайна ложка (ж)	['tʃajna 'lɔʒka]
soup spoon	столова ложка (ж)	[sto'lɔwa 'lɔʒka]
fork	виделка (ж)	[wi'dɛlka]
knife	ніж (ч)	[niʒ]
tableware (dishes)	посуд (ч)	['pɔsud]
plate (dinner ~)	тарілка (ж)	[ta'rilka]
saucer	блюдце (с)	['blʲudtsɛ]
shot glass	чарка (ж)	['tʃarka]
glass (tumbler)	склянка (ж)	['sklʲanka]
cup	чашка (ж)	['tʃaʃka]
sugar bowl	цукорниця (ж)	['tsukornitsʲa]
salt shaker	сільничка (ж)	[silʲ'nitʃka]
pepper shaker	перечниця (ж)	['pɛrɛtʃnitsʲa]
butter dish	маслянка (ж)	['maslʲanka]
stock pot (deep crock)	каструля (ж)	[kas'trulʲa]
frying pan (skillet)	сковорідка (ж)	[skowo'ridka]
ladle	черпак (ч)	[tʃɛr'pak]
colander	друшляк (ч)	[druʃ'lʲak]

tray (serving ~)	піднос (ч)	[pid'nɔs]
bottle	пляшка (ж)	['plʲaʃka]
jar (glass)	банка (ж)	['banka]
can	бляшанка (ж)	[blʲa'ʃanka]

bottle opener	відкривачка (ж)	[widkri'watʃka]
can opener	відкривачка (ж)	[widkri'watʃka]
corkscrew	штопор (ч)	['ʃtopor]
filter	фільтр (ч)	['filʲtr]
to filter (vt)	фільтрувати	[filʲtru'wati]

| trash, garbage (food waste, etc.) | сміття (с) | [smit'tʲa] |
| trash can (kitchen ~) | відро (с) для сміття | [wid'ro dlʲa smit'tʲa] |

92. Bathroom

bathroom	ванна кімната (ж)	['wana kim'nata]
water	вода (ж)	[wo'da]
faucet	кран (ч)	[kran]
hot water	гаряча вода (ж)	[ha'rʲatʃa wo'da]
cold water	холодна вода (ж)	[ho'lɔdna wo'da]

toothpaste	зубна паста (ж)	[zub'na 'pasta]
to brush one's teeth	чистити зуби	['tʃistiti 'zubi]
toothbrush	зубна щітка (ж)	[zub'na 'ɕitka]

to shave (vi)	голитися	[ho'litisʲa]
shaving foam	піна (ж) для гоління	['pina dlʲa ho'linʲa]
razor	бритва (ж)	['britwa]

to wash (one's hands, etc.)	мити	['miti]
to take a bath	митися	['mitisʲa]
shower	душ (ч)	[duʃ]
to take a shower	приймати душ	[prij'mati duʃ]

bathtub	ванна (ж)	['wana]
toilet (toilet bowl)	унітаз (ч)	[uni'taz]
sink (washbasin)	раковина (ж)	['rakowina]

| soap | мило (с) | ['miɫo] |
| soap dish | мильниця (ж) | ['milʲnitsʲa] |

sponge	губка (ж)	['hubka]
shampoo	шампунь (ч)	[ʃam'punʲ]
towel	рушник (ч)	[ruʃ'nik]
bathrobe	халат (ч)	[ha'lat]

| laundry (laundering) | прання (с) | [pra'nʲa] |
| washing machine | пральна машина (ж) | ['pralʲna ma'ʃina] |

to do the laundry	прати білизну	['prati bi'liznu]
laundry detergent	пральний порошок (ч)	['pralʲnij poro'ʃɔk]

93. Household appliances

TV set	телевізор (ч)	[tɛlɛ'wizor]
tape recorder	магнітофон (ч)	[maɦnito'fɔn]
VCR (video recorder)	відеомагнітофон (ч)	['widɛo maɦnito'fɔn]
radio	приймач (ч)	[prij'matʃ]
player (CD, MP3, etc.)	плеєр (ч)	['plɛɛr]
video projector	відеопроектор (ч)	['widɛo pro'ɛktor]
home movie theater	домашній кінотеатр (ч)	[do'maʃnij kinotɛ'atr]
DVD player	програвач (ч) DVD	[proɦra'watʃ diwi'di]
amplifier	підсилювач (ч)	[pid'silʲuwatʃ]
video game console	гральна приставка (ж)	['ɦralʲna pri'stawka]
video camera	відеокамера (ж)	['widɛo 'kamɛra]
camera (photo)	фотоапарат (ч)	[fotoapa'rat]
digital camera	цифровий фотоапарат (ч)	[tsifro'wij fotoapa'rat]
vacuum cleaner	пилосос (ч)	[pilo'sɔs]
iron (e.g., steam ~)	праска (ж)	['praska]
ironing board	дошка (ж) для прасування	['dɔʃka dlʲa prasu'wanʲa]
telephone	телефон (ч)	[tɛlɛ'fɔn]
cell phone	мобільний телефон (ч)	[mo'bilʲnij tɛlɛ'fɔn]
typewriter	писемна машинка (ж)	[pi'sɛmna ma'ʃinka]
sewing machine	швейна машинка (ж)	['ʃwɛjna ma'ʃinka]
microphone	мікрофон (ч)	[mikro'fɔn]
headphones	навушники (мн)	[na'wuʃniki]
remote control (TV)	пульт (ч)	[pulʲt]
CD, compact disc	CD-диск (ч)	[si'di disk]
cassette, tape	касета (ж)	[ka'sɛta]
vinyl record	платівка (ж)	[pla'tiwka]

94. Repairs. Renovation

renovations	ремонт (ч)	[rɛ'mɔnt]
to renovate (vt)	робити ремонт	[ro'biti rɛ'mɔnt]
to repair, to fix (vt)	ремонтувати	[rɛmontu'wati]
to put in order	привести до ладу	[pri'wɛsti do 'ladu]
to redo (do again)	переробляти	[pɛrɛrob'lʲati]
paint	фарба (ж)	['farba]

to paint (~ a wall)	фарбувати	[farbu'wati]
house painter	маляр (ч)	['malʲar]
paintbrush	пензлик (ч)	['pɛnzlik]

| whitewash | побілка (ж) | [po'bilka] |
| to whitewash (vt) | білити | [bi'liti] |

wallpaper	шпалери (мн)	[ʃpa'lɛri]
to wallpaper (vt)	поклеїти шпалерами	[pok'lɛjiti ʃpa'lɛrami]
varnish	лак (ч)	[lak]
to varnish (vt)	покривати лаком	[pokri'wati 'lakom]

95. Plumbing

water	вода (ж)	[wo'da]
hot water	гаряча вода (ж)	[ha'rʲatʃa wo'da]
cold water	холодна вода (ж)	[ho'lɔdna wo'da]
faucet	кран (ч)	[kran]

drop (of water)	крапля (ж)	['kraplʲa]
to drip (vi)	крапати	['krapati]
to leak (ab. pipe)	протікати	[proti'kati]
leak (pipe ~)	протікання (с)	[proti'kanʲa]
puddle	калюжа (ж)	[ka'lʲuʒa]

pipe	труба (ж)	[tru'ba]
valve (e.g., ball ~)	вентиль (ч)	['wɛntilʲ]
to be clogged up	засмітитись	[zasmi'titisʲ]

tools	інструменти (мн)	[instru'mɛnti]
adjustable wrench	розвідний ключ (ч)	[roz'widnij klʲutʃ]
to unscrew (lid, filter, etc.)	відкрутити	[widkru'titi]
to screw (tighten)	закручувати	[za'krutʃuwati]

to unclog (vt)	прочищати	[protʃi'çati]
plumber	сантехнік (ч)	[san'tɛhnik]
basement	підвал (ч)	[pid'wal]
sewerage (system)	каналізація (ж)	[kanali'zatsiʲa]

96. Fire. Conflagration

fire (accident)	пожежа (ж)	[po'ʒɛʒa]
flame	полум'я (с)	['pɔlumʲla]
spark	іскра (ж)	['iskra]
smoke	дим (ч)	[dim]
(emissions from fire)		

| torch (flaming stick) | смолоскип (ч) | [smolos'kip] |
| campfire | багаття (с) | [ba'hattʲa] |

gas, gasoline	бензин (ч)	[bɛn'zin]
kerosene (type of fuel)	керосин (ч)	[kɛro'sin]
flammable (adj)	горючий	[ɦo'rʲutʃij]
explosive (adj)	вибухонебезпечний	[wibuɦonɛbɛz'pɛtʃnij]
NO SMOKING	**ПАЛИТИ ЗАБОРОНЕНО**	[pa'liti zabo'rɔnɛno]

safety	безпека (ж)	[bɛz'pɛka]
danger	небезпека (ж)	[nɛbɛz'pɛka]
dangerous (adj)	небезпечний	[nɛbɛz'pɛtʃnij]

to catch fire	загорітися	[zaɦo'ritisʲa]
explosion	вибух (ч)	['wibuɦ]
to set fire	підпалити	[pidpa'liti]
arsonist	підпалювач (ч)	[pid'palʲuwatʃ]
arson	підпал (ч)	['pidpal]

to blaze (vi)	палати	[pa'lati]
to burn (to be on fire)	горіти	[ɦo'riti]
to burn down	згоріти	[zɦo'riti]

to call the fire department	викликати пожежників	[wikli'kati po'ʒɛʒnikiw]
firefighter, fireman	пожежник (ч)	[po'ʒɛʒnik]
fire truck	пожежна машина (ж)	[po'ʒɛʒna ma'ʃina]
fire department	пожежна команда (ж)	[po'ʒɛʒna ko'manda]
fire truck ladder	висувна драбина (ж)	[wisuw'na dra'bina]

fire hose	шланг (ч)	[ʃlanɦ]
fire extinguisher	вогнегасник (ч)	[woɦnɛ'ɦasnik]
helmet	каска (ж)	['kaska]
siren	сирена (ж)	[si'rɛna]

to cry (for help)	кричати	[kri'tʃati]
to call for help	кликати на допомогу	['klikati na dopo'mɔɦu]
rescuer	рятувальник (ч)	[rʲatu'walʲnik]
to rescue (vt)	рятувати	[rʲatu'wati]

to arrive (vi)	приїхати	[pri'jihati]
to extinguish (vt)	тушити	[tu'ʃiti]
water	вода (ж)	[wo'da]
sand	пісок (ч)	[pi'sɔk]

ruins (destruction)	руїни (мн)	[ru'jini]
to collapse (building, etc.)	повалитися	[powa'litisʲa]

to fall down (vi)	обвалитися	[obwa'litisʲa]
to cave in (ceiling, floor)	завалитися	[zawa'litisʲa]

piece of debris	уламок (ч)	[u'lamok]
ash	попіл (ч)	['popil]

to suffocate (die)	задихнутися	[zadih'nutisʲa]
to be killed (perish)	загинути	[za'ɦinuti]

HUMAN ACTIVITIES

Job. Business. Part 1

97. Banking

bank	банк (ч)	[bank]
branch (local office of a bank)	відділення (с)	[wid'dilɛnʲa]
bank clerk, consultant	консультант (ч)	[konsulʲ'tant]
manager (director)	керівник (ч)	[kɛriw'nik]
bank account	рахунок (ч)	[ra'hunok]
account number	номер (ч) рахунка	['nɔmɛr ra'hunka]
checking account	поточний рахунок (ч)	[po'tɔʧnij ra'hunok]
savings account	накопичувальний рахунок (ч)	[nako'piʧuwalʲnij ra'hunok]
to open an account	відкрити рахунок	[wid'kriti ra'hunok]
to close the account	закрити рахунок	[za'kriti ra'hunok]
to deposit into the account	покласти на рахунок	[pok'lasti na ra'hunok]
to withdraw (vt)	зняти з рахунку	['znʲati z ra'hunku]
deposit	внесок (ч)	['wnɛsok]
to make a deposit	зробити внесок	[zro'biti 'wnɛsok]
wire transfer	переказ (ч)	[pɛ'rɛkaz]
to wire, to transfer	зробити переказ	[zro'biti pɛ'rɛkaz]
sum	сума (ж)	['suma]
How much?	Скільки?	['skilʲki]
signature	підпис (ч)	['pidpis]
to sign (vt)	підписати	[pidpi'sati]
credit card	кредитна картка (ж)	[krɛ'ditna 'kartka]
code (PIN code)	код (ч)	[kod]
credit card number	номер (ч) кредитної картки	['nɔmɛr krɛ'ditnoji 'kartki]
ATM	банкомат (ч)	[banko'mat]
check	чек (ч)	[ʧɛk]
to write a check	виписати чек	['wipisati 'ʧɛk]
checkbook	чекова книжка (ж)	['ʧɛkowa 'kniʒka]
loan (bank ~)	кредит (ч)	[krɛ'dit]

to apply for a loan	звертатися за кредитом	[zwɛr'tatisʲa za krɛ'ditom]
to get a loan	брати кредит	['brati krɛ'dit]
to give a loan	надавати кредит	[nada'wati krɛ'dit]
guarantee	застава (ж)	[za'stawa]

98. Telephone. Phone conversation

telephone	телефон (ч)	[tɛlɛ'fɔn]
cell phone	мобільний телефон (ч)	[mo'bilʲnij tɛlɛ'fɔn]
answering machine	автовідповідач (ч)	[awtowidpowi'datʃ]

| to call (by phone) | зателефонувати | [zatɛlɛfonu'wati] |
| phone call | дзвінок (ч) | [dzwi'nɔk] |

to dial a number	набрати номер	[nab'rati 'nɔmɛr]
Hello!	Алло!	[a'lɔ]
to ask (vt)	запитати	[zapi'tati]
to answer (vi, vt)	відповісти	[widpo'wisti]

to hear (vt)	чути	['tʃuti]
well (adv)	добре	['dɔbrɛ]
not well (adv)	погано	[po'ɦano]
noises (interference)	перешкоди (мн)	[pɛrɛʃ'kɔdi]

receiver	трубка (ж)	['trubka]
to pick up (~ the phone)	зняти трубку	['znʲati 'trubku]
to hang up (end a call)	покласти трубку	[pok'lasti t'rubku]

busy (engaged)	зайнятий	['zajnʲatij]
to ring (ab. phone)	дзвонити	[dzwo'niti]
telephone book	телефонна книга (ж)	[tɛlɛ'fona 'kniɦa]

local (adj)	місцевий	[mis'tsɛwij]
local call	місцевий зв'язок (ч)	[mis'tsɛwij 'zwʲazok]
long-distance (~ call)	міжміський	[miʒmisʲ'kij]
long-distance call	міжміський зв'язок (ч)	[miʒmisʲ'kij 'zwʲazok]
international (adj)	міжнародний	[miʒna'rɔdnij]
international call	міжнародний зв'язок (ч)	[miʒna'rɔdnij 'zwʲazok]

99. Cell phone

cell phone	мобільний телефон (ч)	[mo'bilʲnij tɛlɛ'fɔn]
display	дисплей (ч)	[dis'plɛj]
button	кнопка (ж)	['knɔpka]
SIM card	SIM-карта (ж)	[sim 'karta]
battery	батарея (ж)	[bata'rɛʲa]
to be dead (battery)	розрядитися	[rozrʲa'ditisʲa]

charger	зарядний пристрій (ч)	[zaˈrʲadnij ˈpristrij]
menu	меню (с)	[mɛˈnʲu]
settings	настройки (мн)	[naˈstrɔjki]
tune (melody)	мелодія (ж)	[mɛˈlɔdiʲa]
to select (vt)	вибрати	[ˈwibrati]

calculator	калькулятор (ч)	[kalʲkuˈlʲator]
voice mail	автовідповідач (ч)	[awtowidpowiˈdatʃ]
alarm clock	будильник (ч)	[buˈdilʲnik]
contacts	телефонна книга (ж)	[tɛlɛˈfɔna ˈkniɦa]

| SMS (text message) | SMS-повідомлення (с) | [ɛsɛˈmɛs powiˈdɔmlɛnʲa] |
| subscriber | абонент (ч) | [aboˈnɛnt] |

100. Stationery

| ballpoint pen | авторучка (ж) | [awtoˈrutʃka] |
| fountain pen | ручка-перо (с) | [ˈrutʃka pɛˈrɔ] |

pencil	олівець (ч)	[oliˈwɛts]
highlighter	маркер (ч)	[ˈmarkɛr]
felt-tip pen	фломастер (ч)	[floˈmastɛr]

| notepad | блокнот (ч) | [blokˈnɔt] |
| agenda (diary) | щоденник (ч) | [ɕoˈdɛnik] |

ruler	лінійка (ж)	[liˈnijka]
calculator	калькулятор (ч)	[kalʲkuˈlʲator]
eraser	гумка (ж)	[ˈɦumka]
thumbtack	кнопка (ж)	[ˈknɔpka]
paper clip	скріпка (ж)	[ˈskripka]

glue	клей (ч)	[klɛj]
stapler	степлер (ч)	[ˈstɛplɛr]
hole punch	діркопробивач (ч)	[dirkoprobiˈwatʃ]
pencil sharpener	стругачка (ж)	[struˈɦatʃka]

Job. Business. Part 2

newspaper	газета (ж)	[ɦa'zɛta]
magazine	журнал (ч)	[ʒur'nal]
press (printed media)	преса (ж)	['prɛsa]
radio	радіо (с)	['radio]
radio station	радіостанція (ж)	[radios'tantsiˈa]
television	телебачення (с)	[tɛlɛ'batʃɛnˈa]
presenter, host	ведучий (ч)	[wɛ'dutʃij]
newscaster	диктор (ч)	['diktor]
commentator	коментатор (ч)	[komɛn'tator]
journalist	журналіст (ч)	[ʒurna'list]
correspondent (reporter)	кореспондент (ч)	[korɛspon'dɛnt]
press photographer	фотокореспондент (ч)	['foto korɛspon'dɛnt]
reporter	репортер (ч)	[rɛpor'tɛr]
editor	редактор (ч)	[rɛ'daktor]
editor-in-chief	головний редактор (ч)	[ɦolow'nij rɛ'daktor]
to subscribe (to ...)	передплатити	[pɛrɛdpla'titi]
subscription	передплата (ж)	[pɛrɛdp'lata]
subscriber	передплатник (ч)	[pɛrɛdp'latnik]
to read (vi, vt)	читати	[tʃi'tati]
reader	читач (ч)	[tʃi'tatʃ]
circulation (of a newspaper)	наклад (ч)	['naklad]
monthly (adj)	щомісячний	[ɕo'misˈatʃnij]
weekly (adj)	щотижневий	[ɕotiʒ'nɛwij]
issue (edition)	номер (ч)	['nɔmɛr]
new (~ issue)	свіжий	['swiʒij]
headline	заголовок (ч)	[zaɦo'lɔwok]
short article	замітка (ж)	[za'mitka]
column (regular article)	рубрика (ж)	['rubrika]
article	стаття (ж)	[stat'tˈa]
page	сторінка (ж)	[sto'rinka]
reportage, report	репортаж (ч)	[rɛpor'taʒ]
event (occurrence, happening)	подія (ж)	[po'diˈa]
sensation (news)	сенсація (ж)	[sɛn'satsiˈa]

scandal	скандал (ч)	[skan'dal]
scandalous (adj)	скандальний	[skan'dalʲnij]
great (~ scandal)	гучний	[ɦutʃ'nij]

show (e.g., cooking ~)	передача (ж)	[pɛrɛ'datʃa]
interview	інтерв'ю (с)	[intɛr'wʲlu]
live broadcast	пряма трансляція (ж)	[prʲa'ma trans'lʲatsʲia]
channel	канал (ч)	[ka'nal]

102. Agriculture

agriculture	сільське господарство (с)	[silʲsʲ'kɛ ɦospo'darstwo]
peasant (masc.)	селянин (ч)	[sɛlʲa'nin]
peasant (fem.)	селянка (ж)	[sɛ'lʲanka]
farmer	фермер (ч)	['fɛrmɛr]

| tractor (farm ~) | трактор (ч) | ['traktor] |
| combine, harvester | комбайн (ч) | [kom'bajn] |

plow	плуг (ч)	[pluɦ]
to plow (vi, vt)	орати	[o'rati]
plowland	рілля (ж)	[ri'lʲa]
furrow (in a field)	борозна (ж)	[boroz'na]

to sow (vi, vt)	сіяти	['sʲiati]
seeder	сівалка (ж)	[si'walka]
sowing (process)	посів (ч)	[po'siw]

| scythe | коса (ж) | [ko'sa] |
| to mow, to scythe | косити | [ko'siti] |

| spade (tool) | лопата (ж) | [lo'pata] |
| to till (vt) | копати, вскопувати | [ko'pati], ['wskɔpuwati] |

hoe	сапка (ж)	['sapka]
to hoe, to weed	полоти	[po'lɔti]
weed (plant)	бур'ян (ч)	[bu'rʲlan]

watering can	лійка (ж)	['lijka]
to water (~ plants, irrigate)	поливати	[poli'wati]
watering (act)	поливання (с)	[poli'wanʲa]

| pitchfork | вила (мн) | ['wila] |
| rake | граблі (мн) | [ɦra'bli] |

fertilizer	добриво (с)	['dɔbriwo]
to fertilize (vt)	удобрювати	[u'dɔbrʲuwati]
manure (animal ~)	гній (ч)	[ɦnij]
field	поле (с)	['pɔlɛ]

meadow	лука (ж)	['luka]
vegetable garden	город (ч)	[ɦo'rɔd]
orchard (e.g., apple ~)	сад (ч)	[sad]

to graze (vt)	пасти	['pasti]
herder (herdsman)	пастух (ч)	[pas'tuh]
pasture	пасовище (с)	[paso'wiɕɛ]

| cattle breeding | тваринництво (с) | [twa'rinitstwo] |
| sheep farming | вівчарство (с) | [wiw'tʃarstwo] |

plantation	плантація (ж)	[plan'tatsiʲa]
row (garden bed ~s)	грядка (ж)	['ɦrʲadka]
hothouse	парник (ч)	[par'nik]

| drought (lack of rain) | посуха (ж) | ['pɔsuha] |
| dry (~ summer) | посушливий | [po'suʃliwij] |

grain	зерно (с), зернові (мн)	[zɛr'nɔ], [zɛrno'wi]
cereal crops	зернові (мн)	[zɛrno'wi]
to harvest, to gather	збирати	[zbi'rati]

miller (person)	мірошник (ч)	[mi'rɔʃnik]
mill (e.g., gristmill)	млин (ч)	[mlin]
to grind (grain)	молотити	[molo'titi]
flour	борошно (с)	['bɔroʃno]
straw	солома (ж)	[so'lɔma]

103. Building. Building process

construction site	будівництво (с)	[budiw'nitstwo]
to build (vt)	будувати	[budu'wati]
construction worker	будівельник (ч)	[budi'wɛlʲnik]

project	проект (ч)	[pro'ɛkt]
architect	архітектор (ч)	[arhi'tɛktor]
worker	робітник (ч)	[robit'nik]

foundation (base of a building)	фундамент (ч)	[fun'damɛnt]
roof	дах (ч)	[dah]
foundation pile	паля (ж)	['palʲa]
wall	стіна (ж)	[sti'na]

| reinforcing bars | арматура (ж) | [arma'tura] |
| scaffolding | риштування (мн) | [riʃtu'wanʲa] |

concrete	бетон (ч)	[bɛ'tɔn]
granite	граніт (ч)	[ɦra'nit]
stone	камінь (ч)	['kaminʲ]

brick	цегла (ж)	['tsɛɦla]
sand	пісок (ч)	[pi'sɔk]
cement	цемент (ч)	[tsɛ'mɛnt]
plaster (covering for walls)	штукатурка (ж)	[ʃtuka'turka]
to plaster (vt)	штукатурити	[ʃtuka'turiti]

paint	фарба (ж)	['farba]
to paint (~ a wall)	фарбувати	[farbu'wati]
barrel	бочка (ж)	['bɔtʃka]

crane	кран (ч)	[kran]
to lift, to hoist (vt)	піднімати	[pidni'mati]
to lower (vt)	опускати	[opus'kati]

bulldozer	бульдозер (ч)	[bulʲ'dɔzɛr]
excavator	екскаватор (ч)	[ɛkska'wator]
scoop, bucket	ківш (ч)	[kiwʃ]
to dig (excavate)	копати	[ko'pati]
hard hat	каска (ж)	['kaska]

Professions and occupations

job	робота (ж)	[ro'bɔta]
staff (work force)	колектив, штат (ч)	[kolɛk'tiw], [ʃtat]
personnel	персонал (ч)	[pɛrso'nal]
career	кар'єра (ж)	[ka'rʲɛra]
prospects (chances)	перспектива (ж)	[pɛrspɛk'tiwa]
skills (mastery)	майстерність (ж)	[majs'tɛrnistʲ]
selection (hire, screening)	підбір (ч)	[pid'bir]
employment agency	кадрове агентство (с)	['kadrowɛ a'ɦɛntstwo]
résumé	резюме (с)	[rɛzʲu'mɛ]
job interview	співбесіда (ж)	[spiw'bɛsida]
vacancy, opening	вакансія (ж)	[wa'kansiʲa]
salary, pay	зарплатня (ж)	[zarplat'nʲa]
fixed salary	оклад (ч)	[ok'lad]
pay, compensation	оплата (ж)	[op'lata]
position (job)	посада (ж)	[po'sada]
duty (of an employee)	обов'язок (ч)	[o'bɔwʲazok]
range of duties	коло (с) обов'язків	['kɔlo obo'wʲazkiw]
busy (I'm ~)	зайнятий	['zajnʲatij]
to fire (dismiss)	звільнити	[zwilʲ'niti]
dismissal	звільнення (с)	['zwilʲnɛnʲa]
unemployment	безробіття (с)	[bɛzro'bittʲa]
unemployed (n)	безробітний (ч)	[bɛzro'bitnij]
retirement	пенсія (ж)	['pɛnsiʲa]
to retire (from a job)	вийти на пенсію	['wijti na 'pɛnsiʲu]

director	директор (ч)	[di'rɛktor]
manager (director)	керівник (ч)	[kɛriw'nik]
boss	бос (ч)	[bɔs]
superior	начальник (ч)	[na'tʃalʲnik]
superiors	керівництво (с)	[kɛriw'nitstwo]
president	президент (ч)	[prɛzi'dɛnt]

chairman	голова (ч)	[ɦolo'wa]
deputy (substitute)	заступник (ч)	[za'stupnik]
assistant	помічник (ч)	[pomitʃ'nik]
secretary	секретар (ч)	[sɛkrɛ'tar]
personal assistant	особистий секретар (ч)	[oso'bistij sɛkrɛ'tar]
businessman	бізнесмен (ч)	[biznɛs'mɛn]
entrepreneur	підприємець (ч)	[pidpri'ɛmɛʦ]
founder	засновник (ч)	[zas'nownik]
to found (vt)	заснувати	[zasnu'wati]
incorporator	основоположник (ч)	[osnowopo'loʒnik]
partner	партнер (ч)	[part'nɛr]
stockholder	акціонер (ч)	[akʦio'nɛr]
millionaire	мільйонер (ч)	[milʲo'nɛr]
billionaire	мільярдер (ч)	[miljar'dɛr]
owner, proprietor	власник (ч)	['wlasnik]
landowner	землевласник (ч)	[zɛmlɛw'lasnik]
client	клієнт (ч)	[kli'ɛnt]
regular client	постійний клієнт (ч)	[pos'tijnij kli'ɛnt]
buyer (customer)	покупець (ч)	[poku'pɛʦ]
visitor	відвідувач (ч)	[wid'widuwatʃ]
professional (n)	професіонал (ч)	[profɛsio'nal]
expert	експерт (ч)	[ɛks'pɛrt]
specialist	фахівець (ч)	[fahi'wɛʦ]
banker	банкір (ч)	[ba'nkir]
broker	брокер (ч)	['brɔkɛr]
cashier, teller	касир (ч)	[ka'sir]
accountant	бухгалтер (ч)	[buh'ɦaltɛr]
security guard	охоронник (ч)	[oho'rɔnik]
investor	інвестор (ч)	[in'wɛstor]
debtor	боржник (ч)	[borʒ'nik]
creditor	кредитор (ч)	[krɛdi'tɔr]
borrower	боржник (ч)	[borʒ'nik]
importer	імпортер (ч)	[impor'tɛr]
exporter	експортер (ч)	[ɛkspor'tɛr]
manufacturer	виробник (ч)	[wirob'nik]
distributor	дистриб'ютор (ч)	[distri'bʲutor]
middleman	посередник (ч)	[posɛ'rɛdnik]
consultant	консультант (ч)	[konsulʲ'tant]
sales representative	представник (ч)	[prɛdstaw'nik]
agent	агент (ч)	[a'ɦɛnt]
insurance agent	страховий агент (ч)	[straho'wij a'ɦɛnt]

106. Service professions

cook	кухар (ч)	['kuhar]
chef (kitchen chef)	шеф-кухар (ч)	[ʃɛf 'kuhar]
baker	пекар (ч)	['pɛkar]
bartender	бармен (ч)	[bar'mɛn]
waiter	офіціант (ч)	[ofitsi'ant]
waitress	офіціантка (ж)	[ofitsi'antka]
lawyer, attorney	адвокат (ч)	[adwo'kat]
lawyer (legal expert)	юрист (ч)	[ʲu'rist]
notary public	нотаріус (ч)	[no'tarius]
electrician	електрик (ч)	[ɛ'lɛktrik]
plumber	сантехнік (ч)	[san'tɛhnik]
carpenter	тесля (ч)	['tɛslʲa]
masseur	масажист (ч)	[masa'ʒist]
masseuse	масажистка (ж)	[masa'ʒistka]
doctor	лікар (ч)	['likar]
taxi driver	таксист (ч)	[tak'sist]
driver	шофер (ч)	[ʃo'fɛr]
delivery man	кур'єр (ч)	[ku'rʲɛr]
chambermaid	покоївка (ж)	[poko'jiwka]
security guard	охоронник (ч)	[oho'rɔnik]
flight attendant (fem.)	стюардеса (ж)	[stʲuar'dɛsa]
schoolteacher	вчитель (ч)	['wtʃitɛlʲ]
librarian	бібліотекар (ч)	[biblio'tɛkar]
translator	перекладач (ч)	[pɛrɛkla'datʃ]
interpreter	перекладач (ч)	[pɛrɛkla'datʃ]
guide	гід (ч)	[ɦid]
hairdresser	перукар (ч)	[pɛru'kar]
mailman	листоноша (ч)	[listo'nɔʃa]
salesman (store staff)	продавець (ч)	[proda'wɛts]
gardener	садівник (ч)	[sadiw'nik]
domestic servant	слуга (ч)	[slu'ɦa]
maid (female servant)	служниця (ж)	[sluʒ'nitsʲa]
cleaner (cleaning person)	прибиральниця (ж)	[pribi'ralʲnitsʲa]

107. Military professions and ranks

private	рядовий (ч)	[rʲado'wij]
sergeant	сержант (ч)	[sɛr'ʒant]

| lieutenant | **лейтенант** (ч) | [lɛjtɛ'nant] |
| captain | **капітан** (ч) | [kapi'tan] |

major	**майор** (ч)	[ma'jɔr]
colonel	**полковник** (ч)	[pol'kɔwnik]
general	**генерал** (ч)	[ɦɛnɛ'ral]
marshal	**маршал** (ч)	['marʃal]
admiral	**адмірал** (ч)	[admi'ral]

military (n)	**військовий** (ч)	[wijsʲʲkɔwij]
soldier	**солдат** (ч)	[sol'dat]
officer	**офіцер** (ч)	[ofi'ʦɛr]
commander	**командир** (ч)	[koman'dir]

border guard	**прикордонник** (ч)	[prikor'dɔnik]
radio operator	**радист** (ч)	[ra'dist]
scout (searcher)	**розвідник** (ч)	[roz'widnik]
pioneer (sapper)	**сапер** (ч)	[sa'pɛr]
marksman	**стрілок** (ч)	[stri'lɔk]
navigator	**штурман** (ч)	['ʃturman]

108. Officials. Priests

| king | **король** (ч) | [ko'rɔlʲ] |
| queen | **королева** (ж) | [koro'lɛwa] |

| prince | **принц** (ч) | [prinʦ] |
| princess | **принцеса** (ж) | [prin'ʦɛsa] |

| czar | **цар** (ч) | [ʦar] |
| czarina | **цариця** (ж) | [ʦa'riʦʲa] |

president	**президент** (ч)	[prɛzi'dɛnt]
Secretary (minister)	**міністр** (ч)	[mi'nistr]
prime minister	**прем'єр-міністр** (ч)	[prɛ'm'ɛr mi'nistr]
senator	**сенатор** (ч)	[sɛ'nator]

diplomat	**дипломат** (ч)	[diplo'mat]
consul	**консул** (ч)	['kɔnsul]
ambassador	**посол** (ч)	[po'sɔl]
counselor (diplomatic officer)	**радник** (ч)	['radnik]

official, functionary (civil servant)	**чиновник** (ч)	[ʧi'nɔwnik]
prefect	**префект** (ч)	[prɛ'fɛkt]
mayor	**мер** (ч)	[mɛr]
judge	**суддя** (ч)	[sud'dʲa]
prosecutor (e.g., district attorney)	**прокурор** (ч)	[proku'rɔr]

missionary	місіонер (ч)	[misio'nɛr]
monk	чернець (ч)	[ʧɛr'nɛʦ]
abbot	абат (ч)	[a'bat]
rabbi	рабин (ч)	[ra'bin]

vizier	візир (ч)	[wi'zir]
shah	шах (ч)	[ʃah]
sheikh	шейх (ч)	[ʃɛjh]

109. Agricultural professions

beekeeper	пасічник (ч)	['pasiʧnik]
herder, shepherd	пастух (ч)	[pas'tuh]
agronomist	агроном (ч)	[aɦro'nɔm]
cattle breeder	тваринник (ч)	[twa'rinik]
veterinarian	ветеринар (ч)	[wɛtɛri'nar]

farmer	фермер (ч)	['fɛrmɛr]
winemaker	винороб (ч)	[wino'rɔb]
zoologist	зоолог (ч)	[zo'ɔloɦ]
cowboy	ковбой (ч)	[kow'bɔj]

110. Art professions

actor	актор (ч)	[ak'tɔr]
actress	акторка (ж)	[ak'tɔrka]

singer (masc.)	співак (ч)	[spi'wak]
singer (fem.)	співачка (ж)	[spi'waʧka]

dancer (masc.)	танцюрист (ч)	[tanʦʲu'rist]
dancer (fem.)	танцюристка (ж)	[tanʦʲu'ristka]

performer (masc.)	артист (ч)	[ar'tist]
performer (fem.)	артистка (ж)	[ar'tistka]

musician	музикант (ч)	[muzi'kant]
pianist	піаніст (ч)	[pia'nist]
guitar player	гітарист (ч)	[ɦita'rist]

conductor (orchestra ~)	диригент (ч)	[diri'ɦɛnt]
composer	композитор (ч)	[kompo'zitor]
impresario	імпресаріо (ч)	[imprɛ'sario]

film director	режисер (ч)	[rɛʒi'sɛr]
producer	продюсер (ч)	[pro'dʲusɛr]
scriptwriter	сценарист (ч)	[sʦɛna'rist]
critic	критик (ч)	['kritik]

writer	письменник (ч)	[pisʲˈmɛnik]
poet	поет (ч)	[poˈɛt]
sculptor	скульптор (ч)	[ˈskulʲptor]
artist (painter)	художник (ч)	[huˈdɔʒnik]

juggler	жонглер (ч)	[ʒonˈɦˈlɛr]
clown	клоун (ч)	[ˈklɔun]
acrobat	акробат (ч)	[akroˈbat]
magician	фокусник (ч)	[ˈfɔkusnik]

111. Various professions

doctor	лікар (ч)	[ˈlikar]
nurse	медсестра (ж)	[mɛdsɛstˈra]
psychiatrist	психіатр (ч)	[psihiˈatr]
dentist	стоматолог (ч)	[stomaˈtɔloɦ]
surgeon	хірург (ч)	[hiˈrurɦ]

astronaut	астронавт (ч)	[astroˈnawt]
astronomer	астроном (ч)	[astroˈnɔm]
pilot	льотчик, пілот (ч)	[ˈlʲɔtʧik], [piˈlɔt]

driver (taxi ~, etc.)	водій (ч)	[woˈdij]
engineer (train driver)	машиніст (ч)	[maʃiˈnist]
mechanic	механік (ч)	[mɛˈhanik]

miner	шахтар (ч)	[ʃahˈtar]
worker	робітник (ч)	[robitˈnik]
locksmith	слюсар (ч)	[ˈslʲusar]
joiner (carpenter)	столяр (ч)	[ˈstɔlʲar]
turner (lathe operator)	токар (ч)	[ˈtɔkar]
construction worker	будівельник (ч)	[budiˈwɛlʲnik]
welder	зварювальник (ч)	[ˈzwarʲuwalʲnik]

professor (title)	професор (ч)	[proˈfɛsor]
architect	архітектор (ч)	[arhiˈtɛktor]
historian	історик (ч)	[isˈtɔrik]
scientist	вчений (ч)	[ˈwtʃɛnij]
physicist	фізик (ч)	[ˈfizik]
chemist (scientist)	хімік (ч)	[ˈhimik]

archeologist	археолог (ч)	[arhɛˈɔloɦ]
geologist	геолог (ч)	[ɦɛˈɔloɦ]
researcher (scientist)	дослідник (ч)	[doˈslidnik]

| babysitter | няня (ж) | [ˈnʲanʲa] |
| teacher, educator | вчитель, педагог (ч) | [ˈwtʃitɛlʲ], [pɛdaˈɦoɦ] |

| editor | редактор (ч) | [rɛˈdaktor] |
| editor-in-chief | головний редактор (ч) | [ɦolowˈnij rɛˈdaktor] |

| correspondent | кореспондент (ч) | [korɛspon'dɛnt] |
| typist (fem.) | машиністка (ж) | [maʃi'nistka] |

designer	дизайнер (ч)	[di'zajnɛr]
computer expert	комп'ютерник (ч)	[kom'pʲuternik]
programmer	програміст (ч)	[proɦ'ramist]
engineer (designer)	інженер (ч)	[inʒɛ'nɛr]

sailor	моряк (ч)	[mo'rʲak]
seaman	матрос (ч)	[mat'rɔs]
rescuer	рятувальник (ч)	[rʲatu'walʲnik]

fireman	пожежник (ч)	[po'ʒɛʒnik]
police officer	поліцейський (ч)	[poli'tsɛjsʲkij]
watchman	сторож (ч)	['stɔrɔʒ]
detective	детектив (ч)	[dɛtɛk'tiw]

customs officer	митник (ч)	['mitnik]
bodyguard	охоронець (ч)	[oho'rɔnɛts]
prison guard	охоронець (ч)	[oho'rɔnɛtsʲ]
inspector	інспектор (ч)	[ins'pɛktor]

sportsman	спортсмен (ч)	[sporʦ'mɛn]
trainer, coach	тренер (ч)	['trɛnɛr]
butcher	м'ясник (ч)	[mʲas'nik]
cobbler (shoe repairer)	чоботар (ч)	[tʃobo'tar]
merchant	комерсант (ч)	[komɛr'sant]
loader (person)	вантажник (ч)	[wan'taʒnik]

| fashion designer | модельєр (ч) | [modɛ'ljɛr] |
| model (fem.) | модель (ж) | [modɛlʲ] |

112. Occupations. Social status

| schoolboy | школяр (ч) | [ʃko'lʲar] |
| student (college ~) | студент (ч) | [stu'dɛnt] |

philosopher	філософ (ч)	[fi'lɔsof]
economist	економіст (ч)	[ɛkono'mist]
inventor	винахідник (ч)	[wina'hidnik]

unemployed (n)	безробітний (ч)	[bɛzro'bitnij]
retiree	пенсіонер (ч)	[pɛnsio'nɛr]
spy, secret agent	шпигун (ч)	[ʃpi'ɦun]

prisoner	в'язень (ч)	['wʲazɛnʲ]
striker	страйкар (ч)	[straj'kar]
bureaucrat	бюрократ (ч)	[bʲuro'krat]
traveler (globetrotter)	мандрівник (ч)	[mandriw'nik]
gay, homosexual (n)	гомосексуаліст (ч)	[ɦomosɛksua'list]

| hacker | хакер (ч) | ['hakɛr] |
| hippie | хіпі (ч) | ['hipi] |

bandit	бандит (ч)	[ban'dit]
hit man, killer	найманий вбивця (ч)	['najmanij 'wbiwtsʲa]
drug addict	наркоман (ч)	[narko'man]
drug dealer	наркоторговець (ч)	[narkotor'hɔwɛts]
prostitute (fem.)	проститутка (ж)	[prosti'tutka]
pimp	сутенер (ч)	[sutɛ'nɛr]

sorcerer	чаклун (ч)	[ʧak'lun]
sorceress (evil ~)	чаклунка (ж)	[ʧak'lunka]
pirate	пірат (ч)	[pi'rat]
slave	раб (ч)	[rab]
samurai	самурай (ч)	[samu'raj]
savage (primitive)	дикун (ч)	[di'kun]

Sports

sportsman	спортсмен (ч)	[sportsˈmɛn]
kind of sports	вид (ч) спорту	[wid ˈsportu]
basketball	баскетбол (ч)	[baskɛtˈbɔl]
basketball player	баскетболіст (ч)	[baskɛtboˈlist]
baseball	бейсбол (ч)	[bɛjsˈbɔl]
baseball player	бейсболіст (ч)	[bɛjsboˈlist]
soccer	футбол (ч)	[futˈbɔl]
soccer player	футболіст (ч)	[futboˈlist]
goalkeeper	воротар (ч)	[woroˈtar]
hockey	хокей (ч)	[hoˈkɛj]
hockey player	хокеїст (ч)	[hokɛˈjist]
volleyball	волейбол (ч)	[wolɛjˈbɔl]
volleyball player	волейболіст (ч)	[wolɛjboˈlist]
boxing	бокс (ч)	[boks]
boxer	боксер (ч)	[bokˈsɛr]
wrestling	боротьба (ж)	[borotʲˈba]
wrestler	борець (ч)	[boˈrɛts]
karate	карате (с)	[karaˈtɛ]
karate fighter	каратист (ч)	[karaˈtist]
judo	дзюдо (с)	[dʑʲuˈdɔ]
judo athlete	дзюдоїст (ч)	[dʑʲudoˈjist]
tennis	теніс (ч)	[ˈtɛnis]
tennis player	тенісист (ч)	[tɛniˈsist]
swimming	плавання (с)	[ˈplawanʲa]
swimmer	плавець (ч)	[plaˈwɛts]
fencing	фехтування (с)	[fɛhtuˈwanʲa]
fencer	фехтувальник (ч)	[fɛhtuˈwalʲnik]
chess	шахи (мн)	[ˈʃahi]
chess player	шахіст (ч)	[ʃaˈhist]

| alpinism | альпінізм (ч) | [alʲpiˈnizm] |
| alpinist | альпініст (ч) | [alʲpiˈnist] |

| running | біг (ч) | [biɦ] |
| runner | бігун (ч) | [biˈɦun] |

| athletics | легка атлетика (ж) | [lɛɦˈka atˈlɛtika] |
| athlete | атлет (ч) | [atˈlɛt] |

| horseback riding | кінний спорт (ч) | [ˈkinij ˈspɔrt] |
| horse rider | наїзник (ч) | [naˈjiznik] |

figure skating	фігурне катання (с)	[fiˈɦurnɛ kaˈtanʲa]
figure skater (masc.)	фігурист (ч)	[fiɦuˈrist]
figure skater (fem.)	фігуристка (ж)	[fiɦuˈristka]

powerlifting	важка атлетика (ж)	[waʒˈka atˈlɛtika]
powerlifter	важкоатлет (ч)	[waʒkoatˈlɛt]
car racing	автогонки (мн)	[awtoˈɦonki]
racer (driver)	гонщик (ч)	[ˈɦonɕik]

| cycling | велоспорт (ч) | [wɛloˈspɔrt] |
| cyclist | велосипедист (ч) | [wɛlosipɛˈdist] |

broad jump	стрибки (мн) в довжину	[stribˈki w dowʒiˈnu]
pole vault	стрибки (мн) з жердиною	[stribˈki z ʒɛrˈdinoʲu]
jumper	стрибун (ч)	[striˈbun]

114. Kinds of sports. Miscellaneous

football	американський футбол (ч)	[amɛriˈkansʲkij futˈbɔl]
badminton	бадмінтон (ч)	[badminˈtɔn]
biathlon	біатлон (ч)	[biatˈlɔn]
billiards	більярд (ч)	[biˈlʲjard]

bobsled	бобслей (ч)	[bobˈslɛj]
bodybuilding	бодібілдинг (ч)	[bodiˈbildiɦ]
water polo	водне поло (с)	[ˈwɔdnɛ ˈpolo]
handball	гандбол (ч)	[handˈbɔl]
golf	гольф (ч)	[ɦolʲf]

rowing, crew	гребля (ч)	[ˈɦrɛblʲa]
scuba diving	дайвінг (ч)	[ˈdajwiɦ]
cross-country skiing	лижні гонки (мн)	[ˈliʒni ˈɦonki]
table tennis (ping-pong)	настільний теніс (ч)	[naˈstilʲnij ˈtɛnis]

sailing	парусний спорт (ч)	[ˈparusnij sport]
rally racing	ралі (с)	[ˈrali]
rugby	регбі (с)	[ˈrɛɦbi]

snowboarding	сноуборд (ч)	[snou'bɔrd]
archery	стрільба (ж) з луку	[striĺ'ba z 'luku]

115. Gym

barbell	штанга (ж)	['ʃtanɦa]
dumbbells	гантелі (мн)	[ɦan'tɛli]
training machine	тренажер (ч)	[trɛna'ʒɛr]
exercise bicycle	велотренажер (ч)	[wɛlotrɛna'ʒɛr]
treadmill	бігова доріжка (ж)	[biɦo'wa do'riʒka]
horizontal bar	перекладина (ж)	[pɛrɛk'ladina]
parallel bars	бруси (мн)	['brusi]
vault (vaulting horse)	кінь (ч)	[kinʲ]
mat (exercise ~)	мат (ч)	[mat]
jump rope	скакалка (ж)	[ska'kalka]
aerobics	аеробіка (ж)	[aɛ'robika]
yoga	йога (ж)	['jɔɦa]

116. Sports. Miscellaneous

Olympic Games	Олімпійські ігри (мн)	[olim'pijsʲki 'iɦri]
winner	переможець (ч)	[pɛrɛ'mɔʒɛts]
to be winning	перемагати	[pɛrɛma'ɦati]
to win (vi)	виграти	['wiɦrati]
leader	лідер (ч)	['lidɛr]
to lead (vi)	лідирувати	[li'diruwati]
first place	перше місце (с)	['pɛrʃɛ 'mistsɛ]
second place	друге місце (с)	['druɦɛ 'mistsɛ]
third place	третє місце (с)	['trɛtɛ 'mistsɛ]
medal	медаль (ж)	[mɛ'dalʲ]
trophy	трофей (ч)	[tro'fɛj]
prize cup (trophy)	кубок (ч)	['kubok]
prize (in game)	приз (ч)	[priz]
main prize	головний приз (ч)	[ɦolow'nij priz]
record	рекорд (ч)	[rɛ'kɔrd]
to set a record	встановлювати рекорд	[wsta'nɔwlʲuwati rɛ'kɔrd]
final	фінал (ч)	[fi'nal]
final (adj)	фінальний	[fi'nalʲnij]
champion	чемпіон (ч)	[tʃɛmpi'ɔn]
championship	чемпіонат (ч)	[tʃɛmpio'nat]

stadium	стадіон (ч)	[stadi'ɔn]
stand (bleachers)	трибуна (ж)	[tri'buna]
fan, supporter	фан, вболівальник (ч)	[fan], [wboli'walʲnik]
opponent, rival	супротивник (ч)	[supro'tiwnik]

start (start line)	старт (ч)	[start]
finish line	фініш (ч)	['finiʃ]

defeat	поразка (ж)	[po'razka]
to lose (not win)	програти	[proɦ'rati]

referee	суддя (ч)	[sud'dʲa]
jury (judges)	журі (с)	[ʒu'ri]
score	рахунок (ч)	[ra'ɦunok]
tie	нічия (ж)	[nitʃiˈʲa]
to tie (vi)	зіграти внічию	[zi'ɦrati wnitʃiˈʲu]
point	очко (с)	[otʃ'kɔ]
result (final score)	результат (ч)	[rɛzulʲ'tat]

period	тайм (ч), період (ч)	[tajm], [pɛ'riod]
half-time	перерва (ж)	[pɛ'rɛrwa]
doping	допінг (ч)	['dɔpinɦ]
to penalize (vt)	штрафувати	[ʃtrafu'wati]
to disqualify (vt)	дискваліфікувати	[diskwalifiku'wati]

apparatus	снаряд (ч)	[sna'rʲad]
javelin	спис (ч)	[spis]
shot (metal ball)	ядро (с)	[jad'rɔ]
ball (snooker, etc.)	куля (ж)	['kulʲa]

aim (target)	ціль (ж)	[tsilʲ]
target	мішень (ж)	[mi'ʃɛnʲ]
to shoot (vi)	стріляти	[stri'lʲati]
accurate (~ shot)	влучний	['wlutʃnij]

trainer, coach	тренер (ч)	['trɛnɛr]
to train (sb)	тренувати	[trɛnu'wati]
to train (vi)	тренуватися	[trɛnu'watisʲa]
training	тренування (с)	[trɛnu'wanʲa]

gym	спортзал (ч)	[sport'zal]
exercise (physical)	вправа (ж)	['wprawa]
warm-up (athlete ~)	розминка (ж)	[roz'minka]

Education

school	школа (ж)	[ˈʃkɔla]
principal (headmaster)	директор (ч) школи	[diˈrɛktor ˈʃkɔli]
student (m)	учень (ч)	[ˈutʃɛnʲ]
student (f)	учениця (ж)	[utʃɛˈnitsʲa]
schoolboy	школяр (ч)	[ʃkoˈlʲar]
schoolgirl	школярка (ж)	[ʃkoˈlʲarka]
to teach (sb)	вчити	[ˈwtʃiti]
to learn (language, etc.)	вивчати	[wiwˈtʃati]
to learn by heart	вчити напам'ять	[ˈwtʃiti naˈpamʲatʲ]
to learn (~ to count, etc.)	вчитися	[ˈwtʃitisʲa]
to be in school	вчитися	[ˈwtʃitisʲa]
to go to school	йти до школи	[jti do ˈʃkoli]
alphabet	алфавіт (ч)	[alfaˈwit]
subject (at school)	предмет (ч)	[prɛdˈmɛt]
classroom	клас (ч)	[klas]
lesson	урок (ч)	[uˈrɔk]
recess	перерва (ж)	[pɛˈrɛrwa]
school bell	дзвінок (ч)	[dzwiˈnɔk]
school desk	парта (ж)	[ˈparta]
chalkboard	дошка (ж)	[ˈdɔʃka]
grade	оцінка (ж)	[oˈtsinka]
good grade	добра оцінка (ж)	[ˈdɔbra oˈtsinka]
bad grade	погана оцінка (ж)	[poˈɦana oˈtsinka]
to give a grade	ставити оцінку	[ˈstawiti oˈtsinku]
mistake, error	помилка (ж)	[poˈmilka]
to make mistakes	робити помилки	[roˈbiti ˈpɔmilki]
to correct (an error)	виправляти	[wiprawˈlʲati]
cheat sheet	шпаргалка (ж)	[ʃparˈɦalka]
homework	домашнє завдання (с)	[doˈmaʃnɛ zawˈdanʲa]
exercise (in education)	вправа (ж)	[ˈwprawa]
to be present	бути присутнім	[ˈbuti priˈsutnim]
to be absent	бути відсутнім	[ˈbuti widˈsutnim]
to miss school	пропускати уроки	[propusˈkati uˈrɔki]

to punish (v)	покарати	[poka'rati]
punishment	покарання (c)	[poka'ranʲa]
behavior	поведінка (ж)	[powɛ'dinka]

report card	щоденник (ч)	[ɕo'dɛnik]
pencil	олівець (ч)	[oli'wɛts]
eraser	гумка (ж)	['ɦumka]
chalk	крейда (ж)	['krɛjda]
pencil case	пенал (ч)	[pɛ'nal]

schoolbag	портфель (ч)	[port'fɛlʲ]
pen	ручка (ж)	['rutʃka]
school notebook	зошит (ч)	['zɔʃit]
textbook	підручник (ч)	[pid'rutʃnik]
drafting compass	циркуль (ч)	['tsirkulʲ]

| to make technical drawings | креслити | ['krɛsliti] |
| technical drawing | креслення (c) | ['krɛslɛnʲa] |

poem	вірш (ч)	[wirʃ]
by heart (adv)	напам'ять	[na'pamʲʲatʲ]
to learn by heart	вчити напам'ять	['wtʃiti na'pamʲʲatʲ]

school vacation	канікули (мн)	[ka'nikuli]
to be on vacation	бути на канікулах	['buti na ka'nikulah]
to spend one's vacation	провести канікули	[prowɛs'ti ka'nikuli]

test (e.g., written math ~)	контрольна робота (ж)	[kon'trɔlʲna ro'bɔta]
essay (composition)	твір (ч)	[twir]
dictation	диктант (ч)	[dik'tant]
exam (examination)	іспит (ч)	['ispit]
to take an exam	складати іспити	[skla'dati 'ispiti]
experiment (e.g., chemistry ~)	дослід (ч)	['dɔslid]

118. College. University

academy	академія (ж)	[aka'dɛmiʲa]
university	університет (ч)	[uniwɛrsi'tɛt]
faculty (e.g., ~ of Medicine)	факультет (ч)	[fakulʲ'tɛt]

student (masc.)	студент (ч)	[stu'dɛnt]
student (fem.)	студентка (ж)	[stu'dɛntka]
lecturer (teacher)	викладач (ч)	[wikla'datʃ]

lecture hall, room	аудиторія (ж)	[audi'tɔriʲa]
graduate	випускник (ч)	[wipusk'nik]
diploma	диплом (ч)	[dip'lɔm]

dissertation	дисертація (ж)	[disɛr'tatsiʲa]
study (report)	дослідження (с)	[do'slidʒɛnʲa]
laboratory	лабораторія (ж)	[labora'tɔriʲa]

lecture	лекція (ж)	['lɛktsiʲa]
coursemate	однокурсник (ч)	[odno'kursnik]
scholarship	стипендія (ж)	[sti'pɛndiʲa]
academic degree	вчений ступінь (ч)	['wtʃɛnij 'stupinʲ]

119. Sciences. Disciplines

mathematics	математика (ж)	[matɛ'matika]
algebra	алгебра (ж)	['alɦɛbra]
geometry	геометрія (ж)	[ɦɛo'mɛtriʲa]

astronomy	астрономія (ж)	[astro'nɔmiʲa]
biology	біологія (ж)	[bio'lɔɦiʲa]
geography	географія (ж)	[ɦɛo'ɦrafiʲa]
geology	геологія (ж)	[ɦɛo'lɔɦiʲa]
history	історія (ж)	[is'tɔriʲa]

medicine	медицина (ж)	[mɛdi'tsina]
pedagogy	педагогіка (ж)	[pɛda'ɦɔɦika]
law	право (с)	['prawo]

physics	фізика (ж)	['fizika]
chemistry	хімія (ж)	['himiʲa]
philosophy	філософія (ж)	[filo'sɔfiʲa]
psychology	психологія (ж)	[psiho'lɔɦiʲa]

120. Writing system. Orthography

grammar	граматика (ж)	[ɦra'matika]
vocabulary	лексика (ж)	['lɛksika]
phonetics	фонетика (ж)	[fo'nɛtika]

noun	іменник (ч)	[i'mɛnik]
adjective	прикметник (ч)	[prik'mɛtnik]
verb	дієслово (с)	[dic'slɔwo]
adverb	прислівник (ч)	[pris'liwnik]

pronoun	займенник (ч)	[zaj'mɛnik]
interjection	вигук (ч)	['wiɦuk]
preposition	прийменник (ч)	[prij'mɛnik]

root	корінь (ч) слова	['kɔrinʲ 'slɔwa]
ending	закінчення (с)	[za'kintʃɛnʲa]
prefix	префікс (ч)	['prɛfiks]

| syllable | склад (ч) | ['sklad] |
| suffix | суфікс (ч) | ['sufiks] |

| stress mark | наголос (ч) | ['naɦolos] |
| apostrophe | апостроф (ч) | [a'pɔstrof] |

period, dot	крапка (ж)	['krapka]
comma	кома (ж)	['kɔma]
semicolon	крапка (ж) з комою	['krapka z 'kɔmoʲu]
colon	двокрапка (ж)	[dwo'krapka]
ellipsis	три крапки (мн)	[tri 'krapkɨ]

| question mark | знак (ч) питання | [znak pi'tanʲa] |
| exclamation point | знак (ч) оклику | [znak 'ɔklɨku] |

quotation marks	лапки (мн)	[lap'kɨ]
in quotation marks	в лапках	[w lap'kah]
parenthesis	дужки (мн)	[duʒ'kɨ]
in parenthesis	в дужках	[w duʒ'kah]

hyphen	дефіс (ч)	[dɛ'fis]
dash	тире (с)	[ti'rɛ]
space (between words)	пробіл (ч)	[pro'bil]

| letter | літера (ж) | ['litɛra] |
| capital letter | велика літера (ж) | [wɛ'lika 'litɛra] |

| vowel (n) | голосний звук (ч) | [ɦolos'nɨj zwuk] |
| consonant (n) | приголосний (ч) | ['priɦolosnɨj] |

sentence	речення (с)	['rɛtʃɛnʲa]
subject	підмет (ч)	['pidmɛt]
predicate	присудок (ч)	['prisudok]

line	рядок (ч)	[rʲa'dɔk]
on a new line	з нового рядка	[z no'woɦo rʲad'ka]
paragraph	абзац (ч)	[ab'zaʦ]

word	слово (с)	['slɔwo]
group of words	словосполучення (с)	[slowospo'lutʃɛnʲa]
expression	вислів (ч)	['wisliw]
synonym	синонім (ч)	[si'nɔnim]
antonym	антонім (ч)	[an'tɔnim]

rule	правило (с)	['prawɨlo]
exception	виняток (ч)	['winʲatok]
correct (adj)	правильний	['prawɨlʲnɨj]

conjugation	дієвідміна (ж)	[diɛwid'mina]
declension	відмінювання (с)	[wid'minʲuwanʲa]
nominal case	відмінок (ч)	[wid'minok]
question	питання (с)	[pi'tanʲa]

| to underline (vt) | підкреслити | [pid'krɛsliti] |
| dotted line | пунктир (ч) | [punk'tir] |

121. Foreign languages

language	мова (ж)	['mɔwa]
foreign (adj)	іноземний	[ino'zɛmnij]
foreign language	іноземна мова (ж)	[ino'zɛmna 'mɔwa]
to study (vt)	вивчати	[wiw'tʃati]
to learn (language, etc.)	вчити	['wtʃiti]

to read (vi, vt)	читати	[tʃi'tati]
to speak (vi, vt)	говорити	[howo'riti]
to understand (vt)	розуміти	[rozu'miti]
to write (vt)	писати	[pi'sati]

fast (adv)	швидко	['ʃwidko]
slowly (adv)	повільно	[po'wilʲno]
fluently (adv)	вільно	['wilʲno]

rules	правила (мн)	['prawila]
grammar	граматика (ж)	[ɦra'matika]
vocabulary	лексика (ж)	['lɛksika]
phonetics	фонетика (ж)	[fo'nɛtika]

textbook	підручник (ч)	[pid'rutʃnik]
dictionary	словник (ч)	[slow'nik]
teach-yourself book	самовчитель (ч)	[samow'tʃitɛlʲ]
phrasebook	розмовник (ч)	[roz'mɔwnik]

cassette, tape	касета (ж)	[ka'sɛta]
videotape	відеокасета (ж)	['widɛo ka'sɛta]
CD, compact disc	CD-диск (ч)	[si'di disk]
DVD	DVD (ч)	[diwi'di]

alphabet	алфавіт (ч)	[alfa'wit]
to spell (vt)	говорити по буквах	[howo'riti po 'bukwah]
pronunciation	вимова (ж)	[wi'mɔwa]

accent	акцент (ч)	[ak'tsɛnt]
with an accent	з акцентом	[z ak'tsɛntom]
without an accent	без акценту	[bɛz ak'tsɛntu]

| word | слово (с) | ['slɔwo] |
| meaning | сенс (ч) | [sɛns] |

course (e.g., a French ~)	курси (мн)	['kursi]
to sign up	записатися	[zapi'satisʲa]
teacher	викладач (ч)	[wikla'datʃ]
translation (process)	переклад (ч)	[pɛ'rɛklad]

translation (text, etc.)	переклад (ч)	[pɛˈrɛklad]
translator	перекладач (ч)	[pɛrɛklaˈdatʃ]
interpreter	перекладач (ч)	[pɛrɛklaˈdatʃ]
polyglot	поліглот (ч)	[poliɦˈlɔt]
memory	пам'ять (ж)	[ˈpamʲatʲ]

122. Fairy tale characters

Santa Claus	Санта Клаус (ч)	[ˈsanta ˈklaus]
Cinderella	Попелюшка (ж)	[popɛˈlʲuʃka]
mermaid	русалка (ж)	[ruˈsalka]
Neptune	Нептун	[nɛpˈtun]
magician, wizard	чарівник (ч)	[tʃariwˈnik]
fairy	чарівниця (ж)	[tʃariwˈnitsʲa]
magic (adj)	чарівний	[tʃariwˈnij]
magic wand	чарівна паличка (ж)	[tʃaˈriwna ˈpalitʃka]
fairy tale	казка (ж)	[ˈkazka]
miracle	диво (с)	[ˈdiwo]
dwarf	гном (ч)	[ɦnom]
to turn into …	перетворитися на	[pɛrɛtwoˈritisʲa na]
ghost	привид (ч)	[ˈpriwid]
phantom	примара (ж)	[priˈmara]
monster	чудовисько (с)	[tʃuˈdɔwisko]
dragon	дракон (ч)	[draˈkɔn]
giant	велетень (ч)	[ˈwɛlɛtɛnʲ]

123. Zodiac Signs

Aries	Овен (ч)	[ˈɔwɛn]
Taurus	Телець (ч)	[tɛˈlɛts]
Gemini	Близнюки (мн)	[blizˈnʲuˈki]
Cancer	Рак (ч)	[rak]
Leo	Лев (ч)	[lɛw]
Virgo	Діва (ж)	[ˈdiwa]
Libra	Терези (мн)	[tɛrɛˈzi]
Scorpio	Скорпіон (ч)	[skorpiˈɔn]
Sagittarius	Стрілець (ч)	[striˈlɛts]
Capricorn	Козеріг (ч)	[kozɛˈriɦ]
Aquarius	Водолій (ч)	[wodoˈlij]
Pisces	Риби (мн)	[ˈribi]
character	характер (ч)	[haˈraktɛr]
character traits	риси (мн) характеру	[ˈrisi haˈraktɛru]

behavior	**поведінка** (ж)	[powɛ'dinka]
to tell fortunes	**ворожити**	[woro'ʒiti]
fortune-teller	**гадалка** (ж)	[ɦa'dalka]
horoscope	**гороскоп** (ч)	[ɦoro'skɔp]

Arts

theater	театр (ч)	[tɛ'atr]
opera	опера (ж)	['ɔpɛra]
operetta	оперета (ж)	[opɛ'rɛta]
ballet	балет (ч)	[ba'lɛt]

theater poster	афіша (ж)	[a'fiʃa]
troupe (theatrical performers)	трупа (ж)	['trupa]
tour	гастролі (мн)	[ɦa'strɔli]
to be on tour	гастролювати	[ɦastrolʲu'wati]
to rehearse (vi, vt)	репетирувати	[rɛpɛ'tiruwati]
rehearsal	репетиція (ж)	[rɛpɛ'titsiʲa]
repertoire	репертуар (ч)	[rɛpɛrtu'ar]

performance	вистава (ж)	[wis'tawa]
theatrical show	спектакль (ч)	[spɛk'taklʲ]
play	п'єса (ж)	['pʲɛsa]

ticket	квиток (ч)	[kwi'tɔk]
box office (ticket booth)	квиткова каса (ж)	[kwit'kɔwa 'kasa]
lobby, foyer	хол (ч)	[hol]
coat check (cloakroom)	гардероб (ч)	[ɦardɛ'rɔb]
coat check tag	номерок (ч)	[nomɛ'rɔk]
binoculars	бінокль (ч)	[bi'nɔklʲ]
usher	контролер (ч)	[kontro'lɛr]

orchestra seats	партер (ч)	[par'tɛr]
balcony	балкон (ч)	[bal'kɔn]
dress circle	бельетаж (ч)	[bɛlʲʲɛ'taʒ]
box	ложа (ж)	['lɔʒa]
row	ряд (ч)	[rʲad]
seat	місце (с)	['mistsɛ]

audience	публіка (ж)	['publika]
spectator	глядач (ч)	[ɦlʲa'datʃ]
to clap (vi, vt)	плескати	[plɛs'kati]
applause	аплодисменти (мн)	[aplodis'mɛnti]
ovation	овації (мн)	[o'watsiji]

stage	сцена (ж)	['stsɛna]
curtain	завіса (ж)	[za'wisa]
scenery	декорація (ж)	[dɛko'ratsiʲa]

backstage	**куліси** (мн)	[ku'lisi]
scene (e.g., the last ~)	**дія** (ж)	['diʲa]
act	**акт** (ч)	[akt]
intermission	**антракт** (ч)	[an'trakt]

125. Cinema

actor	**актор** (ч)	[ak'tɔr]
actress	**акторка** (ж)	[ak'tɔrka]
movies (industry)	**кіно**	[ki'nɔ]
movie	**кіно** (с)	[ki'nɔ]
episode	**серія** (ж)	['sɛriʲa]
detective movie	**детектив** (ч)	[dɛtɛk'tiw]
action movie	**бойовик** (ч)	[boʲo'wik]
adventure movie	**пригодницький фільм** (ч)	[pri'ɦɔdnitskij filʲm]
sci-fi movie	**фантастичний фільм** (ч)	[fantas'titʃnij filʲm]
horror movie	**фільм** (ч) **жахів**	[filʲm 'ʒahiw]
comedy movie	**кінокомедія** (ж)	[kinoko'mɛdiʲa]
melodrama	**мелодрама** (ж)	[mɛlod'rama]
drama	**драма** (ж)	['drama]
fictional movie	**художній фільм** (ч)	[hu'dɔʒnij filʲm]
documentary	**документальний фільм** (ч)	[dokumɛn'talʲnij filʲm]
cartoon	**мультфільм** (ч)	[mulʲt'filʲm]
silent movies	**німе кіно** (с)	[ni'mɛ ki'nɔ]
role (part)	**роль** (ж)	[rolʲ]
leading role	**головна роль** (ж)	[ɦolow'na rolʲ]
to play (vi, vt)	**грати**	['ɦrati]
movie star	**кінозірка** (ж)	[kino'zirka]
well-known (adj)	**відомий**	[wi'dɔmij]
famous (adj)	**знаменитий**	[znamɛ'nitij]
popular (adj)	**популярний**	[popu'lʲarnij]
script (screenplay)	**сценарій** (ч)	[stsɛ'narij]
scriptwriter	**сценарист** (ч)	[stsɛna'rist]
movie director	**режисер** (ч)	[rɛʒi'sɛr]
producer	**продюсер** (ч)	[pro'dʲusɛr]
assistant	**асистент** (ч)	[asis'tɛnt]
cameraman	**оператор** (ч)	[opɛ'rator]
stuntman	**каскадер** (ч)	[kaska'dɛr]
double (body double)	**дублер** (ч)	[dub'lɛr]
to shoot a movie	**знімати фільм**	[zni'mati filʲm]
audition, screen test	**проби** (мн)	['prɔbi]

shooting	зйомки (мн)	['z⁷ɔmki]
movie crew	знімальна група (ж)	[zni'malʲna 'ɦrupa]
movie set	знімальний майданчик (ч)	[zni'malʲnij maj'danʧik]
camera	кінокамера (ж)	[kino'kamɛra]
movie theater	кінотеатр (ч)	[kinotɛ'atr]
screen (e.g., big ~)	екран (ч)	[ɛk'ran]
to show a movie	показувати фільм	[po'kazuwati filʲm]
soundtrack	звукова доріжка (ж)	[zwuko'wa do'riʒka]
special effects	спеціальні ефекти (мн)	[spɛtsi'alʲni ɛ'fɛkti]
subtitles	субтитри (мн)	[sub'titri]
credits	титри (мн)	['titri]
translation	переклад (ч)	[pɛ'rɛklad]

126. Visual arts

art	мистецтво (с)	[mis'tɛtstwo]
fine arts	образотворчі мистецтва (мн)	[obrazot'wɔrʧi mis'tɛtstwa]
art gallery	арт-галерея (ж)	[art ɦalɛ'rɛʲa]
art exhibition	виставка (ж) картин	['wistawka kar'tin]
painting (art)	живопис (ч)	[ʒi'wɔpis]
graphic art	графіка (ж)	['ɦrafika]
abstract art	абстракціонізм (ч)	[abstraktsio'nizm]
impressionism	імпресіонізм (ч)	[imprɛsio'nizm]
picture, painting	картина (ж)	[kar'tina]
drawing	малюнок (ч)	[ma'lʲunok]
poster	плакат (ч)	[pla'kat]
illustration (picture)	ілюстрація (ж)	[ilʲust'ratsiʲa]
miniature	мініатюра (ж)	[minia'tʲura]
copy (replica of painting, etc.)	копія (ж)	['kɔpiʲa]
reproduction	репродукція (ж)	[rɛpro'duktsiʲa]
mosaic	мозаїка (ж)	[mo'zajika]
stained glass window	вітраж (ч)	[wit'raʒ]
fresco	фреска (ж)	['frɛska]
engraving	гравюра (ж)	[ɦra'wʲura]
bust (sculpture)	бюст (ч)	[bʲust]
sculpture	скульптура (ж)	[skulʲp'tura]
statue	статуя (ж)	['statuʲa]
plaster of Paris	гіпс (ч)	[ɦips]
plaster (as adj)	з гіпсу	[z 'ɦipsu]
portrait	портрет (ч)	[port'rɛt]

self-portrait	автопортрет (ч)	[awtopor'trɛt]
landscape painting	пейзаж (ч)	[pɛj'zaʒ]
still life	натюрморт (ч)	[natʲur'mɔrt]
caricature	карикатура (ж)	[karika'tura]
sketch	нарис (ч)	['naris]
paint	фарба (ж)	['farba]
watercolor paint	акварель (ж)	[akwa'rɛlʲ]
oil (paint)	масло (с)	['maslo]
pencil	олівець (ч)	[oli'wɛʦ]
India ink	туш (ж)	[tuʃ]
charcoal	вугілля (с)	[wu'ɦilʲa]
to draw (vi, vt)	малювати	[malʲu'wati]
to paint (vi, vt)	малювати	[malʲu'wati]
to pose (vi)	позувати	[pozu'wati]
artist's model (masc.)	натурник (ч)	[na'turnik]
artist's model (fem.)	натурниця (ж)	[na'turniʦʲa]
artist (painter)	художник (ч)	[hu'dɔʒnik]
work of art	витвір (ч) мистецтва	['witwir mis'tɛʦtwa]
masterpiece	шедевр (ч)	[ʃɛ'dɛwr]
studio (artist's workroom)	майстерня (ж)	[majs'tɛrnʲa]
canvas (cloth)	полотно (с)	[polot'nɔ]
easel	мольберт (ч)	[molʲ'bɛrt]
palette	палітра (ж)	[pa'litra]
frame (picture ~, etc.)	рама (ж)	['rama]
restoration	реставрація (ж)	[rɛstaw'raʦʲa]
to restore (vt)	реставрувати	[rɛstawru'wati]

127. Literature & Poetry

literature	література (ж)	[litɛra'tura]
author (writer)	автор (ч)	['awtor]
pseudonym	псевдонім (ч)	[psɛwdo'nim]
book	книга (ж)	['kniɦa]
volume	том (ч)	[tɔm]
table of contents	зміст (ч)	[zmist]
page	сторінка (ж)	[sto'rinka]
main character	головний герой (ч)	[ɦolow'nij ɦɛ'rɔj]
autograph	автограф (ч)	[aw'tɔɦraf]
short story	оповідання (с)	[opowi'danʲa]
story (novella)	повість (ж)	['pɔwistʲ]
novel	роман (ч)	[ro'man]
work (writing)	твір (ч)	[twir]
fable	байка (ж)	['bajka]

detective novel	детектив (ч)	[dɛtɛk'tiw]
poem (verse)	вірш (ч)	[wirʃ]
poetry	поезія (ж)	[po'ɛziʲa]
poem (epic, ballad)	поема (ж)	[po'ɛma]
poet	поет (ч)	[po'ɛt]

fiction	белетристика (ж)	[bɛlɛt'ristika]
science fiction	наукова фантастика (ж)	[nau'kɔwa fan'tastika]
adventures	пригоди (мн)	[pri'ɦɔdi]
educational literature	учбова література (ж)	[utʃ'bɔwa litɛra'tura]
children's literature	дитяча література (ж)	[di'tʲatʃa litɛra'tura]

128. Circus

circus	цирк (ч)	[tsirk]
traveling circus	цирк-шапіто (ч)	[tsirk ʃapi'tɔ]
program	програма (ж)	[proɦ'rama]
performance	вистава (ж)	[wis'tawa]

act (circus ~)	номер (ч)	['nɔmɛr]
circus ring	арена (ж)	[a'rɛna]

pantomime (act)	пантоміма (ж)	[panto'mima]
clown	клоун (ч)	['klɔun]
acrobat	акробат (ч)	[akro'bat]
acrobatics	акробатика (ж)	[akro'batika]
gymnast	гімнаст (ч)	[ɦim'nast]
acrobatic gymnastics	гімнастика (ж)	[ɦim'nastika]
somersault	сальто (с)	['salʲto]

athlete (strongman)	атлет (ч)	[at'lɛt]
tamer (e.g., lion ~)	приборкувач (ч)	[pri'bɔrkuwatʃ]
rider (circus horse ~)	наїзник (ч)	[na'jiznik]
assistant	асистент (ч)	[asis'tɛnt]
stunt	трюк (ч)	[trʲuk]
magic trick	фокус (ч)	['fɔkus]
conjurer, magician	фокусник (ч)	['fɔkusnik]

juggler	жонглер (ч)	[ʒonɦ'lɛr]
to juggle (vi, vt)	жонглювати	[ʒonɦlʲu'wati]
animal trainer	дресирувальник (ч)	[drɛsiru'walʲnik]
animal training	дресура (ж)	[drɛ'sura]
to train (animals)	дресирувати	[drɛsiru'wati]

129. Music. Pop music

music	музика (ж)	['muzika]
musician	музикант (ч)	[muzi'kant]

| musical instrument | музичний інструмент (ч) | [mu'zitʃnij instru'mɛnt] |
| to play … | грати на… | ['ɦrati na] |

guitar	гітара (ж)	[ɦi'tara]
violin	скрипка (ж)	['skripka]
cello	віолончель (ж)	[wiolon'tʃɛlʲ]
double bass	контрабас (ч)	[kontra'bas]
harp	арфа (ж)	['arfa]

piano	піаніно (с)	[pia'nino]
grand piano	рояль (ч)	[ro'ʲalʲ]
organ	орган (ч)	[or'ɦan]

wind instruments	духові інструменти (мн)	[duho'wi instru'mɛnti]
oboe	гобой (ч)	[ɦo'bɔj]
saxophone	саксофон (ч)	[sakso'fɔn]
clarinet	кларнет (ч)	[klar'nɛt]
flute	флейта (ж)	['flɛjta]
trumpet	труба (ж)	[tru'ba]

accordion	акордеон (ч)	[akordɛ'ɔn]
drum	барабан (ч)	[bara'ban]
duo	дует (ч)	[du'ɛt]
trio	тріо (с)	['trio]
quartet	квартет (ч)	[kwar'tɛt]
choir	хор (ч)	[hor]
orchestra	оркестр (ч)	[or'kɛstr]

pop music	поп-музика (ж)	[pop 'muzika]
rock music	рок-музика (ж)	[rok 'muzika]
rock group	рок-група (ж)	[rok 'ɦrupa]
jazz	джаз (ч)	[dʒaz]

| idol | кумир (ч) | [ku'mir] |
| admirer, fan | шанувальник (ч) | [ʃanu'walʲnik] |

concert	концерт (ч)	[kon'tsɛrt]
symphony	симфонія (ж)	[sim'fɔniʲa]
composition	твір (ч)	[twir]
to compose (write)	створити	[stwo'riti]

singing (n)	спів (ч)	[spiw]
song	пісня (ж)	['pisnʲa]
tune (melody)	мелодія (ж)	[mɛ'lɔdiʲa]
rhythm	ритм (ч)	[ritm]
blues	блюз (ч)	[blʲuz]

sheet music	ноти (мн)	['nɔti]
baton	паличка (ж)	['palitʃka]
bow	смичок (ч)	[smi'tʃɔk]
string	струна (ж)	[stru'na]
case (e.g., guitar ~)	футляр (ч)	[fut'lʲar]

Rest. Entertainment. Travel

130. Trip. Travel

tourism, travel	туризм (ч)	[tu'rizm]
tourist	турист (ч)	[tu'rist]
trip, voyage	мандрівка (ж)	[mand'riwka]
adventure	пригода (ж)	[pri'ɦɔda]
trip, journey	поїздка (ж)	[po'jizdka]
vacation	відпустка (ж)	[wid'pustka]
to be on vacation	бути у відпустці	['butɨ u wid'pusttsi]
rest	відпочинок (ч)	[widpo'tʃinok]
train	поїзд (ч)	['pɔjizd]
by train	поїздом	['pɔjizdom]
airplane	літак (ч)	[li'tak]
by airplane	літаком	[lita'kɔm]
by car	автомобілем	[awtomo'bilɛm]
by ship	кораблем	[korab'lɛm]
luggage	багаж (ч)	[ba'ɦaʒ]
suitcase	валіза (ж)	[wa'liza]
luggage cart	візок (ч) для багажу	[wi'zɔk dlʲa baɦa'ʒu]
passport	паспорт (ч)	['pasport]
visa	віза (ж)	['wiza]
ticket	квиток (ч)	[kwi'tɔk]
air ticket	авіаквиток (ч)	[awiakwi'tɔk]
guidebook	путівник (ч)	[putiw'nik]
map (tourist ~)	карта (ж)	['karta]
area (rural ~)	місцевість (ж)	[mis'tsɛwistʲ]
place, site	місце (с)	['mistsɛ]
exotica (n)	екзотика (ж)	[ɛk'zɔtika]
exotic (adj)	екзотичний	[ɛkzo'titʃnij]
amazing (adj)	дивовижний	['diwowiʒnij]
group	група (ж)	['ɦrupa]
excursion, sightseeing tour	екскурсія (ж)	[ɛks'kursiʲa]
guide (person)	екскурсовод (ч)	[ɛkskurso'wɔd]

131. Hotel

hotel, inn	готель (ч)	[ɦo'tɛlʲ]
motel	мотель (ч)	[mo'tɛlʲ]
three-star (~ hotel)	три зірки	[tri 'zirki]
five-star	п'ять зірок	[pʲʲatʲ zi'rɔk]
to stay (at a hotel, etc.)	зупинитися	[zupi'nitisʲa]
room	номер (ч)	['nɔmɛr]
single room	одномісний номер (ч)	[odno'misnij nomɛr]
double room	двомісний номер (ч)	[dwo'misnij 'nɔmɛr]
to book a room	бронювати номер	[bronʲu'wati 'nɔmɛr]
half board	напівпансіон (ч)	[napiwpansi'ɔn]
full board	повний пансіон (ч)	['pɔwnij pansi'ɔn]
with bath	з ванною	[z 'wanoʲu]
with shower	з душем	[z 'duʃɛm]
satellite television	супутникове телебачення (с)	[su'putnikowɛ tɛlɛ'batʃɛnʲa]
air-conditioner	кондиціонер (ч)	[kondiʦio'nɛr]
towel	рушник (ч)	[ruʃ'nik]
key	ключ (ч)	[klʲutʃ]
administrator	адміністратор (ч)	[admini'strator]
chambermaid	покоївка (ж)	[poko'jiwka]
porter, bellboy	носильник (ч)	[no'silʲnik]
doorman	портьє (ч)	[por'tʲɛ]
restaurant	ресторан (ч)	[rɛsto'ran]
pub, bar	бар (ч)	[bar]
breakfast	сніданок (ч)	[sni'danok]
dinner	вечеря (ж)	[wɛ'tʃɛrʲa]
buffet	шведський стіл (ч)	['ʃwɛdsʲkij stil]
lobby	вестибюль (ч)	[wɛsti'bʲulʲ]
elevator	ліфт (ч)	[lift]
DO NOT DISTURB	НЕ ТУРБУВАТИ	[nɛ turbu'wati]
NO SMOKING	ПАЛИТИ ЗАБОРОНЕНО	[pa'liti zabo'rɔnɛno]

132. Books. Reading

book	книга (ж)	['kniɦa]
author	автор (ч)	['awtor]
writer	письменник (ч)	[pisʲ'mɛnik]
to write (~ a book)	написати	[napi'sati]
reader	читач (ч)	[tʃi'tatʃ]

| to read (vi, vt) | читати | [tʃi'tati] |
| reading (activity) | читання (с) | [tʃi'tanʲa] |

| silently (to oneself) | про себе | [pro 'sɛbɛ] |
| aloud (to read ~) | вголос | ['wɦɔlos] |

to publish (vt)	видавати	[wida'wati]
publishing (process)	примірник (ч)	[pri'mirnik]
publisher	видавець (ч)	[wida'wɛts]
publishing house	видавництво (с)	[widaw'nitstwo]

to come out (ab. new book)	вийти	['wijti]
release (of a new book)	вихід (ч)	['wihid]
print run	наклад (ч)	['naklad]

| bookstore | книгарня (ж) | [kni'ɦarnʲa] |
| library | бібліотека (ж) | [biblio'tɛka] |

story (novella)	повість (ж)	['pɔwistʲ]
short story	оповідання (с)	[opowi'danʲa]
novel	роман (ч)	[ro'man]
detective novel	детектив (ч)	[dɛtɛk'tiw]

memoirs	мемуари (мн)	[mɛmu'ari]
legend	легенда (ж)	[lɛ'ɦɛnda]
myth	міф (ч)	[mif]

poetry, poems	вірші (мн)	['wirʃi]
autobiography	автобіографія (ж)	[awtobio'ɦrafiʲa]
selected works	вибрані роботи (мн)	['wibrani ro'bɔti]
science fiction	наукова фантастика (ж)	[nau'kɔwa fan'tastika]

title	назва (ж)	['nazwa]
introduction	вступ (ч)	[wstup]
title page	титульна сторінка (ж)	['titulʲna sto'rinka]

chapter	розділ (ч)	['rɔzdil]
extract	уривок (ч)	[u'riwok]
episode	епізод (ч)	[ɛpi'zɔd]

plot (storyline)	сюжет (ч)	[sʲu'ʒɛt]
contents	вміст (ч)	[wmist]
table of contents	зміст (ч)	[zmist]
main character	головний герой (ч)	[ɦolow'nij ɦɛ'rɔj]

volume	том (ч)	[tom]
cover	обкладинка (ж)	[ob'kladinka]
binding	палітура (ж)	[pali'tura]
bookmark	закладка (ж)	[za'kladka]
page	сторінка (ж)	[sto'rinka]
to page through	гортати	[ɦor'tati]

margins	поля (мн)	[po'lʲa]
annotation (marginal note, etc.)	позначка (ж)	['pɔznatʃka]
footnote	примітка (ж)	[priˈmitka]
text	текст (ч)	[tɛkst]
type, font	шрифт (ч)	[ʃrift]
misprint, typo	помилка (ж)	[poˈmilka]
translation	переклад (ч)	[pɛˈrɛklad]
to translate (vt)	перекладати	[pɛrɛklaˈdati]
original (n)	оригінал (ч)	[oriɦiˈnal]
famous (adj)	відомий	[wiˈdɔmij]
unknown (not famous)	невідомий	[nɛwiˈdɔmij]
interesting (adj)	цікавий	[tsiˈkawij]
bestseller	бестселер (ч)	[bɛstˈsɛlɛr]
dictionary	словник (ч)	[slowˈnik]
textbook	підручник (ч)	[pidˈrutʃnik]
encyclopedia	енциклопедія (ж)	[ɛntsikloˈpɛdiʲa]

133. Hunting. Fishing

hunting	полювання (с)	[polʲuˈwanʲa]
to hunt (vi, vt)	полювати	[polʲuˈwati]
hunter	мисливець (ч)	[misˈliwɛts]
to shoot (vi)	стріляти	[striˈlʲati]
rifle	рушниця (ж)	[ruʃˈnitsʲa]
bullet (shell)	патрон (ч)	[patˈrɔn]
shot (lead balls)	шріт (ч)	[ʃrit]
jaw trap	капкан (ч)	[kapˈkan]
snare (for birds, etc.)	пастка (ж)	['pastka]
to fall into a jaw trap	потрапити в капкан	[potˈrapiti w kapˈkan]
to lay a jaw trap	ставити капкан	['stawiti kapˈkan]
poacher	браконьєр (ч)	[brakoˈnʲɛr]
game (in hunting)	дичина (ж)	[ditʃiˈna]
hound dog	мисливський пес (ч)	[misˈliwsʲkij pɛs]
safari	сафарі (с)	[saˈfari]
mounted animal	опудало (с)	[oˈpudalo]
fisherman, angler	рибалка (ч)	[riˈbalka]
fishing (angling)	риболовля (ж)	[riboˈlɔwlʲa]
to fish (vi)	ловити рибу	[loˈwiti ˈribu]
fishing rod	вудочка (ж)	['wudotʃka]
fishing line	волосінь (ж)	[woloˈsinʲ]

hook	гачок (ч)	[ɦa'ʧɔk]
float, bobber	поплавець (ч)	[popla'wɛʦ]
bait	наживка (ж)	[na'ʒiwka]

to cast the line	закинути вудочку	[za'kinuti 'wudoʧku]
to bite (ab. fish)	клювати	[klʲu'wati]
catch (of fish)	улов (ч)	[u'lɔw]
ice-hole	ополонка (ж)	[opo'lɔnka]

fishing net	сітка (ж)	['sitka]
boat	човен (ч)	['ʧɔwɛn]
to net (to fish with a net)	ловити	[lo'witi]
to cast the net	закидати сіті	[zaki'dati 'siti]
to haul the net in	витягати сіті	[witʲa'ɦati 'siti]
to fall into the net	потрапити у сіті	[pot'rapiti u 'siti]

whaler (person)	китобій (ч)	[kito'bij]
whaleboat	китобійне судно (с)	[kito'bijnɛ 'sudno]
harpoon	гарпун (ч)	[ɦar'pun]

134. Games. Billiards

billiards	більярд (ч)	[bi'ljard]
billiard room, hall	більярдна (ж)	[bi'ljardna]
ball (snooker, etc.)	більярдна куля (ж)	[bi'ljardna 'kulʲa]

to pocket a ball	загнати кулю	[za'ɦnati 'kulʲu]
cue	кий (ч)	[kij]
pocket	луза (ж)	['luza]

135. Games. Playing cards

playing card	карта (ж)	['karta]
cards	карти (мн)	['karti]
deck of cards	колода (ж)	[ko'lɔda]
trump	козир (ч)	['kɔzir]

diamonds	бубни (мн)	['bubni]
spades	піки (мн)	['piki]
hearts	черви (мн)	['ʧɛrwi]
clubs	трефи (мн)	['trɛfi]

ace	туз (ч)	[tuz]
king	король (ч)	[ko'rɔlʲ]
queen	дама (ж)	['dama]
jack, knave	валет (ч)	[wa'lɛt]
to deal (vi, vt)	здавати	[zda'wati]
to shuffle (cards)	тасувати	[tasu'wati]

lead, turn (n)	хід (ч)	[hid]
point	очко (с)	[oʧˈkɔ]
cardsharp	шулер (ч)	[ˈʃulɛr]

136. Rest. Games. Miscellaneous

to stroll (vi, vt)	прогулюватися	[proˈɦulʲuwatisʲa]
stroll (leisurely walk)	прогулянка (ж)	[proˈɦulʲanka]
car ride	поїздка (ж)	[poˈjizdka]
adventure	пригода (ж)	[priˈɦɔda]
picnic	пікнік (ч)	[pikˈnik]
game (chess, etc.)	гра (ж)	[ɦra]
player	гравець (ч)	[ɦraˈwɛʦ]
game (one ~ of chess)	партія (ж)	[ˈpartiʲa]
collector (e.g., philatelist)	колекціонер (ч)	[kolɛkʦioˈnɛr]
to collect (stamps, etc.)	колекціонувати	[kolɛkʦionuˈwati]
collection	колекція (ж)	[koˈlɛkʦiʲa]
crossword puzzle	кросворд (ч)	[krosˈwɔrd]
racetrack	іподром (ч)	[ipodˈrɔm]
(horse racing venue)		
disco (discotheque)	дискотека (ж)	[diskoˈtɛka]
sauna	сауна (ж)	[ˈsauna]
lottery	лотерея (ж)	[lotɛˈrɛʲa]
camping trip	похід (ч)	[poˈhid]
camp	табір (ч)	[ˈtabir]
camper	турист (ч)	[tuˈrist]
tent (for camping)	намет (ч)	[naˈmɛt]
compass	компас (ч)	[ˈkɔmpas]
to watch (movie, etc.)	дивитися	[diˈwitisʲa]
viewer	телеглядач (ч)	[tɛlɛɦlʲaˈdaʧ]
TV show (TV program)	телепередача (ж)	[ˈtɛlɛ pɛrɛˈdaʧa]

137. Photography

camera (photo)	фотоапарат (ч)	[fotoapaˈrat]
photo, picture	фото (с)	[ˈfɔto]
photographer	фотограф (ч)	[foˈtɔɦraf]
photo studio	фотостудія (ж)	[fotoˈstudiʲa]
photo album	фотоальбом (ч)	[fotoalʲˈbɔm]
camera lens	об'єктив (ч)	[obˀɛkˈtiw]
telephoto lens	телеоб'єктив (ч)	[tɛlɛobˀɛkˈtiw]

| filter | фільтр (ч) | ['filʲtr] |
| lens | лінза (ж) | ['linza] |

optics (high-quality ~)	оптика (ж)	['ɔptika]
diaphragm (aperture)	діафрагма (ж)	[dia'fraɦma]
exposure time (shutter speed)	витримка (ж)	['witrimka]
viewfinder	видошукач (ч)	[widoʃu'katʃ]

digital camera	цифрова камера (ж)	[tsifro'wa 'kamɛra]
tripod	штатив (ч)	[ʃta'tiw]
flash	спалах (ч)	['spalah]

to photograph (vt)	фотографувати	[fotoɦrafu'wati]
to take pictures	знімати	[zni'mati]
to have one's picture taken	фотографуватися	[fotoɦrafu'watisʲa]

focus	різкість (ж)	['rizkistʲ]
to focus (vt)	наводити різкість	[na'wɔditi 'rizkistʲ]
sharp, in focus (adj)	різкий	[riz'kij]
sharpness	різкість (ж)	['rizkistʲ]

| contrast | контраст (ч) | [kon'trast] |
| contrast (as adj) | контрастний | [kon'trastnij] |

picture (photo)	знімок (ч)	['znimok]
negative (n)	негатив (ч)	[nɛɦa'tiw]
film (a roll of ~)	фотоплівка (ж)	[foto'pliwka]
frame (still)	кадр (ч)	[kadr]
to print (photos)	друкувати	[druku'wati]

138. Beach. Swimming

beach	пляж (ч)	[plʲaʒ]
sand	пісок (ч)	[pi'sɔk]
deserted (beach)	пустельний	[pus'tɛlʲnij]

suntan	засмага (ж)	[zas'maɦa]
to get a tan	засмагати	[zasma'ɦati]
tan (adj)	засмаглий	[zas'maɦlij]
sunscreen	крем (ч) для засмаги	[krɛm dlʲa zas'maɦi]

bikini	бікіні (мн)	[bi'kini]
bathing suit	купальник (ч)	[ku'palʲnik]
swim trunks	плавки (мн)	['plawki]

swimming pool	басейн (ч)	[ba'sɛjn]
to swim (vi)	плавати	['plawati]
shower	душ (ч)	[duʃ]
to change (one's clothes)	перевдягатися	[pɛrɛwdʲa'ɦatisʲa]

towel	рушник (ч)	[ruʃˈnik]
boat	човен (ч)	[ˈtʃɔwɛn]
motorboat	катер (ч)	[ˈkatɛr]

water ski	водяні лижі (мн)	[wodʲaˈni ˈliʒi]
paddle boat	водяний велосипед (ч)	[wodʲaˈnij wɛlosiˈpɛd]
surfing	серфінг (ч)	[ˈsɛrfinɦ]
surfer	серфінгіст (ч)	[sɛrfiˈnɦist]

scuba set	акваланг (ч)	[akwaˈlanɦ]
flippers (swim fins)	ласти (мн)	[ˈlasti]
mask (diving ~)	маска (ж)	[ˈmaska]
diver	нирець (ч)	[niˈrɛts]
to dive (vi)	пірнати	[pirˈnati]
underwater (adv)	під водою	[pid woˈdɔʲu]

beach umbrella	парасолька (ж)	[paraˈsɔlʲka]
sunbed (lounger)	шезлонг (ч)	[ʃɛzˈlɔnɦ]
sunglasses	окуляри (мн)	[okuˈlʲari]
air mattress	плавальний матрац (ч)	[ˈplawalʲnij matˈrats]

| to play (amuse oneself) | грати | [ˈɦrati] |
| to go for a swim | купатися | [kuˈpatisʲa] |

beach ball	м'яч (ч)	[mʲatʃ]
to inflate (vt)	надувати	[naduˈwati]
inflatable, air (adj)	надувний	[naduwˈnij]

wave	хвиля (ж)	[ˈɦwilʲa]
buoy (line of ~s)	буй (ч)	[buj]
to drown (ab. person)	тонути	[toˈnuti]

to save, to rescue	рятувати	[rʲatuˈwati]
life vest	рятувальний жилет (ч)	[rʲatuˈwalʲnij ʒiˈlɛt]
to observe, to watch	спостерігати	[spostɛriˈɦati]
lifeguard	рятувальник (ч)	[rʲatuˈwalʲnik]

TECHNICAL EQUIPMENT. TRANSPORTATION

Technical equipment

computer	комп'ютер (ч)	[kom'pʲiutɛr]
notebook, laptop	ноутбук (ч)	[nout'buk]
to turn on	увімкнути	[uwimk'nuti]
to turn off	вимкнути	['wimknuti]
keyboard	клавіатура (ж)	[klawia'tura]
key	клавіша (ж)	['klawiʃa]
mouse	миша (ж)	['miʃa]
mouse pad	килимок (ч) для миші	[kili'mok dlʲa 'miʃi]
button	кнопка (ж)	['knɔpka]
cursor	курсор (ч)	[kur'sɔr]
monitor	монітор (ч)	[moni'tɔr]
screen	екран (ч)	[ɛk'ran]
hard disk	жорсткий диск (ч)	[ʒor'stkij disk]
hard disk capacity	об'єм (ч) жорсткого диска	[ob'ʲɛm ʒorst'kɔɦo 'diska]
memory	пам'ять (ж)	['pamʲatʲ]
random access memory	оперативна пам'ять (ж)	[opɛra'tiwna 'pamʲatʲ]
file	файл (ч)	[fajl]
folder	папка (ж)	['papka]
to open (vt)	відкрити	[wid'kriti]
to close (vt)	закрити	[za'kriti]
to save (vt)	зберегти	[zbɛrɛɦ'ti]
to delete (vt)	видалити	['widaliti]
to copy (vt)	скопіювати	[skopiʲu'wati]
to sort (vt)	сортувати	[sortu'wati]
to transfer (move)	переписати	[pɛrɛpi'sati]
program	програма (ж)	[proɦ'rama]
software	програмне забезпечення (с)	[proɦ'ramnɛ zabɛz'pɛtʃɛnʲia]
programmer	програміст (ч)	[proɦ'ramist]
to program (vt)	програмувати	[proɦramu'wati]

hacker	хакер (ч)	['hakɛr]
password	пароль (ч)	[pa'rɔlʲ]
virus	вірус (ч)	['wirus]
to find, to detect	виявити	['wijawiti]

| byte | байт (ч) | [bajt] |
| megabyte | мегабайт (ч) | [mɛɦa'bajt] |

| data | дані (мн) | ['dani] |
| database | база (ж) даних | ['baza 'daniɦ] |

cable (USB, etc.)	кабель (ч)	['kabɛlʲ]
to disconnect (vt)	від'єднати	[wid'ɛd'nati]
to connect (sth to sth)	під'єднати	[pid'ɛd'nati]

140. Internet. E-mail

Internet	інтернет (ч)	[intɛr'nɛt]
browser	браузер (ч)	['brauzɛr]
search engine	пошуковий ресурс (ч)	[poʃu'kɔwij rɛ'surs]
provider	провайдер (ч)	[pro'wajdɛr]

webmaster	веб-майстер (ч)	[wɛb 'majstɛr]
website	веб-сайт (ч)	[wɛb 'sajt]
web page	веб-сторінка (ж)	[wɛb sto'rinka]

| address (e-mail ~) | адреса (ж) | [ad'rɛsa] |
| address book | адресна книга (ж) | ['adrɛsna 'kniɦa] |

mailbox	поштова скринька (ж)	[poʃ'tɔwa sk'rinʲka]
mail	пошта (ж)	['pɔʃta]
full (adj)	переповнена	[pɛrɛ'pɔwnɛna]

message	повідомлення (с)	[powi'dɔmlɛnʲa]
incoming messages	вхідні повідомлення	[whid'ni powi'dɔmlɛnʲa]
outgoing messages	вихідні повідомлення	[wihidni powi'dɔmlɛnʲa]
sender	відправник (ч)	[wid'prawnik]
to send (vt)	відправити	[wid'prawiti]
sending (of mail)	відправлення (с)	[wid'prawlɛnʲa]

| receiver | одержувач (ч) | [o'dɛrʒuwatʃ] |
| to receive (vt) | отримати | [ot'rimati] |

| correspondence | листування (с) | [listu'wanʲa] |
| to correspond (vi) | листуватися | [listu'watisʲa] |

file	файл (ч)	[fajl]
to download (vt)	скачати	[ska'tʃati]
to create (vt)	створити	[stwo'riti]
to delete (vt)	видалити	['widaliti]

deleted (adj)	**видалений**	['wɪdalɛnij]
connection (ADSL, etc.)	**зв'язок** (ч)	[zwʲa'zɔk]
speed	**швидкість** (ж)	['ʃwɪdkistʲ]
modem	**модем** (ч)	[mo'dɛm]
access	**доступ** (ч)	['dɔstup]
port (e.g., input ~)	**порт** (ч)	[port]
connection (make a ~)	**підключення** (с)	[pid'klʲutʃɛnʲa]
to connect to … (vi)	**підключитися**	[pidklʲu'tʃitisʲa]
to select (vt)	**вибрати**	['wɪbrati]
to search (for …)	**шукати**	[ʃu'kati]

Transpоrtation

airplane	літак (ч)	[li'tak]
air ticket	авіаквиток (ч)	[awiakwi'tɔk]
airline	авіакомпанія (ж)	[awiakom'paniʲa]
airport	аеропорт (ч)	[aɛro'pɔrt]
supersonic (adj)	надзвуковий	[nadzwuko'wij]
captain	командир (ч) корабля	[koman'dir korab'lʲa]
crew	екіпаж (ч)	[ɛki'paʒ]
pilot	пілот (ч)	[pi'lɔt]
flight attendant (fem.)	стюардеса (ж)	[stʲuar'dɛsa]
navigator	штурман (ч)	['ʃturman]
wings	крила (мн)	['krila]
tail	хвіст (ч)	[hwist]
cockpit	кабіна (ж)	[ka'bina]
engine	двигун (ч)	[dwi'ɦun]
undercarriage (landing gear)	шасі (с)	[ʃa'si]
turbine	турбіна (ж)	[tur'bina]
propeller	пропелер (ч)	[pro'pɛlɛr]
black box	чорна скринька (ж)	['ʧɔrna 'skrinʲka]
yoke (control column)	штурвал (ч)	[ʃtur'wal]
fuel	пальне (с)	[palʲ'nɛ]
safety card	інструкція (ж) з безпеки	[in'struktsiʲa z bɛz'pɛki]
oxygen mask	киснева маска (ж)	['kisnɛwa 'maska]
uniform	уніформа (ж)	[uni'fɔrma]
life vest	рятувальний жилет (ч)	[rʲatu'walʲnij ʒi'lɛt]
parachute	парашут (ч)	[para'ʃut]
takeoff	зліт (ч)	[zlit]
to take off (vi)	злітати	[zli'tati]
runway	злітна смуга (ж)	['zlitna 'smuɦa]
visibility	видимість (ж)	['widimistʲ]
flight (act of flying)	політ (ч)	[po'lit]
altitude	висота (ж)	[wiso'ta]
air pocket	повітряна яма (ж)	[po'witrʲana 'jama]
seat	місце (с)	['mistsɛ]
headphones	навушники (мн)	[na'wuʃniki]

folding tray (tray table)	відкидний столик (ч)	[widkid'nij 'stɔlik]
airplane window	ілюмінатор (ч)	[iʎumi'nator]
aisle	прохід (ч)	[pro'hid]

142. Train

train	поїзд (ч)	['pɔjizd]
commuter train	електропоїзд (ч)	[ɛlɛktro'pɔjizd]
express train	швидкий поїзд (ч)	[ʃwid'kij 'pɔjizd]
diesel locomotive	тепловоз (ч)	[tɛplo'wɔz]
steam locomotive	паровоз (ч)	[paro'wɔz]

| passenger car | вагон (ч) | [wa'hɔn] |
| dining car | вагон-ресторан (ч) | [wa'hɔn rɛsto'ran] |

rails	рейки (мн)	['rɛjki]
railroad	залізниця (ж)	[zaliz'nitsʲa]
railway tie	шпала (ж)	['ʃpala]

platform (railway ~)	платформа (ж)	[plat'fɔrma]
track (~ 1, 2, etc.)	колія (ж)	['kɔliʲa]
semaphore	семафор (ч)	[sɛma'fɔr]
station	станція (ж)	['stantsiʲa]

engineer (train driver)	машиніст (ч)	[maʃi'nist]
porter (of luggage)	носильник (ч)	[no'siʎnik]
car attendant	провідник (ч)	[prowid'nik]
passenger	пасажир (ч)	[pasa'ʒir]
conductor	контролер (ч)	[kontro'lɛr]
(ticket inspector)		

| corridor (aisle in train) | коридор (ч) | [kori'dɔr] |
| emergency brake | стоп-кран (ч) | [stop kran] |

compartment	купе (с)	[ku'pɛ]
berth	полиця (ж)	[po'litsʲa]
upper berth	полиця (ж) верхня	[po'litsʲa 'wɛrhnʲa]
lower berth	полиця (ж) нижня	[po'litsʲa 'niʒnʲa]
bed linen, bedding	білизна (ж)	[bi'lizna]

ticket	квиток (ч)	[kwi'tɔk]
schedule	розклад (ч)	['rɔzklad]
information display	табло (с)	[tab'lɔ]

to leave, to depart	від'їжджати	[wid'jiʒ'ʒati]
departure (of a train)	відправлення (с)	[wid'prawlɛnʲa]
to arrive (ab. train)	прибувати	[pribu'wati]
arrival	прибуття (с)	[pribut'tʲa]
to arrive by train	приїхати поїздом	[pri'jihati 'pɔjizdom]
to get on the train	сісти на поїзд	['sisti na 'pɔjizd]

to get off the train	зійти з поїзду	[zij'ti z 'pɔjizdu]
train wreck	катастрофа (ж)	[kata'strɔfa]
to derail (vi)	зійти з рейок	[zij'ti z 'rɛjok]
steam locomotive	паровоз (ч)	[paro'wɔz]
stoker, fireman	кочегар (ч)	[kotʃɛ'ɦar]
firebox	топка (ж)	['tɔpka]
coal	вугілля (с)	[wu'ɦilʲa]

143. Ship

ship	корабель (ч)	[kora'bɛlʲ]
vessel	судно (с)	['sudno]
steamship	пароплав (ч)	[paro'plaw]
riverboat	теплохід (ч)	[tɛplo'hid]
cruise ship	лайнер (ч)	['lajnɛr]
cruiser	крейсер (ч)	['krɛjsɛr]
yacht	яхта (ж)	['ʲahta]
tugboat	буксир (ч)	[buk'sir]
barge	баржа (ж)	['barʒa]
ferry	паром (ч)	[pa'rɔm]
sailing ship	вітрильник (ч)	[wi'trilʲnik]
brigantine	бригантина (ж)	[briɦan'tina]
ice breaker	криголам (ч)	[kriɦo'lam]
submarine	підводний човен (ч)	[pid'wɔdnij 'tʃɔwɛn]
boat (flat-bottomed ~)	човен (ч)	['tʃɔwɛn]
dinghy (lifeboat)	шлюпка (ж)	['ʃlʲupka]
lifeboat	шлюпка (ж) рятувальна	['ʃlʲupka rʲatu'walʲna]
motorboat	катер (ч)	['katɛr]
captain	капітан (ч)	[kapi'tan]
seaman	матрос (ч)	[mat'rɔs]
sailor	моряк (ч)	[mo'rʲak]
crew	екіпаж (ч)	[ɛki'paʒ]
boatswain	боцман (ч)	['bɔtsman]
ship's boy	юнга (ч)	['ʲunɦa]
cook	кок (ч)	[kok]
ship's doctor	судновий лікар (ч)	['sudnowij 'likar]
deck	палуба (ж)	['paluba]
mast	щогла (ж)	['ɕɔɦla]
sail	вітрило (с)	[wi'trilo]
hold	трюм (ч)	[trʲum]
bow (prow)	ніс (ч)	[nis]

stern	корма (ж)	[kor'ma]
oar	весло (с)	[wɛs'lɔ]
screw propeller	гвинт (ч)	[ɦwint]
cabin	каюта (ж)	[ka'ʲuta]
wardroom	кают-компанія (ж)	[ka'ʲut kom'paniʲa]
engine room	машинне відділення (с)	[ma'ʃinɛ wid'dilɛnʲa]
bridge	капітанський місток (ч)	[kapi'tansʲkij mis'tɔk]
radio room	радіорубка (ж)	[radio'rubka]
wave (radio)	хвиля (ж)	['hwilʲa]
logbook	судновий журнал (ч)	['sudnowij ʒur'nal]
spyglass	підзорна труба (ж)	[pi'dzɔrna tru'ba]
bell	дзвін (ч)	[dzwin]
flag	прапор (ч)	['prapor]
hawser (mooring ~)	канат (ч)	[ka'nat]
knot (bowline, etc.)	вузол (ч)	['wuzol]
deckrails	поручень (ч)	['pɔrutʃɛnʲ]
gangway	трап (ч)	[trap]
anchor	якір (ч)	['ʲakir]
to weigh anchor	підняти якір	[pid'nʲatɨ 'jakir]
to drop anchor	кинути якір	['kinuti 'jakir]
anchor chain	якірний ланцюг (ч)	['ʲakirnij lan'ʦʲuɦ]
port (harbor)	порт (ч)	[port]
quay, wharf	причал (ч)	[pri'ʧal]
to berth (moor)	причалювати	[pri'ʧalʲuwati]
to cast off	відчалювати	[wid'ʧalʲuwati]
trip, voyage	подорож (ж)	['pɔdorɔʒ]
cruise (sea trip)	круїз (ч)	[kru'jiz]
course (route)	курс (ч)	[kurs]
route (itinerary)	маршрут (ч)	[marʃ'rut]
fairway (safe water channel)	фарватер (ч)	[far'watɛr]
shallows	мілина (ж)	[mili'na]
to run aground	сісти на мілину	['sisti na mili'nu]
storm	буря (ж)	['burʲa]
signal	сигнал (ч)	[siɦ'nal]
to sink (vi)	тонути	[to'nuti]
Man overboard!	Людина за бортом!	[lʲu'dina za 'bortom!]
SOS (distress signal)	SOS	[sos]
ring buoy	рятувальний круг (ч)	[rʲatu'walʲnij 'kruɦ]

144. Airport

airport	аеропорт (ч)	[aɛro'pɔrt]
airplane	літак (ч)	[li'tak]
airline	авіакомпанія (ж)	[awiakom'paniˈa]
air traffic controller	авіадиспетчер (ч)	[awiadisˈpɛtʃɛr]
departure	виліт (ч)	['wilit]
arrival	приліт (ч), прибуття (с)	[pri'lit], [pribu'tˈa]
to arrive (by plane)	прилетіти	[pri'lɛtiti]
departure time	час (ч) вильоту	[ʧas 'wilʲotu]
arrival time	час (ч) прильоту	[ʧas prilʲotu]
to be delayed	затримуватися	[za'trimuwatisʲa]
flight delay	затримка (ж) вильоту	[za'trimka 'wilʲotu]
information board	інформаційне табло (с)	[informa'ʦijnɛ tab'lɔ]
information	інформація (ж)	[infor'maʦiˈa]
to announce (vt)	оголошувати	[oho'lɔʃuwati]
flight (e.g., next ~)	рейс (ч)	[rɛjs]
customs	митниця (ж)	['mitniʦʲa]
customs officer	митник (ч)	['mitnik]
customs declaration	митна декларація (ж)	['mitna dɛkla'raʦiˈa]
to fill out (vt)	заповнити	[za'pɔwniti]
to fill out the declaration	заповнити декларацію	[za'pɔwniti dɛkla'raʦiˈu]
passport control	паспортний контроль (ч)	['pasportnij kon'trɔlʲ]
luggage	багаж (ч)	[ba'ɦaʒ]
hand luggage	ручний вантаж (ж)	[ruʧˈnij wan'taʒ]
luggage cart	візок (ч) для багажу	[wi'zɔk dlʲa baɦa'ʒu]
landing	посадка (ж)	[po'sadka]
landing strip	посадкова смуга (ж)	[po'sadkowa 'smuɦa]
to land (vi)	сідати	[si'dati]
airstair (passenger steps)	трап (ч)	[trap]
check-in	реєстрація (ж)	[rɛɛ'straʦiˈa]
check-in counter	стійка (ж) реєстрації	['stijka rɛɛ'straʦiji]
to check-in (vi)	зареєструватися	[zarɛɛstru'watisʲa]
boarding pass	посадковий талон (ч)	[po'sadkowij ta'lɔn]
departure gate	вихід (ч)	['wihid]
transit	транзит (ч)	[tran'zit]
to wait (vt)	чекати	[ʧɛ'kati]
departure lounge	зал (ч) очікування	['zal o'ʧikuwanʲa]
to see off	проводжати	[prowo'ʤati]
to say goodbye	прощатися	[pro'ɕatisʲa]

145. Bicycle. Motorcycle

bicycle	велосипед (ч)	[wɛlosi'pɛd]
scooter	моторолер (ч)	[moto'rɔlɛr]
motorcycle, bike	мотоцикл (ч)	[moto'tsikl]
to go by bicycle	їхати на велосипеді	['jihati na wɛlosi'pɛdi]
handlebars	кермо (с)	[kɛr'mɔ]
pedal	педаль (ж)	[pɛ'dalʲ]
brakes	гальма (мн)	['halʲma]
bicycle seat (saddle)	сідло (с)	[sid'lɔ]
pump	насос (ч)	[na'sɔs]
luggage rack	багажник (ч)	[ba'haʒnik]
front lamp	ліхтар (ч)	[lih'tar]
helmet	шолом (ч)	[ʃo'lɔm]
wheel	колесо (с)	['kɔlɛso]
fender	крило (с)	[kri'lɔ]
rim	обвід (ч)	['ɔbwid]
spoke	спиця (ж)	['spitsʲa]

Cars

automobile, car	**автомобіль** (ч), **машина** (ж)	[awtomoˈbilʲ], [maˈʃina]
sports car	**спортивний автомобіль** (ч)	[sporˈtiwnij awtomoˈbilʲ]
limousine	**лімузин** (ч)	[limuˈzin]
off-road vehicle	**позашляховик** (ч)	[pozaʃlʲahoˈwik]
convertible (n)	**кабріолет** (ч)	[kabrioˈlɛt]
minibus	**мікроавтобус** (ч)	[mikroawˈtɔbus]
ambulance	**швидка допомога** (ж)	[ʃwidˈka dopoˈmɔɦa]
snowplow	**снігоприбиральна машина** (ж)	[sniɦopribiˈralʲna maˈʃina]
truck	**вантажівка** (ж)	[wantaˈʒiwka]
tanker truck	**бензовоз** (ч)	[bɛnzoˈwɔz]
van (small truck)	**фургон** (ч)	[furˈɦɔn]
road tractor (trailer truck)	**тягач** (ч)	[tʲaˈɦatʃ]
trailer	**причіп** (ч)	[priˈtʃip]
comfortable (adj)	**комфортабельний**	[komforˈtabɛlʲnij]
used (adj)	**вживаний**	[ˈwʒiwanij]

hood	**капот** (ч)	[kaˈpɔt]
fender	**крило** (с)	[kriˈlɔ]
roof	**дах** (ч)	[dah]
windshield	**вітрове скло** (с)	[witroˈwɛ ˈsklo]
rear-view mirror	**дзеркало** (с) **заднього виду**	[ˈdzɛrkalo ˈzadnʲoɦo ˈwidu]
windshield washer	**омивач** (ч)	[omiˈwatʃ]
windshield wipers	**склоочисники** (мн)	[sklooˈtʃisniki]
side window	**бічне скло** (с)	[ˈbitʃnɛ ˈsklo]
window lift (power window)	**склопідіймач** (ч)	[sklopidijˈmatʃ]
antenna	**антена** (ж)	[anˈtɛna]
sunroof	**люк** (ч)	[lʲuk]
bumper	**бампер** (ч)	[ˈbampɛr]

trunk	багажник (ч)	[ba'haʒnik]
roof luggage rack	багажник	[ba'haʒnik]
door	дверцята (мн)	[dwɛr'tsʲata]
door handle	ручка (ж)	['rutʃka]
door lock	замок (ч)	[za'mɔk]
license plate	номер (ч)	['nɔmɛr]
muffler	глушник (ч)	[ɦluʃ'nik]
gas tank	бензобак (ч)	[bɛnzo'bak]
tailpipe	вихлопна труба (ж)	[wihlop'na tru'ba]
gas, accelerator	газ (ч)	[ɦaz]
pedal	педаль (ж)	[pɛ'dalʲ]
gas pedal	педаль (ж) газу	[pɛ'dalʲ 'ɦazu]
brake	гальмо (с)	[ɦalʲ'mɔ]
brake pedal	педаль (ж) гальма	[pɛ'dalʲ ɦalʲ'ma]
to brake (use the brake)	гальмувати	[ɦalʲmu'wati]
parking brake	стоянкове гальмо (с)	[sto'ʲankowɛ ɦalʲ'mɔ]
clutch	зчеплення (с)	['zt͡ʃɛplɛnʲa]
clutch pedal	педаль (ж) зчеплення	[pɛ'dalʲ 'zt͡ʃɛplɛnʲa]
clutch disc	диск (ч) зчеплення	['disk 'zt͡ʃiplɛnʲa]
shock absorber	амортизатор (ч)	[amorti'zator]
wheel	колесо (с)	['kɔlɛso]
spare tire	запасне колесо (с)	[zapas'nɛ 'kɔlɛso]
tire	покришка (ж), шина (ж)	[po'kriʃka], '[ʃina]
hubcap	ковпак (ч)	[kow'pak]
driving wheels	ведучі колеса (мн)	[wɛ'dut͡ʃi ko'lɛsa]
front-wheel drive (as adj)	передньоприв́дний	[pɛrɛdnʲop'riwidnij]
rear-wheel drive (as adj)	задньоприв́дний	[zadnʲopriwid'nij]
all-wheel drive (as adj)	повноприв́дний	[pownop'riwidnij]
gearbox	коробка (ж) передач	[ko'rɔbka pɛrɛ'dat͡ʃ]
automatic (adj)	автоматичний	[awtoma'tit͡ʃnij]
mechanical (adj)	механічний	[mɛha'nit͡ʃnij]
gear shift	важіль (ч) коробки передач	['waʒilʲ ko'rɔbki pɛrɛ'dat͡ʃ]
headlight	фара (ж)	['fara]
headlights	фари (мн)	['fari]
low beam	ближнє світло (с)	['bliʒnɛ 'switlo]
high beam	дальнє світло (с)	['dalʲnɛ 'switlo]
brake light	стоп-сигнал (ч)	[stop siɦ'nal]
parking lights	габаритні вогні (мн)	[ɦaba'ritni woɦ'ni]
hazard lights	аварійні вогні (мн)	[awa'rijni woɦ'ni]
fog lights	протитуманні фари (мн)	[protitu'mani 'fari]
turn signal	поворотник (ч)	[powo'rɔtnik]
back-up light	задній хід (ч)	['zadnij hid]

148. Cars. Passenger compartment

car interior	салон (ч)	[sa'lɔn]
leather (as adj)	шкіряний	[ʃkirʲa'nij]
velour (as adj)	велюровий	[wɛ'lʲurowij]
upholstery	оббивка (ж)	[ob'biwka]
instrument (gage)	прилад (ч)	['prilad]
dashboard	панель (ж) приладів	[pa'nɛlʲ 'priladiw]
speedometer	спідометр (ч)	[spi'dɔmɛtr]
needle (pointer)	стрілка (ж)	['strilka]
odometer	лічильник (ч) пробігу	[li'tʃilʲnik pro'bihu]
indicator (sensor)	датчик (ч)	['datʃik]
level	рівень (ч)	['riwɛnʲ]
warning light	лампочка (ж)	['lampotʃka]
steering wheel	кермо (с)	[kɛr'mɔ]
horn	сигнал (ч)	[sih'nal]
button	кнопка (ж)	['knɔpka]
switch	перемикач (ч)	[pɛrɛmi'katʃ]
seat	сидіння (с)	[si'dinʲa]
backrest	спинка (ж)	['spinka]
headrest	підголівник (ч)	[pidɦo'liwnik]
seat belt	ремінь (ч) безпеки	['rɛminʲ bɛz'pɛki]
to fasten the belt	пристебнути ремінь	[pristɛb'nuti 'rɛminʲ]
adjustment (of seats)	регулювання (с)	[rɛɦulʲu'wanʲa]
airbag	повітряна подушка (ж)	[po'witrʲana po'duʃka]
air-conditioner	кондиціонер (ч)	[konditsio'nɛr]
radio	радіо (с)	['radio]
CD player	CD-програвач (ч)	[si'di proɦra'watʃ]
to turn on	увімкнути	[uwimk'nuti]
antenna	антена (ж)	[an'tɛna]
glove box	бардачок (ч)	[barda'tʃɔk]
ashtray	попільниця (ж)	[popilʲ'nitsʲa]

149. Cars. Engine

engine	двигун (ч)	[dwi'ɦun]
motor	мотор (ч)	[mo'tɔr]
diesel (as adj)	дизельний	['dizɛlʲnij]
gasoline (as adj)	бензиновий	[bɛn'zinowij]
engine volume	об'єм (ч) двигуна	[o'b'ɛm dwiɦu'na]
power	потужність (ж)	[po'tuʒnistʲ]
horsepower	кінська сила (ж)	['kinsʲka 'sila]

piston	поршень (ч)	['pɔrʃɛnʲ]
cylinder	циліндр (ч)	[ʦiˈlindr]
valve	клапан (ч)	['klapan]

injector	інжектор (ч)	[inˈʒɛktor]
generator (alternator)	генератор (ч)	[ɦɛnɛˈrator]
carburetor	карбюратор (ч)	[karbʲuˈrator]
motor oil	мастило (с) моторне	[masˈtʲilo moˈtɔrnɛ]

radiator	радіатор (ч)	[radiˈator]
coolant	охолоджувальна рідина (ж)	[oɦoˈlɔʤuwalʲna ridiˈna]
cooling fan	вентилятор (ч)	[wɛntiˈlʲator]

starter	стартер (ч)	['startɛr]
ignition	запалювання (с)	[zaˈpalʲuwanʲa]
spark plug	свічка (ж) запалювання	['swiʧka zaˈpalʲuwanʲa]
fuse	запобіжник (ч)	[zapoˈbiʒnik]

battery (accumulator)	акумулятор (ч)	[akumuˈlʲator]
terminal (battery ~)	клема (ж)	['klɛma]
positive terminal	плюс (ч)	[plʲus]
negative terminal	мінус (ч)	['minus]

air filter	повітряний фільтр (ч)	[poˈwitrʲanij 'filʲtr]
oil filter	масляний фільтр (ч)	['maslʲanij 'filʲtr]
fuel filter	паливний фільтр (ч)	['paliwnij 'filʲtr]

150. Cars. Crash. Repair

car crash	аварія (ж)	[aˈwariʲa]
traffic accident	дорожня пригода (ж)	[doˈrɔʒnʲa priˈɦɔda]
to crash (into a wall, etc.)	врізатися	['wrizatisʲa]

to get smashed up	розбитися	[rozˈbitisʲa]
damage	пошкодження (с)	[poʃˈkɔʤɛnʲa]
intact (unscathed)	цілий	[ʦiˈlij]

breakdown	поломка (ж)	[poˈlɔmka]
to break down (vi)	зламатися	[zlaˈmatisʲa]
towrope	буксирний трос (ч)	[bukˈsirnij tros]

puncture	прокол (ч)	[proˈkɔl]
to be flat	спустити	[spusˈtiti]
to pump up	накачати	[nakaˈʧati]
pressure	тиск (ч)	[tisk]
to check (to examine)	перевірити	[pɛrɛˈwiriti]

| repair | ремонт (ч) | [rɛˈmɔnt] |
| auto repair shop | автосервіс (ч) | [awtoˈsɛrwis] |

spare part	запчастина (ж)	[zapt͡ʃasˈtina]
part	деталь (ж)	[dɛˈtalʲ]
bolt (fastener with a nut)	болт (ч)	[bolt]
screw (fastener)	гвинт (ч)	[ɦwint]
nut	гайка (ж)	[ˈɦajka]
washer	шайба (ж)	[ˈʃajba]
bearing (e.g., ball ~)	підшипник (ч)	[pidˈʃipnik]
tube	трубка (ж)	[ˈtrubka]
gasket (head ~)	прокладка (ж)	[prokˈladka]
cable, wire	провід (ч)	[ˈprɔwid]
jack	домкрат (ч)	[domkˈrat]
wrench	гайковий ключ (ч)	[ɦajkoˈwij klʲutʃ]
hammer	молоток (ч)	[moloˈtɔk]
pump	насос (ч)	[naˈsɔs]
screwdriver	викрутка (ж)	[ˈwikrutka]
fire extinguisher	вогнегасник (ч)	[woɦnɛˈɦasnik]
warning triangle	аварійний трикутник (ч)	[awaˈrijnij triˈkutnik]
to stall (vi)	глохнути	[ˈɦlɔhnuti]
stall (n)	зупинка (ж)	[zuˈpinka]
to be broken	бути зламаним	[ˈbuti ˈzlamanim]
to overheat (vi)	перегрітися	[pɛrɛɦˈritisʲa]
to be clogged up	засмітитися	[zasmiˈtitisʲa]
to freeze up (pipes, etc.)	замерзнути	[zaˈmɛrznuti]
to burst (explode, ab. tube)	лопнути	[ˈlɔpnuti]
pressure	тиск (ч)	[tisk]
level	рівень (ч)	[ˈriwɛnʲ]
slack (~ belt)	слабкий	[slabˈkij]
dent	вм'ятина (ж)	[ˈwmʲlatina]
knocking noise (troublesome engine sound)	стукіт (ч)	[ˈstukit]
crack	тріщина (ж)	[ˈtriɕina]
scratch	подряпина (ж)	[podˈrʲlapina]

151. Cars. Road

road	дорога (ж)	[doˈrɔɦa]
highway	автомагістраль (ж)	[awtomaɦiˈstralʲ]
freeway	шосе (с)	[ʃoˈsɛ]
direction (way)	напрямок (ч)	[ˈnaprʲamok]
distance	відстань (ж)	[ˈwidstanʲ]
bridge	міст (ч)	[mist]

parking lot	паркінг (ч)	['parkinɦ]
square	площа (ж)	['plɔɕa]
interchange	розв'язка (ж)	[roz'w'ʲazka]
tunnel	тунель (ч)	[tu'nɛlʲ]

gas station	автозаправка (ж)	[awtoza'prawka]
parking lot	автостоянка (ж)	[awtosto'ʲanka]
gas pump (fuel dispenser)	бензоколонка (ж)	[bɛnzoko'lɔnka]
auto repair shop	автосервіс (ч)	[awto'sɛrwis]
to get gas (to fill up)	заправити	[za'prawiti]
fuel	паливо (с)	['paliwo]
jerrycan	каністра (ж)	[ka'nistra]

asphalt	асфальт (ч)	[as'falʲt]
road markings	розмітка (ж)	[roz'mitka]
curb	бордюр (ч)	[bor'dʲur]
guardrail	огорожа (ж)	[oɦo'rɔʒa]
ditch	кювет (ч)	[kʲu'wɛt]
roadside (shoulder of the road)	узбіччя (с)	[uz'bitʃʲa]
lamppost	стовп (ч)	[stowp]

to drive (a car)	вести	['wɛsti]
to turn (e.g., ~ left)	повертати	[powɛr'tati]
to make a U-turn	розвертатися	[rozwɛr'tatisʲa]
reverse (~ gear)	задній хід (ч)	['zadnij hid]

to honk (vi)	сигналити	[siɦ'naliti]
honk (sound)	звуковий сигнал (ч)	[zwuko'wij siɦ'nal]
to get stuck (to get bogged down)	застрягти	[za'strʲaɦti]
to spin the wheels	буксувати	[buksu'wati]
to cut, to turn off (vt)	глушити	[ɦlu'ʃiti]

speed	швидкість (ж)	['ʃwidkistʲ]
to exceed the speed limit	перевищити швидкість	[pɛrɛ'wiçiti 'ʃwidkistʲ]
to give a ticket	штрафувати	[ʃtrafu'wati]
traffic lights	світлофор (ч)	[switlo'for]
driver's license	посвідчення (с) водія	[pos'widtʃɛnja wodi'ʲa]

grade crossing	переїзд (ч)	[pɛrɛ'jizd]
intersection	перехрестя (с)	[pɛrɛh'rɛstʲa]
crosswalk	пішохідний перехід (ч)	[piʃo'hidnij pɛrɛ'hid]
pedestrian zone	пішохідна зона (ж)	[piʃo'hidna 'zɔna]

PEOPLE. LIFE EVENTS

152. Holidays. Event

celebration, holiday	свято (c)	['swʲato]
national day	національне свято (c)	[natsio'nalʲnɛ 'swʲato]
public holiday	святковий день (ч)	[swʲat'kɔwij dɛnʲ]
to celebrate (vt)	святкувати	[swʲatku'wati]
event (happening)	подія (ж)	[po'dʲiʲa]
event (organized activity)	захід (ч)	['zahid]
banquet (party with lavish meal)	бенкет (ч)	[bɛ'nkɛt]
reception (formal party)	прийом (ч)	[pri'jɔm]
feast	святкування (c)	[swʲatku'wanʲa]
anniversary	річниця (ж)	[rit͡ʃ'nit͡sʲa]
jubilee	ювілей (ч)	[ʲuwi'lɛj]
New Year	Новий рік (ч)	[no'wij rik]
Happy New Year!	З Новим Роком!	[z no'wim 'rɔkom]
Santa Claus	Санта Клаус (ч)	['santa 'klaus]
Christmas	Різдво (c)	[rizd'wɔ]
Merry Christmas!	Щасливого Різдва!	[ɕas'liwoɦo rizd'wa]
fireworks (fireworks show)	салют (ч)	[sa'lʲut]
wedding	весілля (c)	[wɛ'silʲa]
groom	наречений (ч)	[narɛ't͡ʃɛnij]
bride	наречена (ж)	[narɛ't͡ʃɛna]
to invite (vt)	запрошувати	[za'prɔʃuwati]
invitation card	запрошення (c)	[za'prɔʃɛnʲa]
guest	гість (ч)	[ɦistʲ]
to visit (vt)	йти в гості	[jtʲi w 'ɦɔsti]
to meet the guests	зустрічати гостей	[zustri't͡ʃati ɦos'tɛj]
gift, present	подарунок (ч)	[poda'runok]
to give (sth as present)	дарувати	[daru'wati]
to receive gifts	отримувати подарунки	[ot'rimuwati poda'runki]
bouquet (of flowers)	букет (ч)	[bu'kɛt]
congratulations	привітання (c)	[priwi'tanʲa]
to congratulate (vt)	вітати	[wi'tati]

greeting card	вітальна листівка (ж)	[wi'talʲna lis'tiwka]
to send a postcard	надіслати листівку	[nadi'slati lis'tiwku]
to get a postcard	отримати листівку	[ot'rimati lis'tiwku]

toast	тост (ч)	[tost]
to offer (a drink, etc.)	пригощати	[priɦo'çati]
champagne	шампанське (с)	[ʃam'pansʲkɛ]

to enjoy oneself	веселитися	[wɛsɛ'litisʲa]
merriment (gaiety)	веселощі (мн)	[wɛ'sɛloçi]
joy (emotion)	радість (ж)	['radistʲ]

| dance | танець (ч) | ['tanɛʦ] |
| to dance (vi, vt) | танцювати | [tantsʲu'wati] |

| waltz | вальс (ч) | [walʲs] |
| tango | танго (с) | ['tanɦo] |

153. Funerals. Burial

cemetery	цвинтар (ч)	['ʦwintar]
grave, tomb	могила (ж)	[mo'ɦila]
cross	хрест (ч)	[hrɛst]
gravestone	надгробок (ч)	[nad'ɦrɔbok]
fence	огорожа (ж)	[oɦo'rɔʒa]
chapel	каплиця (ж)	[kap'liʦʲa]

| death | смерть (ж) | [smɛrtʲ] |
| to die (vi) | померти | [po'mɛrti] |

| the deceased | покійник (ч) | [po'kijnik] |
| mourning | траур (ч) | ['traur] |

to bury (vt)	ховати	[ho'wati]
funeral home	похоронне бюро (с)	[poɦo'rɔnɛ bʲuro]
funeral	похорон (ч)	['pɔɦoron]

| wreath | вінок (ч) | [wi'nɔk] |
| casket, coffin | труна (ж) | [tru'na] |

| hearse | катафалк (ч) | [kata'falk] |
| shroud | саван (ч) | [sa'wan] |

funeral procession	траурна процесія (ж)	['traurna pro'ʦɛsiʲa]
funerary urn	поховальна урна (ж)	[poɦo'walʲna 'urna]
crematory	крематорій (ч)	[krɛma'tɔrij]

obituary	некролог (ч)	[nɛkro'lɔɦ]
to cry (weep)	плакати	['plakati]
to sob (vi)	ридати	[ri'dati]

154. War. Soldiers

platoon	взвод (ч)	[wzwod]
company	рота (ж)	['rɔta]
regiment	полк (ч)	[polk]
army	армія (ж)	['armiˈa]
division	дивізія (ж)	[diˈwiziˈa]
section, squad	загін (ч)	[zaˈɦin]
host (army)	військо (с)	['wijsˈko]
soldier	солдат (ч)	[solˈdat]
officer	офіцер (ч)	[ofiˈʦɛr]
private	рядовий (ч)	[rˈadoˈwij]
sergeant	сержант (ч)	[sɛrˈʒant]
lieutenant	лейтенант (ч)	[lɛjtɛˈnant]
captain	капітан (ч)	[kapiˈtan]
major	майор (ч)	[maˈjɔr]
colonel	полковник (ч)	[polˈkɔwnik]
general	генерал (ч)	[ɦɛnɛˈral]
sailor	моряк (ч)	[moˈrˈak]
captain	капітан (ч)	[kapiˈtan]
boatswain	боцман (ч)	['bɔʦman]
artilleryman	артилерист (ч)	[artilɛˈrist]
paratrooper	десантник (ч)	[dɛˈsantnik]
pilot	льотчик (ч)	[lˈɔtʃik]
navigator	штурман (ч)	['ʃturman]
mechanic	механік (ч)	[mɛˈɦanik]
pioneer (sapper)	сапер (ч)	[saˈpɛr]
parachutist	парашутист (ч)	[paraʃuˈtist]
reconnaissance scout	розвідник (ч)	[rozˈwidnik]
sniper	снайпер (ч)	['snajpɛr]
patrol (group)	патруль (ч)	[patˈrulˈ]
to patrol (vt)	патрулювати	[patrulˈuˈwati]
sentry, guard	вартовий (ч)	[wartoˈwij]
warrior	воїн (ч)	['wɔjin]
patriot	патріот (ч)	[patriˈɔt]
hero	герой (ч)	[ɦɛˈrɔj]
heroine	героїня (ж)	[ɦɛroˈjinˈa]
traitor	зрадник (ч)	['zradnik]
to betray (vt)	зраджувати	['zradʒuwati]
deserter	дезертир (ч)	[dɛzɛrˈtir]
to desert (vi)	дезертирувати	[dɛzɛrˈtiruwati]
mercenary	найманець (ч)	['najmanɛʦ]

| recruit | новобранець (ч) | [nowo'branɛts] |
| volunteer | доброволець (ч) | [dobro'wɔlɛts] |

dead (n)	убитий (ч)	[u'bitij]
wounded (n)	поранений (ч)	[po'ranɛnij]
prisoner of war	полонений (ч)	[polo'nɛnij]

155. War. Military actions. Part 1

war	війна (ж)	[wij'na]
to be at war	воювати	[woʲu'wati]
civil war	громадянська війна (ж)	[ɦroma'dʲansʲka wij'na]

treacherously (adv)	віроломно	[wiro'lɔmno]
declaration of war	оголошення (с) війни	[oɦo'lɔʃɛnʲa wij'ni]
to declare (~ war)	оголосити	[oɦolo'siti]
aggression	агресія (ж)	[aɦ'rɛsiʲa]
to attack (invade)	нападати	[napa'dati]

to invade (vt)	захоплювати	[za'ɦɔplʲuwati]
invader	загарбник (ч)	[za'ɦarbnik]
conqueror	завойовник (ч)	[zawo'jɔwnik]

defense	оборона (ж)	[obo'rɔna]
to defend (a country, etc.)	обороняти	[oboro'nʲati]
to defend (against …)	оборонятися	[oboro'nʲatisʲa]

enemy, hostile	ворог (ч), противник (ч)	['wɔroɦ], [pro'tiwnik]
adversary	супротивник (ч)	[supro'tiwnik]
enemy (as adj)	ворожий	[wo'rɔʒij]

| strategy | стратегія (ж) | [stra'tɛɦiʲa] |
| tactics | тактика (ж) | ['taktika] |

order	наказ (ч)	[na'kaz]
command (order)	команда (ж)	[ko'manda]
to order (vt)	наказувати	[na'kazuwati]
mission	завдання (с)	[zaw'danʲa]
secret (adj)	таємний	[ta'ɛmnij]

| battle | битва (ж) | ['bitwa] |
| combat | бій (ч) | [bij] |

attack	атака (ж)	[a'taka]
charge (assault)	штурм (ч)	[ʃturm]
to storm (vt)	штурмувати	[ʃturmu'wati]
siege (to be under ~)	облога (ж)	[ob'lɔɦa]

| offensive (n) | наступ (ч) | ['nastup] |
| to go on the offensive | наступати | [nastu'pati] |

| retreat | відступ (ч) | ['widstup] |
| to retreat (vi) | відступати | [widstu'pati] |

| encirclement | оточення (с) | [o'tɔʧɛnʲa] |
| to encircle (vt) | оточувати | [o'tɔʧuwati] |

bombing (by aircraft)	бомбардування (с)	[bombardu'wanʲa]
to drop a bomb	скинути бомбу	['skinuti 'bombu]
to bomb (vt)	бомбардувати	[bombardu'wati]
explosion	вибух (ч)	['wibuh]

shot	постріл (ч)	['pɔstril]
to fire (~ a shot)	вистрілити	['wistriliti]
firing (burst of ~)	стрілянина (ж)	[strilʲa'nina]

to aim (to point a weapon)	цілитися	['ʦilitisʲa]
to point (a gun)	навести	[na'wɛsti]
to hit (the target)	влучити	['wluʧiti]

to sink (~ a ship)	потопити	[poto'piti]
hole (in a ship)	пробоїна (ж)	[pro'bojina]
to founder, to sink (vi)	йти на дно	[jti na dno]

front (war ~)	фронт (ч)	[front]
evacuation	евакуація (ж)	[ɛwaku'aʦiʲa]
to evacuate (vt)	евакуювати	[ɛwakuʲu'waʧi]

trench	окоп (ч), траншея (ж)	[o'kɔp], [tran'ʃɛʲa]
barbwire	колючий дріт (ч)	[ko'lʲuʧij drit]
barrier (anti tank ~)	загородження (с)	[zaɦo'rɔʤɛnʲa]
watchtower	вишка (ж)	['wiʃka]

military hospital	шпиталь (ч)	[ʃpi'talʲ]
to wound (vt)	поранити	[po'raniti]
wound	рана (ж)	['rana]
wounded (n)	поранений (ч)	[po'ranɛnij]
to be wounded	отримати поранення	[ot'rimati po'ranɛnʲa]
serious (wound)	важкий	[waʒ'kij]

156. Weapons

weapons	зброя (ж)	['zbrɔʲa]
firearm	вогнепальна зброя (ж)	[woɦnɛ'palʲna 'zbrɔʲa]
cold weapons (knives, etc.)	холодна зброя (ж)	[ho'lɔdna 'zbrɔʲa]

chemical weapons	хімічна зброя (ж)	[hi'miʧna 'zbrɔʲa]
nuclear (adj)	ядерний	['ʲadɛrnij]
nuclear weapons	ядерна зброя (ж)	['ʲadɛrna 'zbrɔʲa]
bomb	бомба (ж)	['bɔmba]

atomic bomb	атомна бомба (ж)	['atomna 'bɔmba]
pistol (gun)	пістолет (ч)	[pisto'lɛt]
rifle	рушниця (ж)	[ruʃ'nitsʲa]
submachine gun	автомат (ч)	[awto'mat]
machine gun	кулемет (ч)	[kulɛ'mɛt]
muzzle	дуло (с)	['dulo]
barrel	ствол (ч)	[stwol]
caliber	калібр (ч)	[ka'libr]
trigger	курок (ч)	[ku'rɔk]
sight (aiming device)	приціл (ч)	[pri'tsil]
magazine	магазин (ч)	[maɦa'zin]
butt (shoulder stock)	приклад (ч)	[prik'lad]
hand grenade	граната (ж)	[ɦra'nata]
explosive	вибухівка (ж)	[wibu'ɦiwka]
bullet	куля (ж)	['kulʲa]
cartridge	патрон (ч)	[pat'rɔn]
charge	заряд (ч)	[za'rʲad]
ammunition	боєприпаси (мн)	[boɛpri'pasi]
bomber (aircraft)	бомбардувальник (ч)	[bombardu'walʲnik]
fighter	винищувач (ч)	[wi'niɕuwatʃ]
helicopter	вертоліт (ч)	[wɛrto'lit]
anti-aircraft gun	зенітка (ж)	[zɛ'nitka]
tank	танк (ч)	[tank]
tank gun	гармата (ж)	[ɦar'mata]
artillery	артилерія (ж)	[arti'lɛriʲa]
gun (cannon, howitzer)	гармата (ж)	[ɦar'mata]
to lay (a gun)	навести	[na'wɛsti]
mortar	міномет (ч)	[mino'mɛt]
mortar bomb	міна (ж)	['mina]
shell (projectile)	снаряд (ч)	[sna'rʲad]
splinter (shell fragment)	осколок (ч)	[os'kɔlok]
submarine	підводний човен (ч)	[pid'wodnij 'tʃɔwɛn]
torpedo	торпеда (ж)	[tor'pɛda]
missile	ракета (ж)	[ra'kɛta]
to load (~ a gun)	заряджати	[zarʲa'dʒati]
to shoot (vi)	стріляти	[stri'lʲati]
to point at (aim a gun or cannon)	цілитися	['tsilitisʲa]
bayonet	багнет (ч)	[baɦ'nɛt]
rapier	шпага (ж)	['ʃpaɦa]
saber (e.g., cavalry ~)	шабля (ж)	['ʃablʲa]

spear (weapon)	спис (ч)	[spis]
bow	лук (ч)	[luk]
arrow	стріла (ж)	[stri'la]
musket	мушкет (ч)	[muʃ'kɛt]
crossbow	арбалет (ч)	[arba'lɛt]

157. Ancient people

primitive (prehistoric)	первісний	[pɛr'wisnij]
prehistoric (adj)	доісторичний	[doisto'ritʃnij]
ancient (~ civilization)	стародавній	[staro'dawnij]

Stone Age	Кам'яний вік (ч)	[kamʲa'nij wik]
Bronze Age	Бронзовий вік (ч)	['brɔnzowij wik]
Ice Age	льодовиковий період (ч)	[lʲodowi'kɔwij pɛ'riod]

tribe	плем'я (с)	['plɛmʲa]
cannibal	людоїд (ч)	[lʲudo'jid]
hunter	мисливець (ч)	[mis'liwɛts]
to hunt (vi, vt)	полювати	[polʲu'wati]
mammoth	мамонт (ч)	['mamont]

cave	печера (ж)	[pɛ'tʃɛra]
fire	вогонь (ч)	[wo'hɔnʲ]
campfire	багаття (с)	[ba'hattʲa]
cave painting	наскальний малюнок (ч)	[na'skalʲnij ma'lʲunok]

tool (e.g., stone ax)	знаряддя (с) праці	[zna'rʲaddʲa 'pratsi]
spear	спис (ч)	[spis]
stone ax	кам'яна сокира (ж)	[kamʲa'na so'kira]
to be at war	воювати	[woʲu'wati]
to domesticate (vt)	приручати	[priru'tʃati]

idol	ідол (ч)	['idol]
to worship (vt)	поклонятися	[poklo'nʲatisʲa]
superstition	забобони (мн)	[zabo'bɔni]
rite	обряд, ритуал (ч)	[ob'rʲad], [ritu'al]

evolution	еволюція (ж)	[ɛwo'lʲutsiʲa]
development	розвиток (ч)	['rɔzwitok]
disappearance (extinction)	зникнення (с)	['zniknɛnʲa]
to adapt oneself	пристосовуватися	[pristosowu'watisʲa]

archeology	археологія (ж)	[arhɛo'lɔhiʲa]
archeologist	археолог (ч)	[arhɛ'ɔloh]
archeological (adj)	археологічний	[arhɛolo'hitʃnij]

| excavation site | розкопки (мн) | [roz'kɔpki] |
| excavations | розкопки (мн) | [roz'kɔpki] |

| find (object) | знахідка (ж) | [zna'hidka] |
| fragment | фрагмент (ч) | [frah'mɛnt] |

158. Middle Ages

people (ethnic group)	народ (ч)	[na'rɔd]
peoples	народи (мн)	[na'rɔdi]
tribe	плем'я (с)	['plɛmˀla]
tribes	племена (мн)	[plɛmɛ'na]

barbarians	варвари (мн)	['warwari]
Gauls	гали (ч)	['ɦali]
Goths	готи (мн)	['ɦɔti]
Slavs	слов'яни (мн)	[slo'wˀlani]
Vikings	вікінги (мн)	['wikinɦi]

| Romans | римляни (мн) | [rim'lˈani] |
| Roman (adj) | Римський Папа | ['rimsˈkij 'papa] |

Byzantines	візантійці (мн)	[wizan'tijtsi]
Byzantium	Візантія (ж)	[wizan'tiˈa]
Byzantine (adj)	візантійський	[wizan'tijsˈkij]

emperor	імператор (ч)	[impɛ'rator]
leader, chief (tribal ~)	вождь (ч)	[woʒdˈ]
powerful (~ king)	могутній	[mo'ɦutnij]
king	король (ч)	[ko'rɔlˈ]
ruler (sovereign)	правитель (ч)	[pra'witɛlˈ]

knight	лицар (ч)	['liˈsar]
feudal lord	феодал (ч)	[fɛo'dal]
feudal (adj)	феодальний	[fɛo'dalˈnij]
vassal	васал (ч)	[wa'sal]

duke	герцог (ч)	['ɦɛrʦoɦ]
earl	граф (ч)	[ɦraf]
baron	барон (ч)	[ba'rɔn]
bishop	єпископ (ч)	[ɛ'piskop]

armor	лати (мн)	['lati]
shield	щит (ч)	[ɕit]
sword	меч (ч)	[mɛʧ]
visor	забрало (с)	[za'bralo]
chainmail	кольчуга (ж)	[kolˈ'ʧuɦa]

| Crusade | хрестовий похід (ч) | [hrɛs'tɔwij po'hid] |
| crusader | хрестоносець (ч) | [hrɛsto'nɔsɛʦ] |

| territory | територія (ж) | [tɛri'tɔriˈa] |
| to attack (invade) | нападати | [napa'dati] |

| to conquer (vt) | завоювати | [zawoʲu'wati] |
| to occupy (invade) | захопити | [zaho'piti] |

siege (to be under ~)	облога (ж)	[ob'lɔɦa]
besieged (adj)	обложений	[ob'lɔʒɛnij]
to besiege (vt)	облягати	[oblʲa'ɦati]

inquisition	інквізиція (ж)	[inkwi'ziʦiʲa]
inquisitor	інквізитор (ч)	[inkwi'zitor]
torture	катування (с)	[katu'wanʲa]
cruel (adj)	жорстокий	[ʒor'stɔkij]
heretic	єретик (ч)	[ɛ'rɛtik]
heresy	єресь (ж)	['ɛrɛsʲ]

seafaring	мореплавання (с)	[morɛ'plawanʲa]
pirate	пірат (ч)	[pi'rat]
piracy	піратство (с)	[pi'raʦtwo]
boarding (attack)	абордаж (ч)	[abor'daʒ]
loot, booty	здобич (ж)	['zdɔbiʧ]
treasure	скарби (мн)	[skar'bi]

discovery	відкриття (с)	[widkrit'tʲa]
to discover (new land, etc.)	відкрити	[wid'kriti]
expedition	експедиція (ж)	[ɛkspɛ'diʦiʲa]

musketeer	мушкетер (ч)	[muʃkɛ'tɛr]
cardinal	кардинал (ч)	[kardi'nal]
heraldry	геральдика (ж)	[ɦɛ'ralʲdika]
heraldic (adj)	геральдичний	[ɦɛralʲ'diʧnij]

159. Leader. Chief. Authorities

king	король (ч)	[ko'rɔlʲ]
queen	королева (ж)	[koro'lɛwa]
royal (adj)	королівський	[koro'liwsʲkij]
kingdom	королівство (с)	[koro'liwstwo]

| prince | принц (ч) | [prinʦ] |
| princess | принцеса (ж) | [prin'ʦɛsa] |

president	президент (ч)	[prɛzi'dɛnt]
vice-president	віце-президент (ч)	['wiʦɛ prɛzi'dɛnt]
senator	сенатор (ч)	[sɛ'nator]

monarch	монарх (ч)	[mo'narh]
ruler (sovereign)	правитель (ч)	[pra'witɛlʲ]
dictator	диктатор (ч)	[dik'tator]
tyrant	тиран (ч)	[ti'ran]
magnate	магнат (ч)	[maɦ'nat]
director	директор (ч)	[di'rɛktor]

chief	**шеф** (ч)	[ʃɛf]
manager (director)	**керівник** (ч)	[kɛriw'nik]
boss	**бос** (ч)	[bos]
owner	**господар** (ч)	[ɦos'pɔdar]

leader	**вождь** (ч), **лідер** (ч)	[woʒdʲ], ['lidɛr]
head (~ of delegation)	**голова** (ж)	[ɦolo'wa]
authorities	**влада** (ж)	['wlada]
superiors	**керівництво** (с)	[kɛriw'nitstwo]

governor	**губернатор** (ч)	[ɦubɛr'nator]
consul	**консул** (ч)	['kɔnsul]
diplomat	**дипломат** (ч)	[diplo'mat]
mayor	**мер** (ч)	[mɛr]
sheriff	**шериф** (ч)	[ʃɛ'rif]

emperor	**імператор** (ч)	[impɛ'rator]
tsar, czar	**цар** (ч)	[tsar]
pharaoh	**фараон** (ч)	[fara'ɔn]
khan	**хан** (ч)	[ɦan]

160. Breaking the law. Criminals. Part 1

bandit	**бандит** (ч)	[ban'dit]
crime	**злочин** (ч)	['zlɔtʃin]
criminal (person)	**злочинець** (ч)	[zlo'tʃinɛts]

thief	**злодій** (ч)	['zlɔdij]
to steal (vi, vt)	**красти**	['krasti]
stealing (larceny)	**викрадення** (с)	['wikradɛnʲa]
theft	**крадіжка** (ж)	[kra'diʒka]

to kidnap (vt)	**викрасти**	['wikrasti]
kidnapping	**викрадення** (с)	['wikradɛnʲa]
kidnapper	**викрадач** (ч)	[wikra'datʃ]

| ransom | **викуп** (ч) | ['wikup] |
| to demand ransom | **вимагати викуп** | [wima'ɦati 'wikup] |

to rob (vt)	**грабувати**	[ɦrabu'wati]
robbery	**пограбування** (с), **грабіж** (ч)	[poɦrabu'wanʲa], [ɦra'biʒ]
robber	**грабіжник** (ч)	[ɦra'biʒnik]

to extort (vt)	**вимагати**	[wima'ɦati]
extortionist	**вимагач** (ч)	[wima'ɦatʃ]
extortion	**вимагання** (с)	[wima'ɦanʲa]

| to murder, to kill | **вбити** | ['wbiti] |
| murder | **вбивство** (с) | ['wbiwstwo] |

murderer	вбивця (ч)	['wbiwtsʲa]
gunshot	постріл (ч)	['pɔstril]
to fire (~ a shot)	вистрілити	['wistriliti]
to shoot to death	застрелити	[za'strɛliti]
to shoot (vi)	стріляти	[striˈlʲati]
shooting	стрілянина (ж)	[strilʲa'nina]
incident (fight, etc.)	подія (ж)	[po'diʲa]
fight, brawl	бійка (ж)	['bijka]
Help!	Допоможіть! Врятуйте!	[dopomo'ʒitʲ], [wrʲa'tujtɛ!]
victim	жертва (ж)	['ʒɛrtwa]
to damage (vt)	пошкодити	[poʃˈkɔditi]
damage	шкода (ж)	['ʃkɔda]
dead body, corpse	труп (ч)	[trup]
grave (~ crime)	тяжкий	[tʲaˈʒkij]
to attack (vt)	напасти	[na'pasti]
to beat (to hit)	бити	['biti]
to beat up	побити	[po'biti]
to take (rob of sth)	відібрати	[widi'brati]
to stab to death	зарізати	[za'rizati]
to maim (vt)	покалічити	[poka'litʃiti]
to wound (vt)	поранити	[po'raniti]
blackmail	шантаж (ч)	[ʃan'taʒ]
to blackmail (vt)	шантажувати	[ʃantaʒu'wati]
blackmailer	шантажист (ч)	[ʃanta'ʒist]
protection racket	рекет (ч)	['rɛkɛt]
racketeer	рекетир (ч)	[rɛkɛ'tir]
gangster	гангстер (ч)	['hanɦstɛr]
mafia, Mob	мафія (ж)	['mafiʲa]
pickpocket	кишеньковий злодій (ч)	[kiʃɛnʲˈkɔwij 'zlɔdij]
burglar	зломщик (ч)	['zlɔmɕik]
smuggling	контрабанда (ж)	[kontra'banda]
smuggler	контрабандист (ч)	[kontraban'dist]
forgery	підробка (ж)	[pid'rɔbka]
to forge (counterfeit)	підробляти	[pidrob'lʲati]
fake (forged)	фальшивий	[falʲˈʃiwij]

161. Breaking the law. Criminals. Part 2

rape	зґвалтування (c)	[zgwaltu'wanʲa]
to rape (vt)	зґвалтувати	[zgwaltu'wati]
rapist	ґвалтівник (ч)	[gwaltiw'nik]
maniac	маніяк (ч)	[mani'ʲak]
prostitute (fem.)	проститутка (ж)	[prosti'tutka]

prostitution	проституція (ж)	[prostiˈtutsʲa]
pimp	сутенер (ч)	[sutɛˈnɛr]
drug addict	наркоман (ч)	[narkoˈman]
drug dealer	наркоторговець (ч)	[narkotorˈɦowɛts]
to blow up (bomb)	підірвати	[pidirˈwati]
explosion	вибух (ч)	[ˈwibuɦ]
to set fire	підпалити	[pidpaˈliti]
arsonist	підпалювач (ч)	[pidˈpalʲuwatʃ]
terrorism	тероризм (ч)	[tɛroˈrizm]
terrorist	терорист (ч)	[tɛroˈrist]
hostage	заручник (ч)	[zaˈrutʃnik]
to swindle (deceive)	обманути	[obmaˈnuti]
swindle, deception	обман (ч)	[obˈman]
swindler	шахрай (ч)	[ʃaɦˈraj]
to bribe (vt)	підкупити	[pidkuˈpiti]
bribery	підкуп (ч)	[ˈpidkup]
bribe	хабар (ч)	[haˈbar]
poison	отрута (ж)	[otˈruta]
to poison (vt)	отруїти	[otruˈjiti]
to poison oneself	отруїтись	[otruˈjitisʲ]
suicide (act)	самогубство (с)	[samoˈɦubstwo]
suicide (person)	самогубець (ч)	[samoˈɦubɛtsʲ]
to threaten (vt)	погрожувати	[poɦˈrɔʒuwati]
threat	погроза (ж)	[poɦˈrɔza]
to make an attempt	вчинити замах	[wtʃiˈniti ˈzamah]
attempt (attack)	замах (ч)	[ˈzamah]
to steal (a car)	украсти	[ukˈrasti]
to hijack (a plane)	викрасти	[ˈwikrasti]
revenge	помста (ж)	[ˈpɔmsta]
to avenge (get revenge)	мстити	[ˈmstiti]
to torture (vt)	катувати	[katuˈwati]
torture	катування (с)	[katuˈwanʲa]
to torment (vt)	мучити	[ˈmutʃiti]
pirate	пірат (ч)	[piˈrat]
hooligan	хуліган (ч)	[huliˈɦan]
armed (adj)	озброєний	[ozˈbrɔɛnij]
violence	насильство (с)	[naˈsilʲstwo]
illegal (unlawful)	нелегальний	[nɛlɛˈɦalʲnij]
spying (espionage)	шпигунство (с)	[ʃpiˈɦunstwo]
to spy (vi)	шпигувати	[ʃpiɦuˈwati]

162. Police. Law. Part 1

| justice | правосуддя (c) | [prawo'suddʲa] |
| court (see you in ~) | суд (ч) | [sud] |

judge	суддя (ч)	[sud'dʲa]
jurors	присяжні (мн)	[pri'sʲaʒni]
jury trial	суд (ч) присяжних	[sud pri'sʲaʒnih]
to judge, to try (vt)	судити	[su'diti]

lawyer, attorney	адвокат (ч)	[adwo'kat]
defendant	підсудний (ч)	[pid'sudnij]
dock	лава (ж) підсудних	['lawa pid'sudnih]

| charge | обвинувачення (c) | [obwinu'watʃɛnʲa] |
| accused | обвинувачений (ч) | [obwinu'watʃɛnij] |

| sentence | вирок (ч) | ['wirok] |
| to sentence (vt) | присудити | [prisu'diti] |

guilty (culprit)	винуватець (ч)	[winu'watɛts]
to punish (vt)	покарати	[poka'rati]
punishment	покарання (c)	[poka'ranʲa]

fine (penalty)	штраф (ч)	[ʃtraf]
life imprisonment	довічне ув'язнення (c)	[do'witʃnɛ u'wʲaznɛnʲa]
death penalty	смертна кара (ж)	['smɛrtna 'kara]
electric chair	електричний стілець (ч)	[ɛlɛkt'ritʃnij sti'lɛts]
gallows	шибениця (ж)	['ʃibɛnitsʲa]

| to execute (vt) | стратити | ['stratiti] |
| execution | страта (ж) | ['strata] |

| prison, jail | в'язниця (ж) | [wʲaz'nitsʲa] |
| cell | камера (ж) | ['kamɛra] |

escort (convoy)	конвой (ч)	[kon'wɔj]
prison guard	наглядач (ч)	[naɦlʲa'datʃ]
prisoner	в'язень (ч)	['wʲazɛnʲ]

| handcuffs | наручники (мн) | [na'rutʃniki] |
| to handcuff (vt) | надіти наручники | [na'diti na'rutʃniki] |

prison break	втеча (ж)	['wtɛtʃa]
to break out (vi)	утекти	[utɛk'ti]
to disappear (vi)	зникнути	['zniknuti]
to release (from prison)	звільнити	[zwilʲ'niti]
amnesty	амністія (ж)	[am'nistiʲa]

| police | поліція (ж) | [po'litsiʲa] |
| police officer | поліцейський (ч) | [poli'tsɛjsʲkij] |

police station	поліцейський відділок (ч)	[poli'tsɛjsʲkij 'widdilok]
billy club	гумовий кийок (ч)	['ɦumowij ki'jɔk]
bullhorn	рупор (ч)	['rupor]

patrol car	патрульна машина (ж)	[pat'rulʲna ma'ʃina]
siren	сирена (ж)	[si'rɛna]
to turn on the siren	увімкнути сирену	[uwimk'nuti si'rɛnu]
siren call	виття (с) сирени	[wit'tʲa si'rɛni]

crime scene	місце (с) події	['mistsɛ po'diji]
witness	свідок (ч)	['swidok]
freedom	воля (ж)	['wolʲa]
accomplice	спільник (ч)	['spilʲnik]
to flee (vi)	зникнути	['zniknuti]
trace (to leave a ~)	слід (ч)	[slid]

163. Police. Law. Part 2

search (investigation)	розшук (ч)	['rɔzʃuk]
to look for ...	розшукувати	[roz'ʃukuwati]
suspicion	підозра (ж)	[pi'dɔzra]
suspicious (e.g., ~ vehicle)	підозрілий	[pido'zrilij]
to stop (cause to halt)	зупинити	[zupi'niti]
to detain (keep in custody)	затримати	[za'trimati]

case (lawsuit)	справа (ж)	['sprawa]
investigation	розслідування (с)	[roz'sliduwanʲa]
detective	детектив (ч)	[dɛtɛk'tiw]
investigator	слідчий (ч)	['slidtʃij]
hypothesis	версія (ж)	['wɛrsiʲa]

motive	мотив (ч)	[mo'tiw]
interrogation	допит (ч)	['dɔpit]
to interrogate (vt)	допитувати	[do'pituwati]
to question (~ neighbors, etc.)	опитувати	[o'pituwati]
check (identity ~)	перевірка (ж)	[pɛrɛ'wirka]

round-up (raid)	облава (ж)	[ob'lawa]
search (~ warrant)	обшук (ч)	['ɔbʃuk]
chase (pursuit)	погоня (ж)	[po'ɦɔnʲa]
to pursue, to chase	переслідувати	[pɛrɛs'liduwati]
to track (a criminal)	слідкувати	[slidku'wati]

arrest	арешт (ч)	[a'rɛʃt]
to arrest (sb)	заарештувати	[zaarɛʃtu'wati]
to catch (thief, etc.)	спіймати	[spij'mati]
capture	затримання (с)	[za'trimanʲa]
document	документ (ч)	[doku'mɛnt]

proof (evidence)	доказ (ч)	['dɔkaz]
to prove (vt)	доводити	[do'wɔditi]
footprint	слід (ч)	[slid]
fingerprints	відбитки (мн) пальців	[wid'bitkɨ 'palʲʦiw]
piece of evidence	доказ (ч)	['dɔkaz]

alibi	алібі (с)	['alibi]
innocent (not guilty)	невинний	[nɛ'winij]
injustice	несправедливість (ж)	[nɛsprawɛd'liwistʲ]
unjust, unfair (adj)	несправедливий	[nɛsprawɛd'liwij]

criminal (adj)	кримінальний	[krimi'nalʲnij]
to confiscate (vt)	конфіскувати	[konfisku'wati]
drug (illegal substance)	наркотик (ч)	[nar'kɔtik]
weapon, gun	зброя (ж)	['zbrɔʲa]
to disarm (vt)	обеззброїти	[obɛz'zbrɔjiti]
to order (command)	наказувати	[na'kazuwati]
to disappear (vi)	зникнути	['zniknuti]

law	закон (ч)	[za'kɔn]
legal, lawful (adj)	законний	[za'kɔnij]
illegal, illicit (adj)	незаконний	[nɛza'kɔnij]

| responsibility (blame) | відповідальність (ж) | [widpowi'dalʲnistʲ] |
| responsible (adj) | відповідальний | [widpowi'dalʲnij] |

NATURE

The Earth. Part 1

space	космос (ч)	['kɔsmos]
space (as adj)	космічний	[kos'mitʃnij]
outer space	космічний простір (ч)	[kos'mitʃnij 'prɔstir]
world	світ (ч)	[swit]
universe	всесвіт (ч)	['wsɛswit]
galaxy	галактика (ж)	[ɦa'laktika]
star	зірка (ж)	['zirka]
constellation	сузір'я (с)	[su'zirʲa]
planet	планета (ж)	[pla'nɛta]
satellite	супутник (ч)	[su'putnik]
meteorite	метеорит (ч)	[mɛtɛo'rit]
comet	комета (ж)	[ko'mɛta]
asteroid	астероїд (ч)	[astɛ'rɔjid]
orbit	орбіта (ж)	[or'bita]
to revolve (~ around the Earth)	обертатися	[obɛr'tatisʲa]
atmosphere	атмосфера (ж)	[atmos'fɛra]
the Sun	Сонце (с)	['sɔntsɛ]
solar system	Сонячна система (ж)	['sɔnʲatʃna sis'tɛma]
solar eclipse	сонячне затемнення (с)	['sɔnʲatʃnɛ za'tɛmnɛnʲa]
the Earth	Земля (ж)	[zɛm'lʲa]
the Moon	Місяць (ж)	['misʲats]
Mars	Марс (ч)	[mars]
Venus	Венера (ж)	[wɛ'nɛra]
Jupiter	Юпітер (ч)	[ʲu'pitɛr]
Saturn	Сатурн (ч)	[sa'turn]
Mercury	Меркурій (ч)	[mɛr'kurij]
Uranus	Уран (ч)	[u'ran]
Neptune	Нептун (ч)	[nɛp'tun]
Pluto	Плутон (ч)	[plu'tɔn]
the Milky Way	Чумацький Шлях (ч)	[tʃu'matskij ʃlʲah]

the Great Bear (Ursa Major)	**Велика Ведмедиця** (ж)	[wɛ'lika wɛd'mɛditsʲa]
the North Star	**Полярна Зірка** (ж)	[po'lʲarna 'zirka]
Martian	**марсіанин** (ч)	[marsi'anin]
extraterrestrial (n)	**інопланетянин** (ч)	[inoplanɛ'tʲanin]
alien	**прибулець** (ч)	[pri'bulɛts]
flying saucer	**літаюча тарілка** (ж)	[li'taʲutʃa ta'rilka]
spaceship	**космічний корабель** (ч)	[kos'mitʃnij kora'bɛlʲ]
space station	**орбітальна станція** (ж)	[orbi'talʲna 'stantsiʲa]
blast-off	**старт** (ч)	[start]
engine	**двигун** (ч)	[dwi'ɦun]
nozzle	**сопло** (с)	['sɔplo]
fuel	**паливо** (с)	['paliwo]
cockpit, flight deck	**кабіна** (ж)	[ka'bina]
antenna	**антена** (ж)	[an'tɛna]
porthole	**ілюмінатор** (ч)	[ilʲumi'nator]
solar panel	**сонячна батарея** (ж)	['sonʲatʃna bata'rɛʲa]
spacesuit	**скафандр** (ч)	[ska'fandr]
weightlessness	**невагомість** (ж)	[nɛwa'ɦomistʲ]
oxygen	**кисень** (ч)	['kisɛnʲ]
docking (in space)	**стикування** (с)	[stiku'wanʲa]
to dock (vi, vt)	**здійснювати стикування**	['zdijsnʲuwati stiku'wanʲa]
observatory	**обсерваторія** (ж)	[obsɛrwa'toriʲa]
telescope	**телескоп** (ч)	[tɛlɛ'skɔp]
to observe (vt)	**спостерігати**	[spostɛri'ɦati]
to explore (vt)	**досліджувати**	[do'slidʒuwati]

165. The Earth

the Earth	**Земля** (ж)	[zɛm'lʲa]
the globe (the Earth)	**земна куля** (ж)	[zɛm'na 'kulʲa]
planet	**планета** (ж)	[pla'nɛta]
atmosphere	**атмосфера** (ж)	[atmos'fɛra]
geography	**географія** (ж)	[ɦɛo'ɦrafiʲa]
nature	**природа** (ж)	[pri'rɔda]
globe (table ~)	**глобус** (ч)	['ɦlɔbus]
map	**карта** (ж)	['karta]
atlas	**атлас** (ч)	['atlas]
Europe	**Європа** (ж)	[ɛw'rɔpa]
Asia	**Азія** (ж)	['aziʲa]

Africa	**Африка** (ж)	['afrika]
Australia	**Австралія** (ж)	[aw'straliʲa]
America	**Америка** (ж)	[a'mɛrika]
North America	**Північна Америка** (ж)	[piw'nitʃna a'mɛrika]
South America	**Південна Америка** (ж)	[piw'dɛna a'mɛrika]
Antarctica	**Антарктида** (ж)	[antark'tida]
the Arctic	**Арктика** (ж)	['arktika]

166. Cardinal directions

north	**північ** (ж)	['piwnitʃ]
to the north	**на північ**	[na 'piwnitʃ]
in the north	**на півночі**	[na 'piwnotʃi]
northern (adj)	**північний**	[piw'nitʃnij]
south	**південь** (ч)	['piwdɛnʲ]
to the south	**на південь**	[na 'piwdɛnʲ]
in the south	**на півдні**	[na 'piwdni]
southern (adj)	**південний**	[piw'dɛnij]
west	**захід** (ч)	['zahid]
to the west	**на захід**	[na 'zahid]
in the west	**на заході**	[na 'zahodi]
western (adj)	**західний**	['zahidnij]
east	**схід** (ч)	[shid]
to the east	**на схід**	[na 'shid]
in the east	**на сході**	[na 'shɔdi]
eastern (adj)	**східний**	['shidnij]

167. Sea. Ocean

sea	**море** (с)	['mɔrɛ]
ocean	**океан** (ч)	[okɛ'an]
gulf (bay)	**затока** (ж)	[za'tɔka]
straits	**протока** (ж)	[pro'tɔka]
land (solid ground)	**земля, суша** (ж)	[zɛm'lʲa], ['suʃa]
continent (mainland)	**материк** (ч)	[matɛ'rik]
island	**острів** (ч)	['ɔstriw]
peninsula	**півострів** (ч)	[pi'wɔstriw]
archipelago	**архіпелаг** (ч)	[arhipɛ'laɦ]
bay, cove	**бухта** (ж)	['buhta]
harbor	**гавань** (ж)	['ɦawanʲ]
lagoon	**лагуна** (ж)	[la'ɦuna]

cape	мис (ч)	[mis]
atoll	атол (ч)	[a'tɔl]
reef	риф (ч)	[rif]
coral	корал (ч)	[ko'ral]
coral reef	кораловий риф (ч)	[ko'ralowij rif]
deep (adj)	глибокий	[ɦli'bɔkij]
depth (deep water)	глибина (ж)	[ɦlibi'na]
abyss	безодня (ж)	[bɛ'zɔdnʲa]
trench (e.g., Mariana ~)	западина (ж)	[za'padɨna]
current (Ocean ~)	течія (ж)	['tɛtʃʲia]
to surround (bathe)	омивати	[omɨ'watɨ]
shore	берег (ч)	['bɛrɛɦ]
coast	узбережжя (с)	[uzbɛ'rɛzʲa]
flow (flood tide)	приплив (ч)	[prip'liw]
ebb (ebb tide)	відлив (ч)	[wid'liw]
shoal	мілина (ж)	[mili'na]
bottom (~ of the sea)	дно (с)	[dno]
wave	хвиля (ж)	['hwilʲa]
crest (~ of a wave)	гребінь (ч) хвилі	['ɦrɛbinʲ 'hwili]
spume (sea foam)	піна (ж)	[pi'na]
storm (sea storm)	буря (ж)	['burʲa]
hurricane	ураган (ч)	[uraɦan]
tsunami	цунамі (с)	[tsu'nami]
calm (dead ~)	штиль (ч)	[ʃtilʲ]
quiet, calm (adj)	спокійний	[spo'kijnij]
pole	полюс (ч)	['pɔlʲus]
polar (adj)	полярний	[po'lʲarnij]
latitude	широта (ж)	[ʃiro'ta]
longitude	довгота (ж)	[dowɦo'ta]
parallel	паралель (ж)	[para'lɛlʲ]
equator	екватор (ч)	[ɛk'wator]
sky	небо (с)	['nɛbo]
horizon	горизонт (ч)	[ɦori'zɔnt]
air	повітря (с)	[po'witrʲa]
lighthouse	маяк (ч)	[ma'ʲak]
to dive (vi)	пірнати	[pir'nati]
to sink (ab. boat)	затонути	[zato'nuti]
treasure	скарби (мн)	[skar'bi]

168. Mountains

mountain	гора (ж)	[ɦo'ra]
mountain range	гірський ланцюг (ч)	[ɦirsʲ'kij lan'tsʲuɦ]
mountain ridge	гірський хребет (ч)	[ɦirsʲ'kij ɦrɛ'bɛt]
summit, top	вершина (ж)	[wɛr'ʃina]
peak	шпиль (ч)	[ʃpilʲ]
foot (base, ~ of the mountain)	підніжжя (с)	[pid'niʒʲa]
slope (mountainside)	схил (ч)	[shil]
volcano	вулкан (ч)	[wul'kan]
active volcano	діючий вулкан (ч)	['diʲutʃij wul'kan]
dormant volcano	згаслий вулкан (ч)	['zɦaslij wul'kan]
eruption	виверження (с)	['wiwɛrʒɛnʲa]
crater	кратер (ч)	['kratɛr]
magma	магма (ж)	['maɦma]
lava	лава (ж)	['lawa]
molten (~ lava)	розжарений	[roz'ʒarɛnij]
canyon	каньйон (ч)	[kanʲ'jon]
gorge	ущелина (ж)	[u'ɕɛlina]
crevice	розщілина (ж)	[roz'ɕilina]
abyss (chasm)	прірва (ж), обрив (ч)	['prirwa], [ob'riw]
pass, col	перевал (ч)	[pɛrɛ'wal]
plateau	плато (с)	['plato]
cliff	скеля (ж)	['skɛlʲa]
hill	пагорб (ч)	['paɦorb]
glacier	льодовик (ч)	[lʲodo'wik]
waterfall	водоспад (ч)	[wodos'pad]
geyser	гейзер (ч)	['ɦɛjzɛr]
lake	озеро (с)	['ɔzɛro]
plain	рівнина (ж)	[riw'nina]
landscape	краєвид (ч)	[kraɛ'wid]
echo	луна (ж)	[lu'na]
alpinist	альпініст (ч)	[alʲpi'nist]
rock climber	скелелаз (ч)	[skɛlɛ'laz]
to conquer (vt)	підкоряти	[pidko'rʲati]
climb (an easy ~)	підйом (ч)	[pid'jom]

169. Rivers

river	ріка (ж)	['rika]
spring (natural source)	джерело (с)	[dʒɛrɛ'lɔ]

riverbed (river channel)	річище (с)	['ritʃiɕɛ]
basin (river valley)	басейн (ч)	[ba'sɛjn]
to flow into ...	впадати у...	[wpa'dati u...]
tributary	притока (ж)	[pri'tɔka]
bank (river ~)	берег (ч)	['bɛrɛɦ]
current (stream)	течія (ж)	['tɛtʃiʲa]
downstream (adv)	вниз за течією	[wniz za 'tɛtʃiɛʲu]
upstream (adv)	уверх за течією	[u'wɛrh po 'tɛtʃiɛʲu]
inundation	повінь (ж)	['pɔwinʲ]
flooding	повінь (ж)	['pɔwinʲ]
to overflow (vi)	розливатися	[rozli'watisʲa]
to flood (vt)	затоплювати	[za'tɔplʲuwati]
shallow (shoal)	мілина (ж)	[mili'na]
rapids	поріг (ч)	[po'riɦ]
dam	гребля (ж)	['ɦrɛblʲa]
canal	канал (ч)	[ka'nal]
reservoir (artificial lake)	водосховище (с)	[wodo'shɔwiɕɛ]
sluice, lock	шлюз (ч)	[ʃlʲuz]
water body (pond, etc.)	водойма (ж)	[wo'dɔjma]
swamp (marshland)	болото (с)	[bo'lɔto]
bog, marsh	трясовина (ж)	[trʲasowi'na]
whirlpool	вир (ч)	[wir]
stream (brook)	струмок (ч)	[stru'mɔk]
drinking (ab. water)	питний	['pitnij]
fresh (~ water)	прісний	['prisnij]
ice	лід (ч), крига (ж)	[lid], ['kriɦa]
to freeze over	замерзнути	[za'mɛrznuti]
(ab. river, etc.)		

170. Forest

forest, wood	ліс (ч)	[lis]
forest (as adj)	лісовий	[liso'wij]
thick forest	хаща (ж)	['haɕa]
grove	гай (ч)	[ɦaj]
forest clearing	галявина (ж)	[ɦa'lʲawina]
thicket	зарості (мн)	['zarosti]
scrubland	чагарник (ч)	[tʃa'ɦarnik]
footpath (e.g., forest path)	стежина (ж)	[stɛ'ʒina]
gully	яр (ч)	[jar]

tree	дерево (с)	['dɛrɛwo]
leaf	листок (ч)	[lis'tɔk]
leaves (foliage)	листя (с)	['listʲa]
fall of leaves	листопад (ч)	[listo'pad]
to fall (ab. leaves)	опадати	[opa'dati]
top (of the tree)	верхівка (ж)	[wɛr'hiwka]
branch	гілка (ж)	['hilka]
bough	сук (ч)	[suk]
bud (on shrub, tree)	брунька (ж)	['brunʲka]
needle (of a pine tree)	голка (ж)	['hɔlka]
pine cone	шишка (ж)	['ʃiʃka]
tree hollow	дупло (с)	[dup'lɔ]
nest	гніздо (с)	[hniz'dɔ]
trunk	стовбур (ч)	['stɔwbur]
root	корінь (ч)	['kɔrinʲ]
bark	кора (ж)	[ko'ra]
moss	мох (ч)	[moh]
to uproot (remove trees or tree stumps)	корчувати	[kortʃu'wati]
to chop down	рубати	[ru'bati]
to deforest (vt)	вирубувати ліс	[wi'rubuwati lis]
tree stump	пень (ч)	[pɛnʲ]
campfire	багаття (с)	[ba'hattʲa]
forest fire	лісова пожежа (ж)	[liso'wa po'ʒɛʒa]
to extinguish (vt)	тушити	[tu'ʃiti]
forest ranger	лісник (ч)	[lis'nik]
protection	охорона (ж)	[oho'rɔna]
to protect (e.g., ~ nature)	охороняти	[ohoro'nʲati]
poacher	браконьєр (ч)	[brako'nʲɛr]
jaw trap	капкан (ч)	[kap'kan]
to gather, to pick (vt)	збирати	[zbi'rati]
to lose one's way	заблукати	[zablu'kati]

171. Natural resources

natural resources	природні ресурси (мн)	[pri'rɔdni rɛ'sursi]
underground resources	корисні копалини (мн)	['kɔrisni ko'palini]
deposits	поклади (мн)	['pɔkladi]
field (e.g., oilfield)	родовище (с)	[ro'dɔwiɕɛ]
to mine (extract)	добувати	[dobu'wati]
mining (extraction)	добування (с)	[dobu'wanʲa]

ore	руда (ж)	[ru'da]
mine (e.g., coal mine)	копальня (ж)	[ko'palʲnʲa]
shaft (mine ~)	шахта (ж)	['ʃahta]
miner	шахтар (ч)	[ʃah'tar]

| gas (natural ~) | газ (ч) | [ɦaz] |
| gas pipeline | газопровід (ч) | [ɦazopro'wid] |

oil (petroleum)	нафта (ж)	['nafta]
oil pipeline	нафтопровід (ч)	[nafto'prɔwid]
oil well	нафтова вишка (ж)	['naftowa 'wiʃka]
derrick (tower)	свердлова вежа (ж)	[swɛrd'lɔwa 'wɛʒa]
tanker	танкер (ч)	['tankɛr]

sand	пісок (ч)	[pi'sɔk]
limestone	вапняк (ч)	[wap'nʲak]
gravel	гравій (ч)	['ɦrawij]
peat	торф (ч)	[torf]
clay	глина (ж)	['ɦlina]
coal	вугілля (с)	[wu'ɦilʲa]

iron (ore)	залізо (с)	[za'lizo]
gold	золото (с)	['zɔloto]
silver	срібло (с)	['sriblo]
nickel	нікель (ч)	['nikɛlʲ]
copper	мідь (ж)	[midʲ]

zinc	цинк (ч)	['ʦink]
manganese	марганець (ч)	['marɦanɛʦ]
mercury	ртуть (ж)	[rtutʲ]
lead	свинець (ч)	[swi'nɛʦ]

mineral	мінерал (ч)	[minɛ'ral]
crystal	кристал (ч)	[kris'tal]
marble	мармур (ч)	['marmur]
uranium	уран (ч)	[u'ran]

The Earth. Part 2

weather	**погода** (ж)	[po'ɦoda]
weather forecast	**прогноз** (ч) **погоди**	[proɦ'nɔz po'ɦodi]
temperature	**температура** (ж)	[tɛmpɛra'tura]
thermometer	**термометр** (ч)	[tɛr'mɔmɛtr]
barometer	**барометр** (ч)	[ba'rɔmɛtr]
humid (adj)	**вологий**	[wo'lɔɦij]
humidity	**вологість** (ж)	[wolɔɦistʲ]
heat (extreme ~)	**спека** (ж)	['spɛka]
hot (torrid)	**гарячий**	[ɦaʲrʲatʃij]
it's hot	**спекотно**	[spɛ'kɔtno]
it's warm	**тепло**	['tɛplo]
warm (moderately hot)	**теплий**	['tɛplij]
it's cold	**холодно**	['hɔlodno]
cold (adj)	**холодний**	[ho'lɔdnij]
sun	**сонце** (с)	['sɔntsɛ]
to shine (vi)	**світити**	[swi'titi]
sunny (day)	**сонячний**	['sɔnʲatʃnij]
to come up (vi)	**зійти**	[zij'ti]
to set (vi)	**сісти**	['sistʲi]
cloud	**хмара** (ж)	['hmara]
cloudy (adj)	**хмарний**	['hmarnij]
rain cloud	**хмара** (ж)	['hmara]
somber (gloomy)	**похмурий**	[poh'murij]
rain	**дощ** (ч)	[dɔtɕ]
it's raining	**йде дощ**	[jdɛ dɔtɕ]
rainy (~ day, weather)	**дощовий**	[dɔtɕo'wij]
to drizzle (vi)	**накрапати**	[nakra'pati]
pouring rain	**проливний дощ** (ч)	[proliw'nij dɔtɕ]
downpour	**злива** (ж)	['zliwa]
heavy (e.g., ~ rain)	**сильний**	['silʲnij]
puddle	**калюжа** (ж)	[ka'lʲuʒa]
to get wet (in the rain)	**мокнути**	['mɔknuti]
fog (mist)	**туман** (ч)	[tu'man]
foggy	**туманний**	[tu'manij]

| snow | сніг (ч) | [sniɦ] |
| it's snowing | йде сніг | [jdɛ sniɦ] |

173. Severe weather. Natural disasters

thunderstorm	гроза (ж)	[ɦro'za]
lightning (~ strike)	блискавка (ж)	['bliskawka]
to flash (vi)	блискати	['bliskati]

thunder	грім (ч)	[ɦrim]
to thunder (vi)	гриміти	[ɦri'miti]
it's thundering	гримить грім	[ɦri'mitʲ ɦrim]

| hail | град (ч) | [ɦrad] |
| it's hailing | йде град | [jdɛ ɦrad] |

| to flood (vt) | затопити | [zato'piti] |
| flood, inundation | повінь (ж) | ['powinʲ] |

earthquake	землетрус (ч)	[zɛmlɛt'rus]
tremor, shock	поштовх (ч)	['pɔʃtowɦ]
epicenter	епіцентр (ч)	[ɛpi'ʦɛntr]

| eruption | виверження (с) | ['wiwɛrʒɛnʲa] |
| lava | лава (ж) | ['lawa] |

twister	смерч (ч)	[smɛrtʃ]
tornado	торнадо (ч)	[tor'nado]
typhoon	тайфун (ч)	[taj'fun]

hurricane	ураган (ч)	[uraɦan]
storm	буря (ж)	['burʲa]
tsunami	цунамі (с)	[ʦu'nami]

cyclone	циклон (ч)	[ʦik'lɔn]
bad weather	негода (ж)	[nɛ'ɦɔda]
fire (accident)	пожежа (ж)	[po'ʒɛʒa]
disaster	катастрофа (ж)	[kata'strɔfa]
meteorite	метеорит (ч)	[mɛtɛo'rit]

avalanche	лавина (ж)	[la'wina]
snowslide	обвал (ч)	[ob'wal]
blizzard	заметіль (ж)	[zamɛ'tilʲ]
snowstorm	завірюха (ж)	[zawi'rʲuha]

Fauna

174. Mammals. Predators

predator	хижак (ч)	[hiˈʒak]
tiger	тигр (ч)	[tiɦr]
lion	лев (ч)	[lɛw]
wolf	вовк (ч)	[wowk]
fox	лисиця (ж)	[liˈsitsʲa]
jaguar	ягуар (ч)	[jaɦuˈar]
leopard	леопард (ч)	[lɛoˈpard]
cheetah	гепард (ч)	[ɦɛˈpard]
black panther	пантера (ж)	[panˈtɛra]
puma	пума (ж)	[ˈpuma]
snow leopard	сніговий барс (ч)	[sniɦoˈwij bars]
lynx	рись (ж)	[risʲ]
coyote	койот (ч)	[koˈjɔt]
jackal	шакал (ч)	[ʃaˈkal]
hyena	гієна (ж)	[ɦiˈɛna]

175. Wild animals

animal	тварина (ж)	[twaˈrina]
beast (animal)	звір (ч)	[zwir]
squirrel	білка (ж)	[ˈbilka]
hedgehog	їжак (ч)	[jiˈʒak]
hare	заєць (ч)	[ˈzaɛts]
rabbit	кріль (ч)	[krilʲ]
badger	борсук (ч)	[borˈsuk]
raccoon	єнот (ч)	[ɛˈnɔt]
hamster	хом'як (ч)	[hoˈmʲʲak]
marmot	бабак (ч)	[baˈbak]
mole	кріт (ч)	[krit]
mouse	миша (ж)	[ˈmiʃa]
rat	щур (ч)	[ɕur]
bat	кажан (ч)	[kaˈʒan]
ermine	горностай (ч)	[ɦornoˈstaj]
sable	соболь (ч)	[ˈsɔbolʲ]

marten	куниця (ж)	[ku'nitsʲa]
weasel	ласка (ж)	['laska]
mink	норка (ж)	['nɔrka]
beaver	бобер (ч)	[bo'bɛr]
otter	видра (ж)	['widra]
horse	кінь (ч)	[kinʲ]
moose	лось (ч)	[losʲ]
deer	олень (ч)	['ɔlɛnʲ]
camel	верблюд (ч)	[wɛr'blʲud]
bison	бізон (ч)	[bi'zɔn]
wisent	зубр (ч)	[zubr]
buffalo	буйвіл (ч)	['bujwil]
zebra	зебра (ж)	['zɛbra]
antelope	антилопа (ж)	[anti'lɔpa]
roe deer	косуля (ж)	[ko'sulʲa]
fallow deer	лань (ж)	[lanʲ]
chamois	сарна (ж)	['sarna]
wild boar	вепр (ч)	[wɛpr]
whale	кит (ч)	[kit]
seal	тюлень (ч)	[tʲu'lɛnʲ]
walrus	морж (ч)	[mɔrʒ]
fur seal	котик (ч)	['kɔtik]
dolphin	дельфін (ч)	[dɛlʲ'fin]
bear	ведмідь (ч)	[wɛd'midʲ]
polar bear	білий ведмідь (ч)	['bilij wɛd'midʲ]
panda	панда (ж)	['panda]
monkey	мавпа (ж)	['mawpa]
chimpanzee	шимпанзе (ч)	[ʃimpan'zɛ]
orangutan	орангутанг (ч)	[oranɦu'tanɦ]
gorilla	горила (ж)	[ɦo'rila]
macaque	макака (ж)	[ma'kaka]
gibbon	гібон (ч)	[ɦi'bɔn]
elephant	слон (ч)	[slon]
rhinoceros	носоріг (ч)	[noso'riɦ]
giraffe	жирафа (ж)	[ʒirafa]
hippopotamus	бегемот (ч)	[bɛɦɛ'mɔt]
kangaroo	кенгуру (ч)	[kɛnɦu'ru]
koala (bear)	коала (ч)	[ko'ala]
mongoose	мангуст (ч)	[ma'nɦust]
chinchilla	шиншила (ж)	[ʃin'ʃila]
skunk	скунс (ч)	[skuns]
porcupine	дикобраз (ч)	[diko'braz]

176. Domestic animals

cat	кішка (ж)	['kiʃka]
tomcat	кіт (ч)	[kit]
dog	собака, пес (ч)	[so'baka], [pɛs]
horse	кінь (ч)	[kinʲ]
stallion (male horse)	жеребець (ч)	[ʒɛrɛ'bɛts]
mare	кобила (ж)	[ko'bila]
cow	корова (ж)	[ko'rɔwa]
bull	бик (ч)	[bik]
ox	віл (ч)	[wil]
sheep (ewe)	вівця (ж)	[wiw'tsʲa]
ram	баран (ч)	[ba'ran]
goat	коза (ж)	[ko'za]
billy goat, he-goat	козел (ч)	[ko'zɛl]
donkey	осел (ч)	[o'sɛl]
mule	мул (ч)	[mul]
pig, hog	свиня (ж)	[swi'nʲa]
piglet	порося (с)	[poro'sʲa]
rabbit	кріль (ч)	[krilʲ]
hen (chicken)	курка (ж)	['kurka]
rooster	півень (ч)	['piwɛnʲ]
duck	качка (ж)	['katʃka]
drake	качур (ч)	['katʃur]
goose	гусак (ч)	[ɦu'sak]
tom turkey, gobbler	індик (ч)	[in'dik]
turkey (hen)	індичка (ж)	[in'ditʃka]
domestic animals	домашні тварини (мн)	[do'maʃni twa'rini]
tame (e.g., ~ hamster)	ручний	[rutʃ'nij]
to tame (vt)	приручати	[priru'tʃati]
to breed (vt)	вирощувати	[wi'rɔɕuwati]
farm	ферма (ж)	['fɛrma]
poultry	свійські птахи (мн)	['swijsʲki pta'hi]
cattle	худоба (ж)	[ɦu'dɔba]
herd (cattle)	стадо (с)	['stado]
stable	конюшня (ж)	[ko'nʲuʃnʲa]
pigpen	свинарник (ч)	[swi'narnik]
cowshed	корівник (ч)	[ko'riwnik]
rabbit hutch	крільчатник (ч)	[krilʲ'tʃatnik]
hen house	курник (ч)	[kur'nik]

177. Dogs. Dog breeds

dog	собака (ч)	[so'baka]
sheepdog	вівчарка (ж)	[wiw'ʧarka]
German shepherd	німецька вівчарка (ж)	[ni'mɛʦʲka wiw'ʧarka]
poodle	пудель (ч)	['pudɛlʲ]
dachshund	такса (ж)	['taksa]
bulldog	бульдог (ч)	[bulʲ'dɔɦ]
boxer	боксер (ч)	[bok'sɛr]
mastiff	мастиф (ч)	[mas'tif]
Rottweiler	ротвейлер (ч)	[rot'wɛjlɛr]
Doberman	доберман (ч)	[dobɛr'man]
basset	басет (ч)	[ba'sɛt]
bobtail	бобтейл (ч)	[bob'tɛjl]
Dalmatian	далматинець (ч)	[dalma'tinɛʦ]
cocker spaniel	кокер-спанієль (ч)	['kɔkɛr spani'ɛlʲ]
Newfoundland	ньюфаундленд (ч)	[njufaund'lɛnd]
Saint Bernard	сенбернар (ч)	[sɛnbɛr'nar]
husky	хаскі (ч)	[haski]
Chow Chow	чау-чау (ч)	[ʧau ʧau]
spitz	шпіц (ч)	[ʃpiʦ]
pug	мопс (ч)	[mops]

178. Sounds made by animals

barking (n)	гавкіт (ч)	['ɦawkit]
to bark (vi)	гавкати	['ɦawkati]
to meow (vi)	нявкати	['nʲawkati]
to purr (vi)	муркотіти	[murko'titi]
to moo (vi)	мукати	['mukati]
to bellow (bull)	ревіти	[rɛ'witi]
to growl (vi)	ричати	[ri'ʧati]
howl (n)	виття (с)	[wit'tʲa]
to howl (vi)	вити	['witi]
to whine (vi)	скиглити	['skiɦliti]
to bleat (sheep)	бекати	['bɛkati]
to oink, to grunt (pig)	рохкати	['rɔhkati]
to squeal (vi)	верещати	[wɛrɛ'çati]
to croak (vi)	кумкати	['kumkati]
to buzz (insect)	дзижчати	[ʣiʒ'ʧati]
to chirp (crickets, grasshopper)	стрекотати	[strɛko'tati]

179. Birds

bird	птах (ч)	[ptah]
pigeon	голуб (ч)	['ɦolub]
sparrow	горобець (ч)	[ɦoro'bɛts]
tit (great tit)	синиця (ж)	[si'nitsʲa]
magpie	сорока (ж)	[so'rɔka]

raven	ворон (ч)	['wɔron]
crow	ворона (ж)	[wo'rɔna]
jackdaw	галка (ж)	['ɦalka]
rook	грак (ч)	[ɦrak]

duck	качка (ж)	['katʃka]
goose	гусак (ч)	[ɦu'sak]
pheasant	фазан (ч)	[fa'zan]

eagle	орел (ч)	[o'rɛl]
hawk	яструб (ч)	['ʲastrub]
falcon	сокіл (ч)	['sɔkil]
vulture	гриф (ч)	[ɦrif]
condor (Andean ~)	кондор (ч)	['kɔndor]

swan	лебідь (ч)	['lɛbidʲ]
crane	журавель (ч)	[ʒura'wɛlʲ]
stork	чорногуз (ч)	[tʃorno'ɦuz]

parrot	папуга (ч)	[pa'puɦa]
hummingbird	колібрі (ч)	[ko'libri]
peacock	пава (ж)	['pawa]

ostrich	страус (ч)	['straus]
heron	чапля (ж)	['tʃaplʲa]
flamingo	фламінго (с)	[fla'minɦo]
pelican	пелікан (ч)	[pɛli'kan]

| nightingale | соловей (ч) | [solo'wɛj] |
| swallow | ластівка (ж) | ['lastiwka] |

thrush	дрізд (ч)	[drizd]
song thrush	співучий дрізд (ч)	[spi'wutʃij 'drizd]
blackbird	чорний дрізд (ч)	['tʃornij 'drizd]

swift	стриж (ч)	['striʒ]
lark	жайворонок (ч)	['ʒajworonok]
quail	перепел (ч)	['pɛrɛpɛl]

woodpecker	дятел (ч)	['dʲatɛl]
cuckoo	зозуля (ж)	[zo'zulʲa]
owl	сова (ж)	[so'wa]
eagle owl	пугач (ч)	[pu'ɦatʃ]

wood grouse	глухар (ч)	[ɦlu'har]
black grouse	тетерук (ч)	[tɛtɛ'ruk]
partridge	куріпка (ж)	[ku'ripka]

starling	шпак (ч)	[ʃpak]
canary	канарка (ж)	[ka'narka]
hazel grouse	рябчик (ч)	['rʲabtʃik]
chaffinch	зяблик (ч)	['zʲablik]
bullfinch	снігур (ч)	[sni'ɦur]

seagull	чайка (ж)	['tʃajka]
albatross	альбатрос (ч)	[alʲbat'rɔs]
penguin	пінгвін (ч)	[pinɦ'win]

180. Birds. Singing and sounds

to sing (vi)	співати	[spi'wati]
to call (animal, bird)	кричати	[kri'tʃati]
to crow (rooster)	кукурікати	[kuku'rikati]
cock-a-doodle-doo	кукуріку	[kukuri'ku]

to cluck (hen)	кудкудакати	[kudku'dakati]
to caw (crow)	каркати	['karkati]
to quack (duck)	крякати	['krʲakati]

| to cheep (vi) | пискотіти | [pisko'titi] |
| to chirp, to twitter | цвірінькати | [tswi'rinʲkati] |

181. Fish. Marine animals

bream	лящ (ч)	[lʲaɕ]
carp	короп (ч)	['kɔrop]
perch	окунь (ч)	['ɔkunʲ]
catfish	сом (ч)	[som]
pike	щука (ж)	['ɕuka]

| salmon | лосось (ч) | [lo'sɔsʲ] |
| sturgeon | осетер (ч) | [osɛ'tɛr] |

herring	оселедець (ч)	[osɛ'lɛdɛts]
Atlantic salmon	сьомга (ж)	['sʲomɦa]
mackerel	скумбрія (ж)	['skumbrʲia]
flatfish	камбала (ж)	[kamba'la]

zander, pike perch	судак (ч)	[su'dak]
cod	тріска (ж)	[tris'ka]
tuna	тунець (ч)	[tu'nɛts]
trout	форель (ж)	[fo'rɛlʲ]

eel	**вугор** (ч)	[wu'ɦɔr]
electric ray	**електричний скат** (ч)	[ɛlɛkt'ritʃnij skat]
moray eel	**мурена** (ж)	[mu'rɛna]
piranha	**піранья** (ж)	[pi'ranʲa]
shark	**акула** (ж)	[a'kula]
dolphin	**дельфін** (ч)	[dɛlʲ'fin]
whale	**кит** (ч)	[kit]
crab	**краб** (ч)	[krab]
jellyfish	**медуза** (ж)	[mɛ'duza]
octopus	**восьминіг** (ч)	[wosʲmi'niɦ]
starfish	**морська зірка** (ж)	[morsʲ'ka 'zirka]
sea urchin	**морський їжак** (ч)	[morsʲ'kij ji'ʒak]
seahorse	**морський коник** (ч)	[morsʲ'kij 'kɔnik]
oyster	**устриця** (ж)	['ustritsʲa]
shrimp	**креветка** (ж)	[krɛ'wɛtka]
lobster	**омар** (ч)	[o'mar]
spiny lobster	**лангуст** (ч)	[lan'ɦust]

182. Amphibians. Reptiles

snake	**змія** (ж)	[zmi'ʲa]
venomous (snake)	**отруйний**	[ot'rujnij]
viper	**гадюка** (ж)	[ɦa'dʲuka]
cobra	**кобра** (ж)	['kɔbra]
python	**пітон** (ч)	[pi'tɔn]
boa	**удав** (ч)	[u'daw]
grass snake	**вуж** (ч)	[wuʒ]
rattle snake	**гримуча змія** (ж)	[ɦri'mutʃa zmi'ʲa]
anaconda	**анаконда** (ж)	[ana'kɔnda]
lizard	**ящірка** (ж)	['ʲaçirka]
iguana	**ігуана** (ж)	[iɦu'ana]
monitor lizard	**варан** (ч)	[wa'ran]
salamander	**саламандра** (ж)	[sala'mandra]
chameleon	**хамелеон** (ч)	[ɦamɛlɛ'ɔn]
scorpion	**скорпіон** (ч)	[skorpi'ɔn]
turtle	**черепаха** (ж)	[tʃɛrɛ'paha]
frog	**жаба** (ж)	['ʒaba]
toad	**ропуха** (ж)	[ro'puha]
crocodile	**крокодил** (ч)	[kroko'dil]

183. Insects

insect, bug	комаха (ж)	[ko'maɦa]
butterfly	метелик (ч)	[mɛ'tɛlik]
ant	мураха (ж)	[mu'raɦa]
fly	муха (ж)	['muɦa]
mosquito	комар (ч)	[ko'mar]
beetle	жук (ч)	[ʒuk]
wasp	оса (ж)	[o'sa]
bee	бджола (ж)	[bdʒo'la]
bumblebee	джміль (ч)	[dʒmilʲ]
gadfly (botfly)	овід (ч)	['ɔwid]
spider	павук (ч)	[pa'wuk]
spiderweb	павутиння (с)	[pawu'tinʲa]
dragonfly	бабка (ж)	['babka]
grasshopper	коник (ч)	['kɔnik]
moth (night butterfly)	метелик (ч)	[mɛ'tɛlik]
cockroach	тарган (ч)	[tar'ɦan]
tick	кліщ (ч)	[kliɕ]
flea	блоха (ж)	['blɔɦa]
midge	мошка (ж)	['mɔʃka]
locust	сарана (ж)	[sara'na]
snail	равлик (ч)	['rawlik]
cricket	цвіркун (ч)	[ʦwir'kun]
lightning bug	світлячок (ч)	[switlʲa'ʧɔk]
ladybug	сонечко (с)	['sɔnɛʧko]
cockchafer	хрущ (ч)	[ɦruɕ]
leech	п'явка (ж)	['pʲʲawka]
caterpillar	гусениця (ж)	['ɦusɛniʦʲa]
earthworm	черв'як (ч)	[ʧɛr'wʲʲak]
larva	личинка (ж)	[li'ʧinka]

184. Animals. Body parts

beak	дзьоб (ч)	[dzʲob]
wings	крила (мн)	['krila]
foot (bird foot)	лапка (ж)	['lapka]
feathers (plumage)	пір'я (с)	['pirʲʲa]
feather	перо (с)	[pɛ'rɔ]
crest	чубчик (ч)	['ʧubʧik]
gills	зябра (мн)	['zʲabra]
spawn	ікра (ж)	[ik'ra]

larva	**личинка** (ж)	[li'ʧinka]
fin	**плавець** (ч)	[pla'wɛʦ]
scales (e.g., fish ~)	**луска** (ж)	[lus'ka]

fang (canine)	**ікло** (с)	['iklo]
paw (e.g., cat's ~)	**лапа** (ж)	['lapa]
muzzle (snout)	**морда** (ж)	['mɔrda]
maw (cat's ~)	**паща** (ж)	['paɕa]
tail	**хвіст** (ч)	[hwist]
whiskers	**вуса** (мн)	['wusa]

| hoof | **копито** (с) | [ko'pito] |
| horn | **ріг** (ч) | [rifi] |

carapace	**панцир** (ч)	['panʦir]
shell (mollusk ~)	**мушля** (ж)	['muʃlʲa]
eggshell	**шкаралупа** (ж)	[ʃkara'lupa]

| animal's hair (pelage) | **шерсть** (ж) | [ʃɛrstʲ] |
| pelt (hide) | **шкура** (ж) | ['ʃkura] |

185. Animals. Habitats

| habitat | **середовище** (с) **проживання** | [sɛrɛ'dɔwiɕɛ proʒi'wanʲa] |
| migration | **міграція** (ж) | [mifi'raʦiʲa] |

mountain	**гора** (ж)	[ɦo'ra]
reef	**риф** (ч)	[rif]
cliff	**скеля** (ж)	['skɛlʲa]

forest	**ліс** (ч)	[lis]
jungle	**джунглі** (мн)	['ʤunɦli]
savanna	**савана** (ж)	[sa'wana]
tundra	**тундра** (ж)	['tundra]

steppe	**степ** (ч)	['stɛp]
desert	**пустеля** (ж)	[pus'tɛlʲa]
oasis	**оаза** (ж)	[o'aza]

sea	**море** (с)	['mɔrɛ]
lake	**озеро** (с)	['ɔzɛro]
ocean	**океан** (ч)	[okɛ'an]

swamp (marshland)	**болото** (с)	[bo'lɔto]
freshwater (adj)	**прісноводний**	[prisno'wɔdnij]
pond	**ставок** (ч)	[sta'wɔk]
river	**ріка** (ж)	['rika]
den (bear's ~)	**барліг** (ч)	[bar'liɦ]
nest	**гніздо** (с)	[ɦniz'dɔ]

tree hollow	дупло (c)	[dup'lɔ]
burrow (animal hole)	нора (ж)	[no'ra]
anthill	мурашник (ч)	[muraʃˈnik]

Flora

tree	дерево (c)	['dɛrɛwo]
deciduous (adj)	листяне	[listʲaʹnɛ]
coniferous (adj)	хвойне	['hwɔjnɛ]
evergreen (adj)	вічнозелене	[witʃnozɛ'lɛnɛ]

apple tree	яблуня (ж)	[ʲiablunʲa]
pear tree	груша (ж)	['hruʃa]
sweet cherry tree	черешня (ж)	[tʃɛ'rɛʃnʲa]
sour cherry tree	вишня (ж)	['wiʃnʲa]
plum tree	слива (ж)	['sliwa]

birch	береза (ж)	[bɛ'rɛza]
oak	дуб (ч)	[dub]
linden tree	липа (ж)	['lipa]
aspen	осика (ж)	[o'sika]
maple	клен (ч)	[klɛn]

spruce	ялина (ж)	[ja'lina]
pine	сосна (ж)	[sos'na]
larch	модрина (ж)	[mod'rina]
fir tree	ялиця (ж)	[ja'litsʲa]
cedar	кедр (ч)	[kɛdr]

poplar	тополя (ж)	[to'pɔlʲa]
rowan	горобина (ж)	[ɦoro'bina]
willow	верба (ж)	[wɛr'ba]
alder	вільха (ж)	['wilʲha]

| beech | бук (ч) | [buk] |
| elm | в'яз (ч) | [wʲʲaz] |

| ash (tree) | ясен (ч) | [ʲiasɛn] |
| chestnut | каштан (ч) | [kaʃ'tan] |

magnolia	магнолія (ж)	[mań'nɔliʲa]
palm tree	пальма (ж)	['palʲma]
cypress	кипарис (ч)	[kipa'ris]

mangrove	мангрове дерево (c)	['manɦrowɛ 'dɛrɛwo]
baobab	баобаб (ч)	[bao'bab]
eucalyptus	евкаліпт (ч)	[ɛwka'lipt]
sequoia	секвоя (ж)	[sɛk'wɔʲa]

187. Shrubs

bush	кущ (ч)	[kuɕ]
shrub	чагарник (ч)	[ʧaɦarˈnik]
grapevine	виноград (ч)	[winoˈɦrad]
vineyard	виноградник (ч)	[winoˈɦradnik]
raspberry bush	малина (ж)	[maˈlina]
blackcurrant bush	чорна смородина (ж)	[ˈʧɔrna smoˈrɔdina]
redcurrant bush	порічки (мн)	[poˈriʧki]
gooseberry bush	аґрус (ч)	[ˈagrus]
acacia	акація (ж)	[aˈkatsiʲa]
barberry	барбарис (ч)	[barbaˈris]
jasmine	жасмин (ч)	[ʒasˈmin]
juniper	ялівець (ч)	[jaliˈwɛʦ]
rosebush	трояндовий кущ (ч)	[troʲandowij kuɕ]
dog rose	шипшина (ж)	[ʃipˈʃina]

188. Mushrooms

mushroom	гриб (ч)	[ɦrib]
edible mushroom	їстівний гриб (ч)	[jisˈtiwnij ɦrib]
poisonous mushroom	отруйний гриб (ч)	[otˈrujnij ɦrib]
cap	шапка (ж)	[ˈʃapka]
stipe	ніжка (ж)	[ˈniʒka]
cep (Boletus edulis)	білий гриб (ч)	[ˈbilij ˈɦrib]
orange-cap boletus	підосичник (ч)	[pidoˈsiʧnik]
birch bolete	підберезник (ч)	[pidbɛˈrɛznik]
chanterelle	лисичка (ж)	[liˈsiʧka]
russula	сироїжка (ж)	[siroˈjiʒka]
morel	зморшок (ч)	[ˈzmɔrʃok]
fly agaric	мухомор (ч)	[muhoˈmɔr]
death cap	поганка (ж)	[poˈɦanka]

189. Fruits. Berries

fruit	фрукт, плід (ч)	[frukt], [plid]
fruits	фрукти, плоди (мн)	[frukti], [ploˈdi]
apple	яблуко (с)	[ˈʲabluko]
pear	груша (ж)	[ˈɦruʃa]
plum	слива (ж)	[ˈsliwa]
strawberry (garden ~)	полуниця (ж)	[poluˈnitsʲa]

sour cherry	вишня (ж)	['wiʃnʲa]
sweet cherry	черешня (ж)	[ʧɛ'rɛʃnʲa]
grapes	виноград (ч)	[wino'ɦrad]
raspberry	малина (ж)	[ma'lina]
blackcurrant	чорна смородина (ж)	['ʧorna smo'rɔdina]
redcurrant	порічки (мн)	[po'riʧki]
gooseberry	аґрус (ч)	['agrus]
cranberry	журавлина (ж)	[ʒuraw'lina]
orange	апельсин (ч)	[apɛlʲ'sin]
mandarin	мандарин (ч)	[manda'rin]
pineapple	ананас (ч)	[ana'nas]
banana	банан (ч)	[ba'nan]
date	фінік (ч)	['finik]
lemon	лимон (ч)	[li'mɔn]
apricot	абрикос (ч)	[abri'kɔs]
peach	персик (ч)	['pɛrsik]
kiwi	ківі (ч)	['kiwi]
grapefruit	грейпфрут (ч)	[ɦrɛjp'frut]
berry	ягода (ж)	['ʲaɦoda]
berries	ягоди (мн)	['ʲaɦodi]
cowberry	брусниця (ж)	[brus'nitsʲa]
wild strawberry	суниця (ж)	[su'nitsʲa]
bilberry	чорниця (ж)	[ʧor'nitsʲa]

190. Flowers. Plants

flower	квітка (ж)	['kwitka]
bouquet (of flowers)	букет (ч)	[bu'kɛt]
rose (flower)	троянда (ж)	[tro'ʲanda]
tulip	тюльпан (ч)	[tʲulʲ'pan]
carnation	гвоздика (ж)	[ɦwoz'dika]
gladiolus	гладіолус (ч)	[ɦladi'ɔlus]
cornflower	волошка (ж)	[wo'loʃka]
harebell	дзвіночок (ч)	[dzwi'nɔʧok]
dandelion	кульбаба (ж)	[kulʲ'baba]
camomile	ромашка (ж)	[ro'maʃka]
aloe	алое (с)	[a'lɔɛ]
cactus	кактус (ч)	['kaktus]
rubber plant, ficus	фікус (ч)	['fikus]
lily	лілея (ж)	[li'lɛʲa]
geranium	герань (ж)	[ɦɛ'ranʲ]
hyacinth	гіацинт (ч)	[ɦia'tsint]

mimosa	мімоза (ж)	[mi'mɔza]
narcissus	нарцис (ч)	[nar'tsis]
nasturtium	настурція (ж)	[nas'turtsiʲa]
orchid	орхідея (ж)	[orhi'dɛʲa]
peony	півонія (ж)	[pi'wɔniʲa]
violet	фіалка (ж)	[fi'alka]
pansy	братки (мн)	[brat'ki]
forget-me-not	незабудка (ж)	[nɛza'budka]
daisy	стокротки (мн)	[stok'rɔtki]
poppy	мак (ч)	[mak]
hemp	коноплі (мн)	[ko'nɔpli]
mint	м'ята (ж)	['mʲata]
lily of the valley	конвалія (ж)	[kon'waliʲa]
snowdrop	пролісок (ч)	['prɔlisok]
nettle	кропива (ж)	[kropi'wa]
sorrel	щавель (ч)	[ɕa'wɛlʲ]
water lily	латаття (с)	[la'tattʲa]
fern	папороть (ж)	['paporotʲ]
lichen	лишайник (ч)	[li'ʃajnik]
conservatory (greenhouse)	оранжерея (ж)	[oranʒɛ'rɛʲa]
lawn	газон (ч)	[ɦa'zɔn]
flowerbed	клумба (ж)	['klumba]
plant	рослина (ж)	[ros'lina]
grass	трава (ж)	[tra'wa]
blade of grass	травинка (ж)	[tra'winka]
leaf	листок (ч)	[lis'tɔk]
petal	пелюстка (ж)	[pɛ'lʲustka]
stem	стебло (с)	[stɛb'lɔ]
tuber	бульба (ж)	['bulʲba]
young plant (shoot)	паросток (ч)	['parostok]
thorn	колючка (ж)	[ko'lʲutʃka]
to blossom (vi)	цвісти	[tswis'ti]
to fade, to wither	в'янути	['wʲanuti]
smell (odor)	запах (ч)	['zapah]
to cut (flowers)	зрізати	['zrizati]
to pick (a flower)	зірвати	[zir'wati]

191. Cereals, grains

grain	зерно (с)	[zɛr'nɔ]
cereal crops	зернові рослини (мн)	[zɛrno'wi ros'lini]

ear (of barley, wheat, etc.)	колос (ч)	['kɔlos]
wheat	пшениця (ж)	[pʃɛ'nitsʲa]
rye	жито (с)	['ʒito]
oats	овес (ч)	[o'wɛs]
millet	просо (с)	['prɔso]
barley	ячмінь (ч)	[jatʃ'minʲ]
corn	кукурудза (ж)	[kuku'rudza]
rice	рис (ч)	[ris]
buckwheat	гречка (ж)	['ɦrɛtʃka]
pea plant	горох (ч)	[ɦo'rɔh]
kidney beans	квасоля (ж)	[kwa'sɔlʲa]
soy	соя (ж)	['sɔʲa]
lentil	сочевиця (ж)	[sotʃɛ'witsʲa]
beans	боби (мн)	[bo'bɨ]

REGIONAL GEOGRAPHY

192. Politics. Government. Part 1

politics	політика (ж)	[po'litika]
political (adj)	політичний	[poli'titʃnij]
politician	політик (ч)	[po'litik]

state (country)	держава (ж)	[dɛr'ʒawa]
citizen	громадянин (ч)	[ɦromadʲa'nin]
citizenship	громадянство (с)	[ɦroma'dʲanstwo]

| national emblem | національний герб (ч) | [natsio'nalʲnij 'ɦɛrb] |
| national anthem | державний гімн (ч) | [dɛr'ʒawnij ɦimn] |

government	уряд (ч)	['urʲad]
head of state	керівник (ч) країни	[kɛriw'nik kra'jini]
parliament	парламент (ч)	[par'lamɛnt]
party	партія (ж)	['partiʲa]

| capitalism | капіталізм (ч) | [kapita'lizm] |
| capitalist (adj) | капіталістичний | [kapitalis'titʃnij] |

| socialism | соціалізм (ч) | [sotsia'lizm] |
| socialist (adj) | соціалістичний | [sotsialis'titʃnij] |

communism	комунізм (ч)	[komu'nizm]
communist (adj)	комуністичний	[komunis'titʃnij]
communist (n)	комуніст (ч)	[komu'nist]

democracy	демократія (ж)	[dɛmok'ratiʲa]
democrat	демократ (ч)	[dɛmok'rat]
democratic (adj)	демократичний	[dɛmokra'titʃnij]
Democratic party	демократична партія (ж)	[dɛmokra'titʃna 'partiʲa]

| liberal (n) | ліберал (ч) | [libɛ'ral] |
| liberal (adj) | ліберальний | [libɛ'ralʲnij] |

| conservative (n) | консерватор (ч) | [konsɛr'wator] |
| conservative (adj) | консервативний | [konsɛrwa'tiwnij] |

republic (n)	республіка (ж)	[rɛs'publika]
republican (n)	республіканець (ч)	[rɛspubli'kanɛts]
Republican party	республіканська партія (ж)	[rɛspubli'kansʲka 'partiʲa]

| elections | вибори (мн) | ['wibori] |

to elect (vt)	**обирати**	[obi'rati]
elector, voter	**виборець** (ч)	['wiborɛts]
election campaign	**виборча компанія** (ж)	['wibortʃa kom'paniʲa]
voting (n)	**голосування** (с)	[ɦolosu'wanʲa]
to vote (vi)	**голосувати**	[ɦolosu'wati]
suffrage, right to vote	**право** (с) **голосу**	['prawo 'ɦolosu]
candidate	**кандидат** (ч)	[kandi'dat]
to be a candidate	**балотуватися**	[balotu'watisʲa]
campaign	**кампанія** (ж)	[kam'paniʲa]
opposition (as adj)	**опозиційний**	[opozi'tsijnij]
opposition (n)	**опозиція** (ж)	[opo'zitsiʲa]
visit	**візит** (ч)	[wi'zit]
official visit	**офіційний візит** (ч)	[ofi'tsijnij wi'zit]
international (adj)	**міжнародний**	[miʒna'rodnij]
negotiations	**переговори** (мн)	[pɛrɛɦo'wori]
to negotiate (vi)	**вести переговори**	['wɛsti pɛrɛɦo'wori]

193. Politics. Government. Part 2

society	**суспільство** (с)	[sus'pilʲstwo]
constitution	**конституція** (ж)	[konsti'tutsiʲa]
power (political control)	**влада** (ж)	['wlada]
corruption	**корупція** (ж)	[ko'ruptsiʲa]
law (justice)	**закон** (ч)	[za'kɔn]
legal (legitimate)	**законний**	[za'kɔnij]
justice (fairness)	**справедливість** (ж)	[sprawɛd'liwistʲ]
just (fair)	**справедливий**	[sprawɛd'liwij]
committee	**комітет** (ч)	[komi'tɛt]
bill (draft law)	**законопроект** (ч)	[zakonopro'ɛkt]
budget	**бюджет** (ч)	[bʲu'dʒɛt]
policy	**політика** (ж)	[po'litika]
reform	**реформа** (ж)	[rɛ'fɔrma]
radical (adj)	**радикальний**	[radi'kalʲnij]
power (strength, force)	**сила** (ж)	['sila]
powerful (adj)	**могутній**	[mo'ɦutnij]
supporter	**прибічник** (ч)	[pri'bitʃnik]
influence	**вплив** (ч)	[wpliw]
regime (e.g., military ~)	**режим** (ч)	[rɛ'ʒim]
conflict	**конфлікт** (ч)	[kon'flikt]
conspiracy (plot)	**змова** (ж)	['zmɔwa]

provocation	провокація (ж)	[prowo'katsi'a]
to overthrow (regime, etc.)	скинути	['skinuti]
overthrow (of a government)	повалення (с)	[po'walɛni'a]
revolution	революція (ж)	[rɛwo'liutsi'a]
coup d'état	переворот (ч)	[pɛrɛwo'rɔt]
military coup	військовий переворот (ч)	[wijsi'kɔwij pɛrɛwo'rɔt]
crisis	криза (ж)	['kriza]
economic recession	економічний спад (ч)	[ɛkono'mitʃnij spad]
demonstrator (protester)	демонстрант (ч)	[dɛmon'strant]
demonstration	демонстрація (ж)	[dɛmon'stratsi'a]
martial law	воєнний стан (ч)	[wo'ɛnij stan]
military base	військова база (ж)	[wijsi'kɔwa 'baza]
stability	стабільність (ж)	[sta'bili'nisti]
stable (adj)	стабільний	[sta'bili'nij]
exploitation	експлуатація (ж)	[ɛksplua'tatsi'a]
to exploit (workers)	експлуатувати	[ɛkspluatu'wati]
racism	расизм (ч)	[ra'sizm]
racist	расист (ч)	[ra'sist]
fascism	фашизм (ч)	[fa'ʃizm]
fascist	фашист (ч)	[fa'ʃist]

194. Countries. Miscellaneous

foreigner	іноземець (ч)	[ino'zɛmɛts]
foreign (adj)	іноземний	[ino'zɛmnij]
abroad (in a foreign country)	за кордоном	[za kor'dɔnom]
emigrant	емігрант (ч)	[ɛmih'rant]
emigration	еміграція (ж)	[ɛmih'ratsi'a]
to emigrate (vi)	емігрувати	[ɛmihru'wati]
the West	Захід (ч)	['zahid]
the East	Схід (ч)	[shid]
the Far East	Далекий Схід (ч)	[da'lɛkij shid]
civilization	цивілізація (ж)	[tsiwili'zatsi'a]
humanity (mankind)	людство (с)	['li'udstwo]
the world (earth)	світ (ч)	[swit]
peace	мир (ч)	[mir]
worldwide (adj)	світовий	[swito'wij]
homeland	батьківщина (ж)	[bati'kiw'çina]
people (population)	народ (ч)	[na'rɔd]

population	**населення** (с)	[na'sɛlɛnʲa]
people (a lot of ~)	**люди** (мн)	['lʲudi]
nation (people)	**нація** (ж)	['natsiʲa]
generation	**покоління** (с)	[poko'linʲa]
territory (area)	**територія** (ж)	[tɛri'toriʲa]
region	**регіон** (ч)	[rɛɦi'ɔn]
state (part of a country)	**штат** (ч)	[ʃtat]
tradition	**традиція** (ч)	[tra'ditsiʲa]
custom (tradition)	**звичай** (ч)	['zwitʃaj]
ecology	**екологія** (ж)	[ɛko'lɔɦiʲa]
Indian (Native American)	**індіанець** (ч)	[indi'anɛts]
Gypsy (masc.)	**циган** (ч)	[tsi'ɦan]
Gypsy (fem.)	**циганка** (ж)	[tsi'ɦanka]
Gypsy (adj)	**циганський**	[tsi'ɦansʲkij]
empire	**імперія** (ж)	[im'pɛriʲa]
colony	**колонія** (ж)	[ko'lɔniʲa]
slavery	**рабство** (с)	['rabstwo]
invasion	**навала** (ж)	[na'wala]
famine	**голодомор** (ч)	[ɦolodo'mɔr]

195. Major religious groups. Confessions

religion	**релігія** (ж)	[rɛ'liɦiʲa]
religious (adj)	**релігійний**	[rɛli'ɦijnij]
faith, belief	**віра** (ж)	['wira]
to believe (in God)	**вірити**	['wiriti]
believer	**віруючий** (ч)	['wiruʲutʃij]
atheism	**атеїзм** (ч)	[atɛ'jizm]
atheist	**атеїст** (ч)	[atɛ'jist]
Christianity	**християнство** (с)	[hristiʲ'anstwo]
Christian (n)	**християнин** (ч)	[hristiʲ'anin]
Christian (adj)	**християнський**	[hristiʲ'ansʲkij]
Catholicism	**Католицизм** (ч)	[katoli'tsizm]
Catholic (n)	**католик** (ч)	[ka'tɔlik]
Catholic (adj)	**католицький**	[kato'litskij]
Protestantism	**Протестантство** (с)	[protɛs'tantstwo]
Protestant Church	**Протестантська церква** (ж)	[protɛs'tantsʲka 'tsɛrkwa]
Protestant (n)	**протестант** (ч)	[protɛs'tant]
Orthodoxy	**Православ'я** (с)	[prawo'slaw'ʲa]
Orthodox Church	**Православна церква** (ж)	[prawos'lawna 'tsɛrkwa]

Orthodox (n)	православний (ч)	[prawo'slawnij]
Presbyterianism	Пресвітеріанство (с)	[prɛswitɛri'anstwo]
Presbyterian Church	Пресвітеріанська церква (ж)	[prɛswitɛri'ansʲka 'tsɛrkwa]
Presbyterian (n)	пресвітеріанин (ч)	[prɛswitɛri'anin]
Lutheranism	Лютеранська церква (ж)	[lʲutɛ'ransʲka 'tsɛrkwa]
Lutheran (n)	лютеранин (ч)	[lʲutɛ'ranin]
Baptist Church	Баптизм (ч)	[bap'tizm]
Baptist (n)	баптист (ч)	[bap'tist]
Anglican Church	Англіканська церква (ж)	[anɦli'kansʲka 'tsɛrkwa]
Anglican (n)	англіканець (ч)	[anɦli'kanɛtsʲ]
Mormonism	Мормонство (с)	[mor'mɔnstwo]
Mormon (n)	мормон (ч)	[mor'mɔn]
Judaism	Іудаїзм (ч)	[iuda'jizm]
Jew (n)	іудей (ч)	[iu'dɛj]
Buddhism	Буддизм (ч)	[bud'dizm]
Buddhist (n)	буддист (ч)	[bud'dist]
Hinduism	Індуїзм (ч)	[indu'jizm]
Hindu (n)	індуїст (ч)	[indu'jist]
Islam	Іслам (ч)	[is'lam]
Muslim (n)	мусульманин (ч)	[musulʲ'manin]
Muslim (adj)	мусульманський	[musulʲ'mansʲkij]
Shiah Islam	Шиїзм (ч)	[ʃi'jizm]
Shiite (n)	шиїт (ч)	[ʃi'jit]
Sunni Islam	Сунізм (ч)	[su'nizm]
Sunnite (n)	суніт (ч)	[su'nit]

196. Religions. Priests

priest	священик (ч)	[swʲa'ɕɛnik]
the Pope	Папа Римський	['papa 'rimsʲkij]
monk, friar	чернець (ч)	[tʃɛr'nɛts]
nun	черниця (ж)	[tʃɛr'nitsʲa]
pastor	пастор (ч)	['pastor]
abbot	абат (ч)	[a'bat]
vicar (parish priest)	вікарій (ч)	[wi'karij]
bishop	єпископ (ч)	[ɛ'piskop]
cardinal	кардинал (ч)	[kardi'nal]

preacher	проповідник (ч)	[propo'widnik]
preaching	проповідь (ж)	['prɔpowidʲ]
parishioners	парафіяни (мн)	[parafiʲani]

| believer | віруючий (ч) | ['wiruʲutʃij] |
| atheist | атеїст (ч) | [atɛ'jist] |

197. Faith. Christianity. Islam

| Adam | Адам (ч) | [a'dam] |
| Eve | Єва (ж) | ['ɛwa] |

God	Бог (ч)	[bɔɦ]
the Lord	Господь (ч)	[ɦɔs'pɔdʲ]
the Almighty	Всесильний (ч)	[wsɛ'silʲnij]

sin	гріх (ч)	[ɦrih]
to sin (vi)	грішити	[ɦri'ʃiti]
sinner (masc.)	грішник (ч)	['ɦriʃnik]
sinner (fem.)	грішниця (ж)	['ɦriʃnitsʲa]

| hell | пекло (с) | ['pɛklo] |
| paradise | рай (ч) | [raj] |

| Jesus | Ісус (ч) | [i'sus] |
| Jesus Christ | Ісус Христос (ч) | [i'sus hris'tɔs] |

the Holy Spirit	Святий Дух (ч)	[swʲa'tij duh]
the Savior	Спаситель (ч)	[spa'sitɛlʲ]
the Virgin Mary	Богородиця (ж)	[boɦo'rɔditsʲa]

the Devil	диявол (ч)	[diʲawol]
devil's (adj)	диявольський	[diʲawolʲsʲkij]
Satan	Сатана (ч)	[sata'na]
satanic (adj)	сатанинський	[sata'ninsʲkij]

angel	ангел (ч)	['anɦɛl]
guardian angel	ангел-охоронець (ч)	['anɦɛl oho'rɔnɛts]
angelic (adj)	ангельський	['anɦɛlʲsʲkij]

apostle	апостол (ч)	[a'pɔstol]
archangel	архангел (ч)	[ar'hanɦɛl]
the Antichrist	антихрист (ч)	[an'tihrist]

Church	церква (ж)	['tsɛrkwa]
Bible	Біблія (ж)	['bibliʲa]
biblical (adj)	біблійний	[bib'lijnij]

| Old Testament | Старий Завіт (ч) | [sta'rij za'wit] |
| New Testament | Новий Завіт (ч) | [no'wij za'wit] |

Gospel	**Євангеліє** (c)	[ɛ'wanɦɛliɛ]
Holy Scripture	**Священне Писання** (c)	[swʲa'ɕɛnɛ pi'sanʲa]
Heaven	**Небо** (c)	['nɛbo]
commandment	**заповідь** (ж)	['zapowidʲ]
prophet	**пророк** (ч)	[pro'rɔk]
prophecy	**пророцтво** (c)	[pro'rɔtstwo]
Allah	**Аллах** (ч)	[a'lah]
Mohammed	**Магомет** (ч)	[maɦo'mɛt]
the Koran, Quran	**Коран** (ч)	[ko'ran]
mosque	**мечеть** (ж)	[mɛ'tʃɛtʲ]
mullah	**мула** (ч)	[mu'la]
prayer	**молитва** (ж)	[mo'litwa]
to pray (vi, vt)	**молитися**	[mo'litisʲa]
pilgrimage	**паломництво** (c)	[pa'lɔmnitstwo]
pilgrim	**паломник** (ч)	[pa'lɔmnik]
Mecca	**Мекка** (ж)	['mɛkka]
church	**церква** (ж)	['tsɛrkwa]
temple	**храм** (ч)	[hram]
cathedral	**собор** (ч)	[so'bɔr]
gothic (adj)	**готичний**	[ɦo'titʃnij]
synagogue	**синагога** (ж)	[sina'ɦɔɦa]
mosque	**мечеть** (ж)	[mɛ'tʃɛtʲ]
chapel	**каплиця** (ж)	[kap'litsʲa]
abbey	**абатство** (c)	[a'batstwo]
monastery	**монастир** (ч)	[monas'tir]
bell (church ~s)	**дзвін** (ч)	[dzwin]
bell tower	**дзвіниця** (ж)	[dzwi'nitsʲa]
to ring (ab. bells)	**дзвонити**	[dzwo'niti]
cross	**хрест** (ч)	[hrɛst]
cupola (roof)	**купол** (ч)	['kupol]
icon	**ікона** (ж)	[i'kɔna]
soul	**душа** (ж)	[du'ʃa]
fate (destiny)	**доля** (ж)	['dɔlʲa]
evil (n)	**зло** (c)	[zlo]
good (n)	**добро** (c)	[dob'rɔ]
vampire	**вампір** (ч)	[wam'pir]
witch (evil ~)	**відьма** (ж)	['widʲma]
demon	**демон** (ч)	['dɛmon]
spirit	**дух** (ч)	[duh]
redemption (giving us ~)	**спокута** (ж)	[spo'kuta]
to redeem (vt)	**спокутувати**	[spo'kutuwati]

church service, mass	**служба** (ж)	['sluʒba]
to say mass	**служити**	[slu'ʒiti]
confession	**сповідь** (ж)	['spɔwidʲ]
to confess (vi)	**сповідатися**	[spowi'datisʲa]

saint (n)	**святий** (ч)	[swʲa'tij]
sacred (holy)	**священний**	[swʲa'ɕɛnij]
holy water	**свята вода** (ж)	[swʲa'ta wo'da]

ritual (n)	**ритуал** (ч)	[ritu'al]
ritual (adj)	**ритуальний**	[ritu'alʲnij]
sacrifice	**жертвування** (с)	['ʒɛrtwuwanʲa]

superstition	**забобони** (мн)	[zabo'bɔni]
superstitious (adj)	**забобонний**	[zabo'bɔnij]
afterlife	**загробне життя** (с)	[zaɦ'rɔbnɛ ʒit'tʲa]
eternal life	**вічне життя** (с)	['witʃnɛ ʒit'tʲa]

MISCELLANEOUS

198. Various useful words

background (green ~)	фон (ч)	[fon]
balance (of the situation)	баланс (ч)	[ba'lans]
barrier (obstacle)	перепона (ж)	[pɛrɛ'pona]
base (basis)	база (ж)	['baza]
beginning	початок (ч)	[po'ʧatok]
category	категорія (ж)	[katɛ'ɦoriʲa]
cause (reason)	причина (ж)	[pri'ʧina]
choice	вибір (ч)	['wibir]
coincidence	збіг (ч)	[zbiɦ]
comfortable (~ chair)	зручний	[zruʧʲnij]
comparison	порівняння (с)	[poriw'nʲanʲa]
compensation	компенсація (ж)	[kompɛn'satsiʲa]
degree (extent, amount)	ступінь (ч)	['stupinʲ]
development	розвиток (ч)	['rɔzwitok]
difference	різниця (ж)	[riz'nitsʲa]
effect (e.g., of drugs)	ефект (ч)	[ɛ'fɛkt]
effort (exertion)	зусилля (с)	[zu'silʲa]
element	елемент (ч)	[ɛlɛ'mɛnt]
end (finish)	закінчення (с)	[za'kinʧɛnʲa]
example (illustration)	приклад (ч)	['priklad]
fact	факт (ч)	[fakt]
frequent (adj)	приватний	[pri'watnij]
growth (development)	зростання (с)	[zros'tanʲa]
help	допомога (ж)	[dopo'mɔɦa]
ideal	ідеал (ч)	[idɛ'al]
kind (sort, type)	вид (ч)	[wid]
labyrinth	лабіринт (ч)	[labi'rint]
mistake, error	помилка (ж)	[po'milka]
moment	момент (ч)	[mo'mɛnt]
object (thing)	об'єкт (ч)	[o'b'ɛkt]
obstacle	перешкода (ж)	[pɛrɛʃ'koda]
original (original copy)	оригінал (ч)	[oriɦi'nal]
part (~ of sth)	частина (ж)	[ʧas'tina]
particle, small part	частка, частина (ж)	['ʧastka], [ʧas'tina]
pause (break)	пауза (ж)	['pauza]

position	позиція (ж)	[po'zitsiˈa]
principle	принцип (ч)	['printsip]
problem	проблема (ж)	[prob'lɛma]
process	процес (ч)	[pro'tsɛs]
progress	прогрес (ч)	[proɦ'rɛs]
property (quality)	властивість (ж)	[wlas'tiwistʲ]
reaction	реакція (ж)	[rɛ'aktsiˈa]
risk	ризик (ч)	['rizik]
secret	таємниця (ж), секрет (ч)	[taɛm'nitsʲa], [sɛk'rɛt]
series	серія (ж)	['sɛriˈa]
shape (outer form)	форма (ж)	['fɔrma]
situation	ситуація (ж)	[situ'atsiˈa]
solution	рішення (с)	['riʃɛnʲa]
standard (adj)	стандартний	[stan'dartnij]
standard (level of quality)	стандарт (ч)	[stan'dart]
stop (pause)	перерва (ж)	[pɛ'rɛrwa]
style	стиль (ч)	[stilʲ]
system	система (ж)	[sis'tɛma]
table (chart)	таблиця (ж)	[tab'litsʲa]
tempo, rate	темп (ч)	[tɛmp]
term (word, expression)	термін (ч)	['tɛrmin]
thing (object, item)	річ (ж)	[ritʃ]
truth (e.g., moment of ~)	істина (ж)	['istina]
turn (please wait your ~)	черга (ж)	['ʧɛrɦa]
type (sort, kind)	тип (ч)	[tip]
urgent (adj)	терміновий	[tɛrmi'nɔwij]
urgently (adv)	терміново	[tɛrmi'nɔwo]
utility (usefulness)	користь (ж)	['kɔristʲ]
variant (alternative)	варіант (ч)	[wari'ant]
way (means, method)	спосіб (ч)	['spɔsib]
zone	зона (ж)	['zɔna]

54508192R00114